World Economics Association

Book Series

Volume 10

Ideas Towards a New
International Financial Architecture

Titles produced by the World Economics Association & College Publications

Volume 1:
The Economics Curriculum. Towards a Radical Reformation. Maria Alejandra Madi and Jack Reardon, eds.
Volume 2:
Finance as Warfare. Michael Hudson
Volume 3:
Developing an Economics for the Post-crisis World. Steve Keen
Volume 4:
On the Use and Misuse of Theories and Models in Mainstream Economics. Lars Pålsson Syll
Volume 5:
Green Capitalism. The God that Failed. Richard Smith
Volume 6:
40 Critical Pointers for Students of Economics. Stuart Birks
Volume 7:
The European Crisis. Victor Beker and Beniamino Moro, eds.
Volume 8:
A Philosophical Framework for Rethinking Theoretical Economics and Philosophy of Economics. Gustavo Marqués
Volume 9:
Narrative Fixation in Economics. Edward Fullbrook
Volume 10:
Ideas Towards a New International Financial Architecture. Oscar Ugarteche, Alicia Payana and Maria Alejandra Madi, eds

The **World Economics Association (WEA)** was launched on May 16, 2011. Already over 13,000 economists and related scholars have joined. This phenomenal success has come about because the WEA fills a huge gap in the international community of economists – the absence of a professional organization which is truly international and pluralist.

The World Economics Association seeks to increase the relevance, breadth and depth of economic thought. Its key qualities are worldwide membership and governance, and inclusiveness with respect to: (a) the variety of theoretical perspectives; (b) the range of human activities and issues which fall within the broad domain of economics; and (c) the study of the world's diverse economies.

The Association's activities centre on the development, promotion and diffusion of economic research and knowledge and on illuminating their social character.

The WEA publishes 20+ books a year, three open-access journals (*Economic Thought, World Economic Review* and *Real-World Economics Review*), a bi-monthly newsletter, blogs, holds global online conferences, runs a textbook commentaries project and an eBook library.

www.worldeconomicassociation.org

Ideas Towards a New International Financial Architecture

Edited by

Oscar Ugarteche
Alicia Payana
and
Maria Alejandra Madi

© Individual Authors, WEA and College Publications 2017.

All rights reserved.

ISBN 978-1-84890-238-1 print
ISBN 978-1-911156-15-4 eBook-PDF

Published by College Publications (London) on behalf of the World Economics Association (Bristol)

http://www.worldeconomicsassociation.org
http://www.collegepublications.co.uk

Cover photo by Kyla Rushman
Cover design by Laraine Welch
Printed by Lightning Source, Milton Keynes, UK

Foreword

The current volume is one of the outcomes from a conference on the *Ideas towards a new international financial architecture?*

http://itnifa2015.weaconferences.net

It was led by Oscar Ugarteche and Alicia Puyana and took place in May-July 2015. The problems and issues around the international financial structure are among the most pressing ones in the profession. Moreover, their ramifications spread throughout economies and societies.

The WEA (worldeconomicsassociation.org) was launched in May 2011. It has now some 13,000 members from 150 countries. The WEA seeks to increase the relevance, breadth and depth of economic thought. Its key qualities are worldwide membership and governance, and inclusiveness with respect to: (a) the variety of theoretical perspectives; (b) the range of human activities and issues which fall within the broad domain of economics; and (c) the study of the world's diverse economies. Its commitments listed in the WEA Manifesto include: *plurality; competence; reality and relevance; diversity; openness; outreach; ethical conduct; global democracy.* The WEA makes full use of the digital technologies in the pursuit of these commitments.

The WEA's current activities include the following:

(1) Three Open Access journals: *Economic Thought. (ET); World Economic Review (WER)* and *Real World Economics Review* (RWER). They are all open journals and *Economic Thought* uses an Open Peer Review system. Hard copies of these journals are issued in collaboration with College Publications and available via Amazon;

(2) A blog;

(3) a bimonthly Newsletter;

(4) Online conferences and a Textbook Commentaries Project and

(5) WEA eBooks – a digital-age book publishing project launched in February 2015. This new platform offers academic economics books potentially larger readerships than they now usually have and enables their publication and distribution within weeks of submission. WEA eBooks has already published 17 books, including books by Michael Hudson, Steve Keen, Herman Daly, Asad Zaman and Lars Pålsson Syll.

Maria Alejandra Madi
December 2015

Website worldeconomicsassociation.org

Executive committee

Juan Carlos Moreno Brid, Mexico, UN Economic Com. for Latin America and the Caribbean
C. P. Chandrasekhar, India, Jawaharlal Nehru University
Ping Chen, China, Peking University and Fudan University
Edward Fullbrook, UK, University of the West of England
James K. Galbraith, USA, University of Texas at Austin
Grazia Ietto-Gillies, Italy / UK, London South Bank University
Steve Keen, Australia, University of Western Sydney
Richard C. Koo, Japan, Nomura Research Institute
Tony Lawson, UK, Cambridge University
Peter Radford, USA, Radford Free Press
Dani Rodrik, USA, Harvard University

Acknowledgements

We are grateful to the World Economics Association for giving us the opportunity to lead an online conference on the economics curriculum and to develop this book from it.

We benefitted from many of the open comments that the conference attracted and we would like to thank many of the contributors to the debate, such as: *Jessie Henshaw, Morrison Bonpasse, M.M. van Wijck, Roy Langston, John Craig, Carlos Marichal, Charles Fasola, David Chester, Gerson Lima, James Wood, Marco Saba, Delton Chen, Tim Knight, Peter Shaw and Francisco Cantamutto.*

A special thanks to Jake McMurchie and Malgorzata Dereniowska for all their support during the Conference organization and through the Discussion Forum.

Preface

Bretton Woods constitutes an attempt, unprecedented in the history of capitalism, to create an international financial architecture sensibly regulated and with the participation of all member countries of the world. Since the early 1970s, with the final breakdown of the dollar standard, this ambitious architecture definitively fell into crisis. Thus, Bretton Woods institutions became completely incapable of ensuring the stability of the global financial system in order to achieve a balanced economic developments and greater equity among nations.

More recently, the outbreak of the global financial crisis in 2008 revealed the need, but also the urgency, of moving forward in an exhaustive review of the international financial architecture. The dismantling of regulations since the 1970s, and the lack of new ones, suitable for financial innovations developed in recent decades, has contributed to an uncontrolled advance of derivatives and financial vehicles that hide the true risk of their underlying assets. These sophisticated financial instruments, able to elude the control of national authorities, were an essential element of the global financial crisis, which is already several years old and has not yet found any solutions.

If private sector's finances lack an appropriate regulatory framework, the same applies to the indebtedness of countries, which has also fallen prisoner to global financial markets through the issuance of securities that are bought and sold in speculative financial markets. Within this context, the growth of sovereign states' debt boosted significantly in recent years, reaching records of default in remarkable cases of countries with unsustainable debt levels. It is again the legal gap in the global financial architecture which leaves sovereign states without effective tools to deal with the problem. Lack of financial regulation has led to a new actor in the international financial system: vulture funds. They are speculative investment funds based in tax havens that specialize in attacking countries or companies in distress, either on the eve of falling into default, or after bankruptcy. Their *modus operandi* consists of bringing legal actions in order to obtain windfall profits through special court decisions.

Vulture funds have gained greater importance – becoming a real danger to the stability of the international financial system – since the decision taken by the US Supreme Court in June 2014 to not hear the Argentine case against vulture funds, ratifying District Judge Griesa's decisions. In this way, a completely unprecedented and harmful interpretation of the *pari passu* clause, a boilerplate clause in debt securities, generated a further blow to the chances of countries to restructure their sovereign debt in a successfully and orderly manner.

Since then, however, the concern of the international community at any level, including financial institutions, countries, forums and experts, has been unanimous. In this way, a truly international movement that raises the need to stop vulture funds' practices, has been created. Indeed, the adoption by the United Nations General Assembly of the Nine Principles for Sovereign Debt Restructuring last September appears as an essential step forward.

The discussion among experts and the dissemination of their ideas, by means of seminars, conferences and publications, is definitely a necessary step towards the building of a new international financial architecture that may stop vulture funds' predatory behaviour, as part of the construction of a more rational and fairer financial system. It is the joint action of experts, multilateral financial organizations and sovereign States which can create the conditions to develop the necessary structures to definitely transform the international financial architecture, which should meet the needs of the production system and contribute to putting an end to the supremacy of finances and speculation over real economies.

The Argentine Government appreciates the efforts to carry out this publication which undoubtedly represents a contribution to the current debate.

Dr Axel Kicillof, Minister of Finance. Argentina
Buenos Aires, September 11th, 2015

Contents

Introduction   1

Chapter 1: The Need for a New International Financial   3
Architecture
by Oscar Ugarteche, Alicia Puyana and Maria Alejandra Madi

Part I - The great crisis and policy challenges   19

Chapter 2: The great global financial crises: official   21
investigations, past and present, 1929-2011
by Carlos Marichal

Chapter 3: A new financial governance model for the new   47
global economy of the 21st century
by Constantine E. Passaris

Chapter 4: Public debt is economic nonsense   77
by Gerson P. Lima

Part II- Rethinking the international financial architecture   101

Chapter 5: Re-engineering the economic processes   103
by Tim Knight

Chapter 6: Infrastructure without debt   123
by Ellen Brown, J.D. and Uli Kortsch

Chapter 7: Globalization and an international monetary   147
clearing union
by Paul Davidson

Chapter 8: A new international financial architecture: The   179
regional versus the global view?
by Oscar Ugarteche

Conclusions   209

Concluding remarks: A new world is possible and necessary   211
by *Alicia Puyana and Oscar Ugarteche*

About the editors and authors   217

Contents

Introduction

Part 1

Chapter 1

Chapter 2

Part 2

Chapter 3

Chapter 4

Chapter 5

Chapter 6

About the author

INTRODUCTION

CHAPTER 1
The need for a new international financial architecture

Oscar Ugarteche, Alicia Puyana and Maria Alejandra Madi

1. Setting the scene

The international financial architecture is made up of institutions, practices and instruments. Most institutions were designed in the 1940s, at the time when stable exchange rates were central and financing the reconstruction of the post war world, essential. Since then Bretton Woods I (BWI) demised in 1971 and the World Bank shifted in the 1980s from project based financing to programme based financing, centring on economic policy and institutional reforms.

During the last forty years, most governments around the world have supported the long-run process of financial expansion that turned out to be characterized as the "financialization" of the capitalist economy (Chesnais, 1998). In this historical scenario, monopoly-finance capital became increasingly dependent on bubbles that, both in credit and capital markets, proved to be global sources of endogenous financial fragility. Financial and currency crises have also revealed that monetary and supervisory authorities do not cope with the complexity of the global, profit-seeking, innovative and speculative portfolios of investors and banks.

New financial instruments began to operate at least since 1995 on a risk elimination basis with no new international institutions on their side to overlook, supervise or regulate them. The operate by means of insurance operations such as credit default swaps, interest rate swaps and currency swaps, which make it possible for bankers to undertake greater risks, given the fact that each operation can have a derivative instrument attached that hedges risks. The derivative instrument essentially transfers property of the instrument from the creditor to the holder of such instrument in the event a credit, interest rate or exchange rate risk materializes. But in 2007 many economic agents stopped paying bad loans at the same time and soon derivatives were not able to cope. It was realized that derivatives serve to hedge individual operations but fail to hedge the system. Thus, it became public knowledge that first, there was no precise information regarding neither the size of the derivatives market nor who its holders were, and second, that the Bank for International Settlements in Basel registered the amount of $687 trillion which was twelve times higher than the world gross domestic product (GDP) and many times higher than the GDP of the United States and Great Britain which, being international financial centres, concentrate the bulk of these instruments.

All of a sudden, since 2007, the world was facing a US financial crisis led by its own investment banks, which had carried out "very innovative", hardly solid and, let alone, ethical operations, because the end customers did not know the risks involved in these new structured instruments, i.e. they did not know how their resources were being invested by pension or investment funds. It became evident that commercial banks were not performing very strong risk ratings before offering a credit since, being a transaction that was going to be sold almost immediately, there was no reason to do so. In this way, commercial banks did not have large heavy portfolios while a crisis of large proportions that ended up being spread to the rest of the world was unfolding.

Indeed, the shift from a reserve-based finance to hedging in the 1990s released resources from commercial banks that no longer had to save reserves for bad debts. At the same time, it relieved bankers from their responsibility in loans since banking became an activity in which commissions, rather than the profits obtained from each loan, are the main source of revenue for banks and bankers. The latter no longer had to take responsibility for loans.

The point of the international financial architecture is to bring its institutions, practices and instruments not only into international borrowing and lending but also into debt problems and solutions including the new elements at play which has made the system more complicated.

The need for a new international financial architecture

Dealing with international financial problems has required policy conditionality since the 1970s. The link between the new instruments and policy conditionality is unclear, not so between sovereign borrowing and new "rescue" lending. The problem is that in some cases the sovereign problem results from financial rescues derived from the use of new instruments that failed or simply from excess speculation that led to financial bubbles. Nevertheless, the requirement of policy conditionality is still at the base of new lending in times of stress. And it is related to depressing consumption and churning the economies from consumer led into the export led model, even in Europe where consumption reflects about 70% of European GDP.

Besides, there is a mixture of types of creditors and loans not reflected in any way in the existing debt resolution mechanisms leading to the need for new mechanisms, some of which are now under discussion at the UN General Assembly (i.e. Argentina's proposal for a sovereign debt restructuration mechanism). Looking back, the debt problems faced by practically all countries at some time in their history before 1944 had mechanisms of resolution. They were not linked to any conditionality and were related to the London and Paris bond markets through what was known as the Corporation of Foreign Bondholders (1872-1955) that served to bring together all creditors holding bonds, with the debtor at the time of negotiations. However, these mechanisms turned out to be inefficient after the creation of the concept of bilateral loans in World War I, the emergence of multilateral loans through BWI in the 1940s, the expansion of the commercial bank sovereign loans in the 1960s and the return of the bond market in the 1980s.

2. Beyond the 2007–2008 crisis

Considering this background, the existing international financial architecture that left over institutions from the Bretton Woods period proved to be useless to prevent or warn about the 2007-2008 crisis. The financial stage of the US financial crisis started in August 2007 and spread through the financial sector until by end-September 2008, the Lehman Brothers investment bank – one of the oldest firms in Wall Street – filed for bankruptcy. Almost one year had elapsed since the New York Stock Exchange had started to

Ideas towards a new international financial architecture?

plummet and almost one year and a half since the news had spread that bad quality mortgage loans had been sold and purchased in the financial market by investment banks that pooled them as bonds and then resold them in the market under the seductive name of structured investment vehicles. Then, it was made public that the bankers making these bad loans were collecting large bonuses for the total amount borrowed, notwithstanding the fact that they later sold them, and that investment bankers were also receiving large bonuses for re-selling these new instruments. And upon the question, does anybody look at the quality of loans when these are sold in the market? There came the timid answer that risk rating agencies are responsible for that. The latter are paid by loan sellers, i.e. the issuing banks, and therefore have a duty towards them, thus leaving a question mark on the impartiality of these agencies.

It then became evident that the market had been operating, at least since 1995, on a risk elimination basis, by means of insurance operations such as credit default swaps, interest rate swaps and currency swaps, which made it possible for bankers to undertake greater risks, given the fact that each operation could have a derivative instrument attached that hedged risks. The derivative instrument essentially transfers property of the instrument from the creditor to the holder of such instrument in the event a credit, interest rate or exchange rate risk materializes. But many economic agents stopped paying these bad loans at the same time and soon derivatives were not able to cope. It was realized that derivatives serve to hedge operations but fail to hedge the system. Thus, it became public knowledge that first, there was no precise information regarding neither the size of the derivatives market nor who its holders were, and second, that the Bank for International Settlements (BIS) in Basel registered the amount of $687 trillion which was twelve times higher than the world GDP and many times higher than the GDP of the United States and Great Britain which, being international financial centres, concentrate the bulk of these instruments.

As the crisis unfolded between 2007 and 2008, it became apparent that the international transfer of these risks was almost epidemiological. So long as European and Japanese investment banks had purchased these instruments, they were also infected by the bad quality of sub-prime loans. They had purchased them in the belief that they were Vehicle Performance

Enhancer (VPE) and it turned out that they were additional rubbish. Furthermore, evidence showed that there were no records as to who had purchased those instruments and little was known except from sensing that problems would arise with investment banks around the world affecting their profitability.

When the New York stock markets collapsed losing half their capitalisation value this spread around all stock markets almost simultaneously. At that time, investment banks noticed that they did not know what kind of investment portfolio they had and commercial banks then stopped lending them money for their current operations. This gave rise to a credit crunch that was spread to interbank operations in general, thus having a strong impact on international trade, which dropped by 30 per cent in the second semester of 2008 and led to a sharp economic contraction in the US and Europe but affecting all trading partners in 2009.

The financial deregulation first implemented by industrialized countries after 1971, following the end of the Bretton Woods agreement, is essential to understand the current crisis. This was accelerated after 1980 and the stage was set up for what is referred to by Toporowski (2008) as "financialization", thus moving financial intermediation to stock markets and away from the banking sector. On the one hand, this brought exchange rate volatility as a result of flexible exchange rates and, on the other hand, great interest rate volatility as a result of floating interest rates and commodity prices (Marichal, 2010). Investment banks have played a major role since they acted as if they were immune to credit risks once they sold their loans in the stock market, not considering the fact that liquidity may cause the financial system to collapse. The financialization impacted on productive firms in two complementary ways: on the one hand, interest payments shrank profits, therefore downsizing investment; and on the other hand, even productive firms found themselves keen on financial investing, since that offered yields few productive investments could meet (Duménil and Lévy, 2011). In both features, less investment ultimately reduced employment and wages of the very indebted population. That's how highly financierized enterprises added volatility into the productive structure, exceeding the effects of speculation from financial markets. When derivatives were presented, no one knew the real risk involved.

Ideas towards a new international financial architecture?

The market shift from reserve-based to hedging-based finance made totally incomprehensible the speculative bubbles that started to appear in 1996 and finally burst in 2007 and 2008. Between January 1996 and October 2007, the Dow Jones industrial average, for instance, rose from 5,117 to 14,165 points, nearly three times the market cap value while the US was registering very low average GDP growth rates. Greenspan referred to this as an "irrational exuberance". On the other hand, savings grew substantially in developing economies as a result of the exporting model while mature economies registered increased deficit. A change in the international financial system indeed took place when the US Treasury decided to borrow money from the rest of the world, thus becoming the world's biggest debtor in the early 21st century. This has turned the old US dollar into an unstable currency and has encouraged the search for new reserve currencies, in view of the fact that deficit economies have weak currencies and that the impact of having it as world currency makes prices unstable at global level (Ocampo, 2014).

Behind the October 2008 crisis there lie factors such as derivatives, excessive deregulation, lack of financial surveillance, privatization of banks, self-assessment criteria included in the Basel II Accord and speculation. The financial market segmentation and the fragmentation of production jointly generate instability and promote the proliferation of massive speculation. The "new" financial products made financial assets pledgeable, thus issuing more secured debt and building a house of cards that was twelve times bigger than the real economy by October 2008. It is clear that derivatives and the over-the-counter market are key factors in the current financial crisis. The financial system is based on complex products that go beyond derivatives and together are hard to regulate and understand. These result from the lack of a specific collective goal that goes beyond the profit increases at unsustainable rates, which in this context give rise to a new script in order to search for new or reformed institutions and instruments that adapt to and address social development and economic growth needs. During boom periods, to put it in Kregel (2009) words, other agents are dragged into the game, making it highly unstable until its unsustainability is indeed identified and the market contracts, thus forcing agents to leave the market and lose money obtained from speculation.

3. The outcomes of the global crisis and the current global financial scenario

The existing international financial architecture has proved useless to solve the crisis. Only when a new presidential grouping (G20) meeting was called in London in March 2009, the issues on how to coordinate countercyclical policies and inject resources into the economies were discussed. At the time, a United Nations high level Commission was named to propose reforms to the international financial architecture. The results of what became known as the Stiglitz Commission came to light in April 2010 but were shunned in light of the non-acceptance of the principle of global solutions for global problems, by some large UN member countries. Some European countries and the US still insist on national solutions meaning to say, the use of local regulatory agencies in the international financial field. The political and ideological struggle between austerity-defendant Germany and the money-easing US on behalf of how to cope with the crisis played a relevant role on this lack of coordination (Farrel and Quiggin, 2012).

At the same time the economic problems facing the major G7 economies force a rethink into what is to be considered a reserve currency. Moreover, the concept of the Special Drawing Rights (SDR) and its components must be reconsidered and so must its function as additional international liquidity and its workings. It is perhaps the time to rethink if BWI under a new voting structure could be of use or if under the circumstances it is time to explore new regional institutions with new regional SDRs or a global SDR with 192 member currencies assigned regionally according to world GDP and world trade weights.

In addition to the currency challenges, a growing global concern has enhanced changes in the regime of prudential banking regulation founded on the ratio of a bank's capital to its risk-adjusted assets (Altman and Saunders, 2001). In the aftermath of the crisis, American and European banks increased write-downs on loans while credit losses put pressure on profitability (BIS, 2012). Besides, the reduction of leverage and new strategies related to risks – credit, currency, interest, liquidity – have been adopted to avoid further pressure on capital requirements.

Ideas towards a new international financial architecture?

Looking back, Capital Accord Basel II shaped an institutional set up where banks' capital adequacy aimed to improve the efficiency of financial markets in the allocation of resources. However, Basel II "codes and patterns" – based on capital adjustment to risk – proved to enhance asset-liability management (ALM), or even, balance sheet management, to reduce legally capital requirements. At the pragmatic level, ALM involves new management practices and techniques to manage risks that arise due to imbalances in assets and liabilities (Saunders, 1994). At the macroeconomic level, Basel II supported the *status quo*, that is to say, the expansion of universal banks, private money and liquid capital markets under the World Trade Organization's defense of the financial services liberalization (Guttmann, 1998).

The lesson learned after the 2007-2008 global crisis is that bank capital requirements are not sufficient to foster financials' stability. As a matter of fact, the concern about the weaknesses in the regulatory framework has arisen. First, segmented supervisory authorities do not cope with the universal scope of banks. Second, new regulatory frameworks are generally proposed after banking innovations (Campilongo *et al.*, 2000).

In response to the crisis, the financial supervisory authorities have been looking for setting new rules within Capital Accord Basel III that could make the financial system more resilient accordingly regulatory changes. Among other issues, 1) banks will need to hold larger capital requirements against further potential losses, 2) financial products' approval would involve extensive disclosure requirements, 3) banks would be induced to negotiate standardized products, 4) liquidity requirements and leverage constraints will also be considered. Nevertheless, lower risk-weighted assets and higher capital ratios represent a challenge for increasing profitability (BIS, 2012).

Eight years have elapsed since the crisis emerged in 2007. The impact on the real sector as well as the financial sector is still being felt with no regrets from leading financial institutions or Central Bank's authorities. As a matter of fact, the idea of autonomous monetary management collapsed under the 2008 global financial crisis, as it became clear that the central banks' actions are not independent from private and public pressures. The social conflicts that emerged within the markets shifted to the political sphere and proved to challenge money as a public good – since livelihoods have been subordinated to the bailouts of the financial systems. Besides, the increasing growth of sovereign-debts has imposed the adoption of austerity programs which burden that mainly rely on workers and taxpayers.

Indeed, the tensions between the local and the global have been brought to the forefront. The leading financial problems are being dealt with at a national level. Since 2010, the U.S. Securities and Exchange Commission (SEC) has put large fines on Too Big to Fail (TBTF) banks' wrongdoings in the definition of the LIBOR (London Interbank Offered Rates), the commodity markets, the exchange markets and the fraudulent sale of collateralized dent obligations with credit risk approval from the large three American credit rating agencies, while European regulators have done some of the same. Simultaneously, vulture funds attacked Argentina and made evident a nonsense of having the last creditor obtain better payment terms than the first, breaking the usual understanding of the *pari passu* principle while a New York judge held the country hostage to his decisions.

Finally, all the G7 economies have come to reflect over 100% public debt on GDP ratios with only one approach to the solution to this problem: austerity. Fiscal measures regarding surplus, tax increases and expenditure cuts, turn out to be highlighted in the macroeconomic stabilization attempt. The consequence has been the sharp increase of the debt indexes and the depression of economic activity. Consequently, the current era of austerity certainly affects day-to-day life of citizens. Indeed, austerity programs subordinate the whole policy decision process that turns out to look for a realignment of relative prices (mainly real wages) and further structural reforms (mainly in the public sector and the labor market).

As a matter of fact, the labor market has become a key variable in macroeconomic policies based on austerity programs. Longer working hours, job destruction, turnover, outsourcing, workforce displacement, job reduction and loss of rights are part of the spectrum of management practices that emerge from the austerity guidelines. This scenario, characterized by precarious jobs, enhances the vulnerability of workers, mainly young people.

11

Ideas towards a new international financial architecture?

Following austerity programs, countries like Greece and Brazil, among others, must undergo painful adjustments over next years, mainly through deflationary policies that favor the reduction of the relative unit of labor costs. Wage cuts may prove to be devastating, not only socially and politically, but economically as well. Therefore, fiscal austerity could become a risky long-term strategy as a tighter fiscal policy would certainly result in even weaker economic growth rates and higher public debt/GDP rates.

As Keynes pointed out in his analysis of the monetary economy of production, there is a contradiction of money as a public good and a private good that overwhelms the central banks' actions in periods of crisis. As a result of the choice to adopt austerity programs and support the investors' credibility agenda, many governments have disappointed their citizens on behalf of less spending on social policies, low growth and increasing social inequalities. The current policies carried out to save financial firms have actually exacerbated the very roots of the crisis, by sustaining the impoverishment of the working force, inducing them to start a new indebtedness upraise once again. The strong inequality resulting of this process has necessarily negative impacts on growth, as recent discussions on inequality have shown, even if they do not enhance on the crisis debate (Picketty, 2014). Everything points out the need for a serious revision of the role of the financial sector in an increasingly unequal society.

4. The book's chapters

The current global financial scenario and what appears as the new international financial architecture poses many questions that need to be addressed:

1) How did the crisis affect the structure of the financial sector in the different regions of the world, what provisions were implemented to manage the impact?
2) Has the financial crisis impacted the financial flows to productive sectors in all regions?

3) Have the regional financial architectures been reformed after the crisis? Do they have any margin of autonomy or are they totally dependent of foreign banks and funds?
4) Can the vulture funds be considered an element of the so called new financial structure to prevent crises or are they one more cause of instability?
5) Are the IMF and the available existing international reserves sufficient to prevent another major crisis?
6) Can the IMF be reformed given European and US reluctance to do so?
7) How should a debt work out mechanism function in the new global scenario?
8) Are there lessons from the Latin American debt crisis of the 1980's valuable for current crisis, such as the European?
9) Are austerity programs the appropriate policy measures to prevent financial crisis such as the 2008 one?

In order to give answers to these issues, Part I deals with the great crisis and current policy challenges. In Chapter 2, Carlos Marichal reviews a set of enquiries and reports that were realized and published as a result of the major financial crises since 1929 till 2011. In accordance to the author, these documents generally address the issue of the causes of collapse of bank and capital markets but also shed light on regulations proposed at different points in time to improve financial stability. The chapter begins with reference to official investigations on the crisis of 1929 – and the subsequent bank crises in the Great Depression – and deeps a comparison with the outcomes of the 2008 Global Financial Collapse that have produced the greatest outpouring of these types of investigations and publications. In his opinion, one important avenue for a historical understanding of the great financial debacles of the past consists in a careful evaluation of official literature and documents that can complement the theoretical approaches of economists in search of explanations for these events.

Chapter 3, by Constantine Passaris highlights the need for a realignment in global governance in order to conform to the realities of the new global economy of the 21st century. In his perspective, two milestones sustains his proposal; the emergence of a new global economy and the outcomes of the 2008 financial crisis, which has precipitated the need for a new vision and a new direction for financial governance. Indeed, the institutional architecture of economic governance requires modernization as well as transitional and transformational change since it proved ineffective and inadequate for the new economy. The aim of Passaris is to explore the future architectural governance landscape for the financial industry and the scope and substance of regulatory initiatives and mechanisms that should be designed in order to avert a future financial crisis.

In Chapter 4, Gerson Lima deeps the analysis of current global policy challenges. The author suggests the need for a new theoretical approach to public debt in order to build the foundations of a critique towards austerity programs as they do not lead the public debt to the desired stability. In accordance to the author, mainstream economics treat public debt as if was the same as private companies or consumers, without considering proper macroeconomic effects. Public debt dynamics must consider impacts on expanding aggregate demand and therefore tax revenue: it is mistaken to assume that government can produce a primary surplus to stabilize the public debt ratio to GDP at any point of time. An experiment applied to the United States in the period 1960-2007 does not allow for the rejection of these hypotheses.

Part II presents contributions that aim to rethink the international financial architecture -considering that it is made up of institutions, practices and instruments. Considering recent events and changes in the global economy, authors of this part make an imaginative theoretical effort to make innovative proposals to this new possible financial architecture.

Chapter 5 presents the contribution of Tim Knight, who discusses a new approach to policy making in the current global scenario. The author highlights the need to reconsider several macro-economic principles in order to use a re-engineering approach to economics. His attempt is focused in the definition of a more coherent paradigm for the concepts currently "enclosed" by that expression "money". Accordingly Knight, there are two radically-distinct concepts currently 'enclosed' by the single expression "money" – wealth and currency – with different effects on policy options. In revisiting global economic features, he proposes to restrict currency to its plain use of unite of measure, and therefore nothing but an administrative tool. Its effect in real value creation should be eliminated, since owed-wealth is nothing but a trick hiding the liability side of the balance sheet. In regulating more heavily this borrowed-lent assets creation, speculative bubbles could be avoided.

In Chapter 6, Ellen Brown and Uli Kortsch discuss new perspectives in funding infrastructure projects in the context of the current financial international architecture. In their opinion, this is an urgent policy issue since, over the next five years, the US budget for infrastructure faces a shortfall of $1.6 trillion. Current funding mechanisms in the US, such as the "Highway Trust Fund", are no longer sustainable or are nearly bankrupt. Meanwhile, national austerity has come back to the policy agenda with a general perception that the deficit must be reduced. Authors propose that the US should adopt an infrastructure funding mechanism that is based on a new round of Quantitative Easing. To analyse the challenges, Brown and Kortsch discussed three options in funding infrastructure projects: i) Funding through the Federal Reserve (similar to existing QE rounds); ii) Funding through the Treasury through the printing of US Notes (government-issued money); and iii) Funding through the Treasury by the minting of special coins. The authors show that this approach has historical precedents and a current legislative enablement, and that it will not lead to hyper-inflation.

Professor Paul Davidson analyses the possible national-level solutions to world recession, by promoting exports, which could lead to impoverish-the-neighbour struggle among huge economies (such as the US and China). He states that mainstream economics have no solution whatsoever to this possible outcome, since they stand as an assumption that the world works at full employment all the time. Davidson, from a post-Keynesian approach, proposes the development of an international financial architecture system that could deal with persistent trade imbalances and any international financial crisis in Chapter 7. The author states that this system does not require the establishment of a supranational central bank of the world as Keynes suggested in his "Keynes Plan" at Bretton Woods. Instead, he argues that this new international payment system does not require any nation to surrender the control of either its domestic banking system or the operation of its domestic monetary and fiscal policies to a supranational authority. In accordance to Davidson, the new international institution to be set up under this plan could be labelled the International Monetary Clearing Union (IMCU).

Finally, in Chapter 8, Oscar Ugarteche shows the limitations of the current financial architecture and the emergence of what appears to be a new financial architecture with regional financial frameworks. The author starts by making a brief history of the existing international financial system and its role in international financial regulations. His aim is to show the lack of proper global organisations by highlighting the changes in the governance issues and the massive shift in world economic power. Ugarteche analyses the problem of a country based reserve currency and revises the existing experiences to finally suggest ways forward to strengthen the international financial regulations through regional mechanisms.

Each author presents, in various ways, issues to be considered in order to improve actual globalization. They all somehow consider that the BW remaining institutions lack of reality in their working assumptions, and have – by action or omission- contribute to the 2008 crisis. Taking into account their contributions, the need for a new international financial architecture is called into question.

References

Altman, E. and Saunders, A. (2001) "An analysis and critique of the BIS proposal on capital adequacy and ratings", *Journal of Banking and Finance*, 25 (1), pp. 25–46.

Bank of International Settlement (BIS). (2012) "Post-crisis evolution of the banking sector", In: BIS 82nd Annual Report, Basel: BIS. Available at http://www.bis.org/publ/arpdf/ar2012e6.pdf (accessed on June 25th, 2013).

Campilongo, C. *et al.* (ed.) (2002) *Concorrência e Regulação no Sistema Financeiro*, São Paulo: Max Limonad Editora.

Chesnais, F. (1998) Mundialização financeira e vulnerabilidade sistêmica. In: Chesnais, F. (ed.). *A mundialização financeira- gênese, custos e riscos*. São Paulo: Xamã.

Dermine, J. and Bissada, Y. (2007) *Asset and Liability Management: The Banker's Guide to Value Creation and Risk Control*, London and New York:

Financial Times and Prentice Hall.

Duménil, G. and Lévy, D. (2011) *The crisis of neoliberalism,* Harvard University Press.

Farrell, H. and Quiggin, J. (2012) "Consensus, Dissensus and Economic Ideas: The Rise and Fall of Keynesianism During the Economic Crisis", Draft paper. Available at: www.henryfarrell.net/Keynes.pdf

Fligstein, N. (2001) *The architecture of markets.* New Jersey: Princeton University Press.

Foster, J. B. (2009) "A Failed System: The World Crisis of Capitalist Globalization and its Impact on China", *Monthly Review,* 60(10) (March 2009), pp. 1-23.

Guttmann, R. (1998) As mutações do capital financeiro. In: Chesnais, F. (ed.) *A mundialização financeira- gênese, custos e riscos.* São Paulo: Xamã.

Kregel, J. (2009) *"Managing the Impact of Volatility in International Capital Markets in an Uncertain World",* Levy Economics Institute Working Paper No. 558 Available at SSRN: http://ssrn.com/abstract=1394465 or http://dx.doi.org/10.2139/ssrn.1394465.

Marichal, C. (2010) *Nueva historia de las grandes crisis financieras: una perspectiva global 1873-2008,* Buenos Aires: Debate.

Ocampo, J. A. (2014) "Reforming the Global Reserve System", FES, Policy Analysis brief, at http://library.fes.de/pdf-files/iez/global/10900.pdf

Picketty, T. (2014) *Capital in the Twenty-First Century,* Cambridge, MA: Belknap Press.

Saunders, A. (1994), *Financial Institutions Management: A Modern Perspective*, Burr Ridge, IL: Richard D. Irwin.

Saunders, A. and Cornett, M. (2002) *Financial Institutions Management: A Risk Management Approach,* Columbus: McGraw-Hill College.

The *Economist.* (2011) "The great unknown. Can policymakers fill the gaps in their knowledge about the financial system?", Jan 13th, print edition

Toporowski, J. (2008) "The Economics and Culture of Financialisation", School of Oriental and African Studies, University of London, Department Of Economics Working Papers No.158, April.

Ideas towards a new international financial architecture?

PART I
The great crisis and policy challenges

Ideas towards a new international financial architecture?

CHAPTER 2
The great global financial crises: official investigations, past and present, 1929-2011

Carlos Marichal

1. Introduction

The economic meltdown provoked by the global financial crisis which exploded in 2008-2009 is reflected by big numbers: the loss of almost two trillion dollars by the banking system, the loss of another various trillions in the mortgage and stock markets, and the rise in unemployment by between 50 and 70 million on a worldwide scale between 2008 and 2011. The huge costs these disasters provoked have been discussed at length in the press, in thousands of working papers and in many international investigations, among which one of the first was the UN-sponsored *Stiglitz Commission* on financial reforms that published detailed reports from May and June 2009.[1] In particular, the Commission's emphasis was on understanding how the financial collapse crisis, which originated in the *North*, affected not only the economies of the North Atlantic but also the countries of the *South*.

The controversy is strong and will continue to be so in the future. The reason is that major crises destroy traditional structures and practices in politics and the economic activity and force people to think about new ways of managing financial markets and institutions, as well as new methods of public regulation. It is positive that an intense and wide-ranging debate about these decisive subjects for the future of humanity has emerged. But at the same time, it is clear that there is great resistance to change by various influential corporate lobbies, the more conservative mass media, and the power structures that cling to monopolist or bureaucratic practices and are not

---

[1] The documents of the Stiglitz Commission as well as the declarations of the delegates of dozens of nations who participated in the discussions can be accessed on the Commission's web page: http://www.un.org/ga/econcrisissummit/

Ideas towards a new international financial architecture?

interested in profound reforms or a worldwide democratic discussion on the future management of finances and politics.

A fundamental challenge of this debate consists in understanding why the most important financial markets of the world collapsed and why the principal financial companies and regulatory agencies failed so clearly in the US, where what has been described as a perfect and gigantic storm in September and October 2008 had its epicenter. Many academic studies analyzing the causes have already been published. This challenge consists in thinking about the suggestions for implementing reforms to the banking, monetary, and financial system, nationally as well as internationally.

But let us being by asking: which are the best and the most important sources for understanding the outbreak as well as the immediate causes and consequences of a major financial crisis? They come in various shapes and formats, including empirical, theoretical, legal and political texts and documents. Financial and economic historians have been studying these kinds of texts for decades because it is necessary to combine a large variety of primary and secondary sources in order to fully grasp the complexity of a great financial collapse. It is worthwhile noting that this literature has broadened remarkably in our own day as a result of the most recent crash of 2008, which is now known both familiarly and among experts as the Global Financial Crisis.[2] Indeed, the number of books, documents, articles and working papers on this recent financial cataclysm is not only expanding exponentially but also has become much more accessible worldwide due to the internet, and has even spawned a new kind of electronic publication, the "financial blog", which also attracts great interest. Nonetheless, it should also be recognized that there are important historical antecedents dealing with prior crises that consist not only of books and articles, but also official documents and enquiries that can be identified and studied for many financial crises over the last century and a half.

---

[2] It is interesting to note that in the World Finance Conference held this year in Cyprus, the expression has become a standard reference among the leading financial experts and in paper after paper, the acronym for the 'global financial crisis' used is GFC.

The great global financial crises

Perhaps the first sources of study which historians habitually utilize to reconstruct financial crises of the past are newspapers, particularly the specialized financial press that publish articles providing a first-hand description of the daily events that occur on the outbreak of a major event of this nature. A second source are the more analytical articles that appear somewhat later in economic newsletters or journals (and today in web sites of *working papers* and *blogs*, as well), written in most cases by economists, financial experts or well informed financial journalists. A third source consists of reports circulated by banking institutions, particularly central banks and multilateral financial entities, gradually increasing in volume and regularity over the twentieth century.

But apart from the sources aforementioned, there were (and are) other complementary documents that may have more of a political origin, based on official efforts to "uncover" the causes of financial collapse of banks or stock markets and the key figures considered responsible for the debacle. Whether this objective is fulfilled or if there is actually a "cover-up" depends on a great variety of factors. In this case, historians need to focus on a fourth important repository of information which are the official enquiries realized generally by parliamentary committees or commissions soon published after the crisis that provide much information of interest, including the testimony of a large number of key financial actors. A complementary source – although generally less consulted except by legal experts- are the judicial records of court cases related to embezzlements or frauds by banks or financial agents. Finally, it may be suggested that major pieces of legislation ratified in the wake a result of a financial collapse should also be studied in the light of the important materials contained in parliamentary debates or in the laws themselves and in subsidiary documents.

Our essay focuses on the importance and utility of these kinds of documents, but we focus, in particular, on the official enquiries on the causes of financial crises, the majority of them being the product of legislative commissions of different governments but also in more recent times investigative committees of central banks and multilateral institutions. We begin by looking into the official investigations spurred by the crash of 1929 and the subsequent Great Depression, and then turn to the more numerous official investigations that were generated by the crash of 2008 and the subsequent Great Recession.

2. The crash of 1929: the U.S. Senate investigation of foreign loan defaults (1931) and the Banking and Currency Commission (1933)

As in previous crises, the enormous losses suffered by investors as a result of the stock market crash of 1929 soon also generated considerable pressure to find culprits or scapegoats and to do so through official enquiries. Since it was well known that playing the stock market by investing in private companies or corporations had many risks, attention was initially channeled by the United States press and by bondholder organizations against foreign governments which had issued a large number of dollar bonds and were considered responsible for stoking speculation in New York. Hence, it was not surprising that following the first Latin American defaults in 1931 – including Bolivia, Chile and Peru – many bitter and distressed bondholders in the United States began to organize a campaign to demand a congressional investigation of banker malpractice in the issue and sale of the bonds. The bondholders believed, with some reason, that the New York investment houses engaged in the international loan business had not adequately informed them of the political and economic risks involved in acquiring Latin American government securities.

A number of powerful Washington D.C. politicians agreed with them, and in December, 1931 the U.S. Senate opened hearings on the subject[3]. During the space of four months an impressive roster of New York bankers was publicly cross-examined. The financiers called to Washington included the patrician Thomas Lamont of the House of Morgan, the flamboyant Charles Mitchell, president of the National City Bank, Clarence Dillon of the blue-ribbon firm of Dillon, Read, Otto Kahn of Kuhn, Loeb & Company, James

---

[3] United States. Congress. Senate. Committee on Finance, Sale of Foreign Bonds or Securities in the United States. Hearings before the Committee on Finance, United States Senate, Seventy-second Congress, first session, pursuant to S. Res. 19 a resolution authorizing the Finance committee of the Senate to investigate the sale, flotation, and allocation by banks, banking institutions, corporations, or individuals of foreign bonds or securities in the United States. Accessed Aug 1, 2013 from FRASER, http://fraser.stlouisfed.org/publication/?pid=398

Speyer of Speyer & Company, and many others. Not surprisingly, these individuals denied any wrongdoing and affirmed that by selling the bonds they had simply been pursuing the expansion of United States trade. As Charles Mitchell affirmed: "That the banking interests of this country have floated foreign loans in America is something which should have the praise rather than the criticism of any body of men".[4]

Some of the senators did not appear to be convinced by this argument. Senator Tom Connally replied to Mitchell: "With reference to foreign bonds, you are like the saloon keeper who never drank. His whiskey was made to sell, not to drink".[5] Connally's intention was to suggest that the financiers enticed the investors to buy the bonds without informing them of the possible dangers which such transactions might entail. The bankers, of course, insisted that they were innocent. On the other hand, a number of lower-level employees of the banks divulged much information which revealed the degree of cupidity and amorality of both North American bankers and Latin American politicians. The arguments put forth were similar, in many respects, to those presented before the British Parliament in its investigation of Latin American loans held in 1875. The bankers were judged to be, on the whole, unscrupulous businessmen who did not have the interests of the average investor at heart. It was due largely to their duplicity that the menace of a Latin American financial crisis had not been foreseen.

Despite the withering criticisms vented in the U.S. Senate and in the North American press against the bankers and politicians who had inflated the Latin American loan bubble, the fact was that defaults were not caused so much by speculation as by the depression itself. All Latin American economies and governments depended heavily on the trade cycle and when exports and dropped dramatically in 1930 and 1931, so did imports and as result customs revenue which was the backbone of government income. There was hence no way of maintaining debt service payments. Nonetheless, the whole of issue of Latin American defaults was quite quickly forgotten amidst the calamities generated by the banking crises in the United States and Europe in 1931 and 1932.

---

[4] Senate Committee on Finance, p. 64. Also see Marichal (1989, p.206), which includes the Mitchell quotation.
[5] Senate Committee on Finance, p. 81.

Ideas towards a new international financial architecture?

In 1932 the World Economic Conference was held at Lausanne, Switzerland, with the aim of helping to save the European banks and in particular the largest German financial institutions. Among the most important measures adopted was an agreement by the major powers to forgive most of the old war debts of Germany known as reparations which had been ratified since the Versailles Treaty of 1919: these were slashed from 31,000 million dollars to less than 1 thousand million dollars. The contrast between the generosity extended to Germany and the critiques of the much smaller Latin American debt defaults was striking. Soon however, public opinion in the United States turned against the domestic bankers as a result of thousands of domestic bank failures, and in early 1933 the new administration headed by Franklin Delano Roosevelt took a set of active measures to remedy the situation, declaring a bank holiday that lasted from March to June. Subsequently there followed a variety of investigations which have been of great use for historians seeking to explain the crash of 1929 and the Great Depression.

Inside the United States popular pressure built up in 1932 to investigate the role of bankers in the manipulation of the stock exchange, which was generally considered a cause of the crash of 1929.[6] The hearings organized in 1933 by the United States Senate's Banking and Currency Commission were headed by Ferdinand Pecora, who personally did much of the interrogations of leading financiers, including Richard Whitney, president of the New York Stock Exchange, George Whitney and Thomas Lamont of J.P. Morgan, Albert Wiggin, head of the Chase National Bank and Charles Mitchell of the National City Bank. The transcripts and records included 12,000 printed pages. The work of the committee uncovered the concentrated nature of the top sector of the New York financial community and brought to light unscrupulous practices. The hearings prepared the ground for the ratification of the Banking Act of 1933 (known as the Glass Steagall Act, separating commercial from investment banking), the Securities Act of 1933 and the Securities Exchange Act of 1934.

---

[6] Parts 1-6, April 11-May 25, 1933, were digitized by Internet Archive: United States. Congress. Senate. Committee on Banking and Currency, Stock Exchange Practices. Hearings before the Committee on Banking and Currency Pursuant to S.Res. 84 and S.Res. 56 and S.Res. 97. Accessed Aug 1, 2013 from FRASER, http:fraser.stlouisfed.org/publication/?pid=87

As may be observed, the Senate investigation was not particularly important as opening a way to prosecute the leading New York bankers who escaped scott free from litigation or jail. On the other hand, the hearings did generate a strong current of public opinion favourable to the ratification of major pieces of reform legislation, which in fact established the regulatory and institutional banking and financial architecture that played a most important role the United States from the mid-1930s almost to the end of the twentieth century.

In the case of Great Britain in the early 1930s, Parliament did not open public hearings on the crisis, but the government did order that an official investigation by leading politicians and economists produce an official report on the origins of the stock market crash of 1929 and on the subsequent economic depression in the United Kingdom. The body in charge of this task was that of the Macmillan Committee also known as the *Committee on Finance and Industry* which published a much cited study. Among the most informed members of this investigative body were Ernest Bevin, John Maynard Keynes and Reginald McKenna. The final report was mainly the work of Keynes and made important recommendations, including reforms to the Bank of England. According to an article published on July 17, 1931 in the newspaper *The Spectator*:

> "Lord Macmillan's Committee published its Report on Monday. All of the fourteen members, except Lord Bradbury, take a favourable view of Great Britain's prospects. They hold that monetary policy should seek to raise international prices, at present dangerously low, and should try to maintain the higher level, once attained. The creditor countries must be more willing to lend to, and buy from, the debtor countries – a counsel of perfection, perhaps, for our cautious Protectionist friends in France and the United States. The Committee recommends drastic changes in the Bank of England. Its Banking and Issue Departments should no longer be distinct. It should be empowered to increase its note issue to £400,000,000 and to reduce its minimum gold reserve to £70,000,000 – less than half the present amount – so that more gold might be available for the needs of

poorer countries. Our banks, the Committee holds, should co-operate more fully with our industries, though the suspension of the Darmstedter Bank in Berlin, partly at least because it was heavily involved in the failure of a large woollen company, comes as a simultaneous reminder of the grave risks of the German banking policy thus commended. Lord Bradbury in a dissenting minute bluntly says that no manipulation of currency or credit would cure our diseases – excessive taxation, heavy costs and the general insistence on a higher standard of living than we can afford".[7]

Another important source of official reports on the financial crisis and its consequences is the collection of League of Nations publications of the 1930s, which were quite numerous and detailed. In his classic work titled *Golden Fetters*, Barry Eichengreen registered 12 books or reports prepared by League of Nations' experts dealing with the causes and impacts of the Great Depression (Eichengreen, 1995). The first and perhaps best known study was that drafted by a League of Nations bureau, the World Peace Foundation, and was titled *The Course and Phases of the World Economic Depression: Report Presented to the Assembly of the League of Nations*, Geneva, 1931.

In other countries there were also official investigations, though some of these took time: for example, in Australia there was a major enquiry (a Royal Commission) into banking in 1936–37, as a consequence of the Great Depression, and on the behaviour of the central bank (The Commonwealth Bank) in these years.[8]

---

[7] The quote is taken from the following source accessed August 4, 2013 http://archive.spectator.co.uk/article/18th-july-1931/2/the-macmillan-report-lord-macmillans-committee-on-

[8] Economic historian Alex Millmow (2010), argues that the Royal Commission stimulated the adoption of Keynsian policies by the Australian government and by the Commonwealth Bank Board.

The great global financial crises

3. Official enquiries on the world financial crisis of 2008

While official enquiries have been characteristic after numerous financial crises of the past, never have there been so many as those carried out and published since the financial collapse of 2008. Their findings are significant to understand some of the roots of this global financial collapse but they also have played a role in stimulating new regulations, both national and international. It is to the subject of these, recent official investigations to which we now turn.

The impacts and consequences of the financial and economic crisis that erupted in the United States in September 2008 were so acute and widespread that immediately comparisons began to be made by analysts with the Great Depression of 1929-1933.[9] The breakdown of banks, stock exchanges, and real estate markets, particularly in the United States and much of Europe, caused a severe credit crunch and affected most countries and companies worldwide. It led to a drastic drop in employment which, it is calculated, affected as many as 50 million persons who lost their jobs worldwide in 2009. The collapse also caused a catastrophic decline in stock markets as well as investment in nearly all nations as well as a sudden fall in profit rates and a drastic decline in worldwide production and trade. The magnitude of the crisis was certainly enormous although it was not as long lasting and devastating as the Great Depression, which probably explains why it has frequently been baptized the *Great Recession*.

The financial collapse of 2008 and 2009 came as a major surprise and raised a great number of questions about causes of the collapse, especially because it broke out in the largest and most dynamic financial markets in the world, those of New York and London. A number of economists had foreseen the possibility of new crises in the developing countries, but only few of them had anticipated breakdowns in the economically more advanced nations. The great question then is why did New York and London experience runs and losses of this magnitude? Were there common factors that caused the disarrays in these *capitals of capital?*[10] There certainly

---

[9] The most frequently quoted statistical comparisons can be seen in the graphs Eichengreen 1995 and O'Rourke (2009-2010).
[10] We use the expression from the excellent book by Cassis (2006).

existed particularly close financial links between them, but the size of the collapse and its rapid spill-over to other financial markets of the world indicate a broader range of causes.

It is quite evident that the financial revolution of our age is closely related both to economic globalization and to the new information technologies, which connect different markets by means of a multitude of high-speed transactions. The intensified relationships between banks and other financial service providers in different nations inevitably multiply the risks in case of a crisis in the major markets. But now we also know that the dangers had been increasing considerably since the 1990s due to the introduction of a series of financial innovations, such as the famous derivatives and diverse structured investment products, the object of which consisted in diversifying the risks of investments in bundles of mortgages, primary commodities and an endless number of additional securities. A set of major problems and risks was caused by the fact that the new securities were traded in a vast and new banking market that was barely supervised: some authors have defined it as an *alternative* banking system and others, more negatively, as *shadow banking.*[11] As a result, nobody really knew the real value of these transactions or the nature of the credit chain, in spite of the huge volume. It was a gigantic *black hole,* but even though its dangers were signaled by a fair number of analysts, in practice, it was not regulated by the key central banks, particularly by the Federal Reserve Bank of United States or by the Bank of England, which were at the center of the deepest and most important financial markets in the world.

From the end of the twentieth century the potential danger of a *systemic* collapse augmented, but very few could foresee the possible string of faults in the markets. It was clear, nonetheless, that in the case of an explosion, all main financial centers would be affected on account of the intense globalization process and notable concentration of capitals. One way to describe the highly complex entanglement between the contemporary financial centers is to visualize them like a small galaxy of suns and planet as was illustrated in a magnificent paper and speech of May 2009 by Andrew Haldane (2009), executive director of Financial Stability of the Bank

[11] One of the best and deepest analyses on banks and the crisis as a whole is the work by Dehesa (2010).

of England: his graphs demonstrated that, in 2005, the United States and Great Britain were the two most important financial markets in the world; they were connected by means of many exchanges with all the other large and mid-sized financial markets.

The solar system metaphor helps to explain the dynamics of the contemporary world of finance. As was demonstrated in the 1990s, if a one or more secondary markets collapsed (particularly in the developing countries), a systemic crisis was not probable: the rescue mechanisms put in place after the Asian financial crises of 1997, for example, avoided a world financial panic. On the other hand, if the financial markets at center were to implode, all markets would be affected. In September 2008, the breakdown of Lehman Brothers, at the very center of the major financial center in the world, had devastating effects and caused panic waves among thousands of financial servers that were linked to this investment bank, which then led to the freeze-up of short-term credit markets. The banking collapse which ensued in New York and London riveted all other financial centers and provoked a completely unexpected series of panics on practically all stock exchanges and banks. The rumors of possible bankruptcies of a number of the largest United States investment banks and several commercial banks as well as -and equally important- of major British commercial banks were followed in September and October by news of the collapse of several important banks in Germany, Belgium, the Netherlands, France, as well as virtually the entire banking systems of Ireland and Iceland. It was not clear at the time if the meltdown of financial markets could be reversed, and it was feared that there would be very serious consequences, as this would likely lead to the paralysis of the operations in trade and production in many countries.

The crisis dramatically demonstrated that financial markets everywhere were much more fragile than it had been assumed and that there were gigantic flaws in the anticipation of risks. It is true that other organizations like the Bank for International Settlements (BIS) and the national financial supervisors and regulators had been working on the introduction of new regulations so as to reduce the risks in the banking systems and other financial markets. The Basel II agreements to upgrade bank capital as well as the improvements in banking supervision policies in several EU countries indicated that some progress had been made (Tarullo, 2008). However, the magnitude of the 2008 collapse and, especially, the economic and social consequences – including the numerous bankruptcies of companies and banks, the sharp increase in worldwide unemployment, and the huge losses of wealth – suggested that the diagnostic capacity of the problems had been entirely deficient among central banks, private banks and financial experts. Nonetheless, a review of the official investigations, which have been published since the crisis, suggests that actually there was a clear awareness of the enormous changes in the financial markets but little willpower to actually confront the rapidly increasing risks of a possible explosion.

After the financial downturn of 2007 and the crash of September 2008, came the rescues put in place by treasuries and central banks around the world. Once the depth of the financial and economic losses began to be grasped, there were political pressures to put in place a variety of efforts to carry out and publish *official enquiries* on the causes of the collapse. The first nation to begin such studies was Great Britain, led by the Bank of England, when its director, Mervyn King – with the support of the Treasury- instructed Lord Adair Turner, head of the Financial Services Authority in late October 2008 to produce a report that was published in March 2009 (Financial Services Authority United Kingdom, 2009, pp.16-22).[12] The text identifies the primordial causes of the financial crisis as being generated by 1) severe global macroeconomic imbalances, in which countries like China and Japan had huge commercial and financial surpluses, while other countries like the United States and the United Kingdom had massive deficits; 2) the increase of risky operations by the commercial banks, which had high leverage in their activities; 3) the growth in the use and complexity of securitized credits; 4) inadequate reserve capital held by major banks; 5) excessive trust by the financial community on mathematical models and in the credit rating agencies. The extraordinary statistical graphs that accompany the report indicate that there was detailed awareness in central banks like that of the Bank of England of the enormous changes that had been taking place in contemporary financial markets since the 1990s. But there was also a singularly clear recognition that the mathematical models had led the

---

[12] This document can be consulted in paper and on the internet.

banking experts to believe they had most things under control. The following extracts from the report are indicative:

"The evolution of the securitised credit model was accompanied by a remarkable growth in the relative size of wholesale financial services within the overall economy, with activities internal to the banking system growing far more rapidly than end services to the real economy....

From about 2003 onwards, there were significant increases in the measured on-balance sheet leverage of many commercial and investment banks, driven in some cases by dramatic increases in gross assets and derivative positions...

The increasing scale and complexity of the securitised credit market was obvious to individual participants, to regulators and to academic observers. But the predominant assumption was that increased complexity had been matched by the evolution of mathematically sophisticated and effective techniques for measuring and managing the resulting risks" (Financial Services Authority United Kingdom, 2009, pp.16-22).[13]

The Turner report, however, did not limit itself to analysis of global financial trends as well as innovations in the financial markets in the United States. It also focused on the specifics of developments in Great Britain including the growing current account deficit from 2000 onwards, the great housing mortgage boom in that country, the enormous increase in securitised loans in the mortgage lending business. Furthermore it was remarkably candid with regard to a critique of theoretical propositions and assumptions underlying the supervision and regulation of financial markets in the years preceding the collapse. The following quote is illustrative:

---

[13] We have put the italics on the last part of the citation.

Ideas towards a new international financial architecture?

"At the core of these assumptions has been the theory of efficient and rational markets. Five propositions with implications for regulatory approach have followed:

(i) Market prices are good indicators of rationally evaluated economic value.

(ii) The development of securitised credit, since based on the creation of new and more liquid markets, has improved both allocative efficiency and financial stability.

(iii) The risk characteristics of financial markets can be inferred from mathematical analysis, delivering robust quantitative measures of trading risk.

(iv) Market discipline can be used as an effective tool in constraining harmful risk taking.

(v) Financial innovation can be assumed to be beneficial since market competition would winnow out any innovations which did not deliver value added.

Each of these assumptions is now subject to extensive challenge on both theoretical and empirical grounds, with potential implications for the appropriate design of regulation and for the role of regulatory authorities" (Financial Services Authority United Kingdom, 2009, p. 39).[14]

While covering some of the macro and micro economic causes of the crisis, the Turner report actually directed most of its attention to propose solutions with regards to future financial regulation. The key recommendations in order to avoid future problems included the recommendations to implement more stringent reserve capital requirements, establishing a ceiling for the financial institutions leverage ratio, the need to set up in a counter cyclical regime, the application of financial stress tests to verify the liquidity level of the financial institutions. Other recommendations; the creation of a deposit insurance scheme that would protect all the depositors in case of bankruptcy of their financial institutions; increased supervision of credit rating agencies,

---

[14] We have put the italics on the last part of the citation.

in order to limit their potential conflicts of interest; and the creation of a compensation system in the derivatives trade market that could protect standardized contracts. The Turner report also focused on the need for increased regulatory powers by the *Financial Services Authority*, giving it the capacity to oversee the shadow and offshore banking system activities, as well as redefinition of its tasks to give priority to the overseeing of the biggest banking institutions, of systemic importance, and to put emphasis not only in the process but also on their the business models, strategies, risks and results. Lord Turner's report also stressed the co responsibility of the *Financial Services Authority* and the *Bank of England* in the macro prudential analysis and recommended further international cooperation in order to increase the flux of information between the most important national and international agencies in charge of financial regulation or supervision. In this regard, the report suggested that it could be wise to set up an independent European institution with the capacity to supervise the financial activities in the zone.

Almost simultaneously, the British Parliament initiated a series of investigations, among which several should be cited, such as that carried out by the *Committee of Public Accounts* of the House of Commons regarding the trajectory and dynamics of the banking system of Great Britain before and during the crisis (House of Common, Committee of Public Accounts, 2010)[15]. The interviews with bankers in the hearings are of enormous interest for historians interested in understanding the views of key actors in the financial world during the boom and bust. Similarly, other important documents which included research on the crisis were prepared by a variety of government offices, including for example the document by H.M Treasury titled *Reforming Financial Markets* and presented to Parliament in July 2009 which explains the views of officials regarding the crisis and outlining a large number of new financial regulations considered appropriate for discussion and subsequent legislative reform. A subsequent report with more emphasis on the need to discuss future reforms to the banking system was promoted by the Chancellor of the Exchequer in June 2010 on announcing the creation

---

[15] Twelfth Report of Session 2009–10, published on 9 February 2010, together with formal minutes, oral and written evidence. This document can be consulted in paper and on the internet.

of the Independent Commission on Banking, chaired by Sir John Vickers, which produced its report on November, 2011.

In the United States, government officials as well as members of Congress also moved from late 2008 onwards to investigate and explain the crisis by promoting a large variety of research and legislative reports. For instance, the Department of the Treasury conducted studies into the financial collapse, including the important White Paper, titled *Financial Regulatory Reform*, which was published on June 17, 2009.[16] Many other major pieces of documentation can be found in the website and publication list of the Department of Treasury as well as of other federal government offices. Equally notable was the enormous increase in number and transparency of publications by the Federal Reserve Bank: all speeches by the Chairman, Ben Bernanke, have been published on the internet quickly, as well as speeches and reports by other top level functionaries of the same institution. And the number of working papers on the financial crash has literally exploded, providing a huge amount of published analysis of great interest for researchers.

Perhaps the most extensive research on the origins of the world financial crisis, however, can be found in two major, official enquiries, one conducted under the auspices of the Congress and the second more specifically by the United States Senate. In the first place, it is worthwhile commenting *The Financial Crisis Inquiry Report* which is one of the most significant official documents on the financial crisis that exploded in the United States in September, 2008 and quickly muted into a global financial and economic crash. It is important not only because of what it may tell us about the causes of the crisis, but also because it speaks to the political response to this type of financial catastrophe. The United States Congress set up the Financial Crisis Inquiry Commission as a result of ratification of the Fraud Enforcement and Recovery Act on May 20, 2009, a bare six months after the fall of the house of Lehman Brothers and its worldwide ramifications. During the year 2010 the commission reviewed millions of pages of documents collected as a result of 18 public hearings held all over the United States,

---

[16] United States, Department of the Treasury Financial Regulatory Reform, June 17, 2009: TG-175 -(US Dept of the Treasury), which can be consulted at http://www.financialstability.gov/docs/regs/FinalReport_web.pdf

during which over 700 witnesses were interviewed and questioned, including bankers, investment managers, businessmen, government officials, financial regulators and academic figures. The final report was presented on January 27, 2011 as the "The Financial Crisis Inquiry Commission Report" and later published a few months later as a book which can also be consulted as an e-book on line.[17]

The report focuses on the huge mortgage bubble in the United States and its gradual collapse in 2007 and early 2008 which eventually led to a huge short-circuit in financial markets. The commission was formed by ten members, six Democrats and four Republicans, reflecting the relative strength of these political parties at that time. The report reflected to a considerable degree the economic point of view of each group of constituent members on the causes of the crisis. The final report aimed its artillery against investment banks, private financial mortgage firms and rating agencies. The Democrats on the Commission including its president, Phill Angelides, and commission members, Brooksley Born, Byron Georgiou, Bob Graham, Heather Murren and John W. Thompson, voted in favor of the general conclusions. On the other hand, the four Republicans, vicepresident Bill Thomas and his fellow commissioners, Keith Hennessey, Douglas Holtz-Eakin and Peter J. Wallison were not in agreement and did not recommend publication.

The Democrats and their research assistants argued basically that the crisis was largely the result of the widespread belief among financiers and investors as well as central bankers, regulators, that markets could self-regulate, a view that led many private actors to take very risky positions in financial markets, including extraordinarily high levels of leverage and lack of transparency, at the same time as official regulators displayed a notable lack of vision and of supervisory vigor. The dangers of a debacle were muted by the extensive use of risk coverage in the form of derivatives and of an incredible number of complex financial instruments created to assure firms

---

[17] Apart from the e-book version of *The Financial Crisis Inquiry Report*, which can be found on internet in the US Congress site, most documents and interviews can be researched on a site of the Faculty of Law at Stanford University:
http://fcic.law.stanford.edu/
Another site with documents from the Congress is:
http://www.fcic.gov/hearings/testimony/first-public-meeting-of-the-fcic

and individual investors that they would not lose their shirts. The banks selling the mortgages and derivatives, as well as their clients, apparently believed the tale of inevitable and guaranteed gain. In addition, credit agencies played a major part in impelling the huge wave of financial speculation by providing top ratings for the majority of the risky financial instruments sold. The report also emphasized the excess liquidity provided by the Federal Reserve, the official policies in favor of home construction, including the role of government mortgage agencies. But it also argued that the latter policies were not the real cause of the crisis, which was basically caused by the actions of many domestic private actors in a financial free-for-all that was fraught with enormous and risky speculation, and eventually led to the crash.

Three Republicans on the commission presented a dissenting opinion which was also published in the volume under review. They disagreed with the Democrats, arguing that the US financial markets were not to blame and that the financial actors and institutions which promoted the mortgage boom were also not responsible. Rather – they argued – the huge credit bubble had been generated largely through the international transfer of excess capital to the United States by China as well as the recycling of petrodollars by the Arab states, which caused a lowering of interest rates, and virtually pushed the money into the mortgage business, including subprime mortgages. The subsequent explosion of the housing bubble destabilized banks and other financial institutions and eventually set off the crisis.

Finally, one fourth and more radically conservative Republican, Peter Wallison, who also was on the Commission and clearly appears as a partisan of the *Tea Party*, also presented his conclusions. He argued that he also did not favor publishing the report because the entire fault of the crisis lay at the feet of the government and more particularly of the federal agencies, Fannie Mae and Fannie Mac, which had led private actors astray, by pushing them to take excess risk in the mortgage business.

In summary the Democrats blamed financial deregulation and lack of supervision of the behavior of private financial actors and markets as the major causes of the collapse, while the Republicans held that regulation and supervision were not key causes but rather financial globalization. But perhaps it may be suggested that above and beyond the general conclusions of the report, what may of greatest interest to future historians of the financial crash are the documents of the hearings, which constitute an inestimable source, although not easy to consult.

Of similar importance is the Senate report on the crisis. This document was the result of an investigation carried out by the Permanent Subcommittee on Investigations, which from November, 2008 "initiated a wide-ranging inquiry, issuing subpoenas, conducting over 150 interviews and suppositions, and consulting with dozens of government, academic and private sector experts". The Subcommittee affirmed that it had accumulated and reviewed "tens of millions of pages of documents". The committee was headed senator Carl Levin, Democrat, and senator Tom Coburn, Republican, and included 23 lawyers and clerks that carried out the bulk of the research and hearings, as well as drafting the drafts of the final six hundred page report.

After the preliminary research work was concluded, the Subcommittee held four hearings to examine "four root causes of the financial crisis". At that time it released tens of thousands of pages of evidence, and proceeded to explore in depth the operations of several of the largest banks and institutions involved in the crash. The first case study was of the huge banking firm known as Washington Mutual, which became the largest bank failure in US history, and was later absorbed by J.P. Morgan. The Senate investigation is a scathing document that reveals the extraordinary degree of impropriety and very high risks assumed by the bank directors of this enormous financial company. The report then focuses on review of the role of two of the largest credit rating agencies, Moody's and Standard & Poor in the financial markets before the crisis. Finally, extensive hearings and in-depth studies were carried out on the enormous number of irregularities in the market conduct of two powerful banks, Goldman Sachs and Deutsche Bank, in fomenting the speculation in derivatives and so-called *synthetic* financial instruments which increased risk in all financial markets, but particularly those in the United States in the years 2003-2008. The hearings also reveal an enormous number of irregularities in the conduct of these very powerful financial firms.

As in the case of the Congressional investigation, the Senate placed considerable emphasis on the peculiar and dangerous dynamics of the mortgage markets, in particular, the enormous increase of high-risk instruments, the so-called subprime mortgages, from 2003 onwards. But the Senate subcommittee was most interested in analyzing the microeconomics of the largest financial institutions in the process of creation and massive sale of investment packages containing a complex composition of securities and derivatives.

The acronyms of these products reflect that they represented a new generation of securities: these included financial vehicles whose acronyms were varied, such as CDO, ARM, ABS/CDO, AVM, ABX CMBS, REI, CDS, and SIV, created in the last two decades.[18] As the investigations demonstrated, understanding these instruments requires great expertise in the most sophisticated and arcane of modern banking and finance, and it certainly exceeded the knowledge of the individual investor. This created huge problems of information asymmetry between sellers and buyers. The Senate report transcribed parts of many interviews which demonstrated irregularities and risks involved in these transactions, and concluded by recommending specific regulations of the new financial instruments. It also raised major questions about the issue of banks which are "too big to fail", and therefore involve government rescues in times of crisis. The Senate inquiry clearly demonstrated the dangers inherent to contemporary financial markets as influenced by huge and very difficult to regulate banking giants, which are also not all transparent in their transactions.

Of course, the official enquiries have no monopoly on interpretations and documentation of the crisis, as can be seen in the innumerable books and articles that have been published by journalists, economists and financial experts on the greatest financial crash since the Great Depression, a subject on which probably many more will be written in the future. Nonetheless, as economic historians it is important underline the importance of reviewing and carefully analyzing the official documents and investigations that poured forth quite early after the outbreak of the financial debacle and have continued to do so down to the present. Also of great importance are the *Valukas Report* which contains the records of the court case on Lehman Brothers (some 12,000 pages, placed online in June 2010), or the two

---

[18] A detailed guide written at the time was the book by Das (2005).

thousand pages of Dodd/Frank law Wall Street and consumer Protection Act, signed into law in July 2010, which was accompanied by a huge amount of documentation that is of historical interest.

Apart from the official enquiries carried out in Great Britain and in the United States, it is worthwhile emphasizing that a large number of institutions and countries have promoted enquiries, including, for example, the reports on the financial crisis by committees of the National Assembly of France and by the French ministry of Finance which can be found online. Similarly, it is important to analyze the documents of the Dutch Temporary (Parliamentary) Committee on the Inquiry of Financial System, also known as the 'De Wit Committee' after its chairman, set up by the Dutch Parliament's House of Representatives, which in June 2010 presented its report on the first part of its investigation into the crisis in the Dutch financial system.

Furthermore, as already suggested, the central banks of many countries have published many reports and studies of the crisis. So have multilateral financial organizations such as the International Monetary Fund (IMF), the World Bank, and the Bank of International Settlements, and most of these can be consulted online. On the other hand, there are as yet few critical studies of some of the most important and revealing of these documents, including perhaps most significantly the independent evaluation of the IMF, which provides a truly critical and in-depth analysis of the errors committed by this institution in the years preceding the global financial collapse. The contrast with the World Bank evaluation, which is extremely superficial, is striking.

It is also important to keep in mind the large amount of official research on the social consequences of the financial collapse, as is demonstrated, for example, by the detailed investigations of the International Labor Office on the tragic and drastic impact of the crisis on employment worldwide, which can be reviewed in its annual report of the year 2011. Similarly, the United Nations has sponsored several investigations into the crisis, the best known being the Stiglitz Commission, which in June 2009 published not only the results of its enquiry into causes of the global crisis but also a large raft of recommendations for revising financial regulation and supervision throughout the world.

Ideas towards a new international financial architecture?

In summary, although it may be argued that the Great Recession is now fast becoming history – except in Europe, where it may continue to wreak havoc for some time – its enormous and long-term consequences on a worldwide scale certainly merit the explain a major turning point in modern history. And it is the argument of this essay that greater attention should be devoted in the future to studying and analyzing the key official documents collected and produced by governments, banks, courts and legislatures on this gigantic catastrophe of the contemporary age.

4. In lieu of a conclusion

All major financial over the last two centuries have provoked disbelief because of the suddenness of the catastrophe but also as a result of the enormous costs provoked by economic collapse. This is all too evident in the case of the global financial crisis of 2008/2009: the depth of the financial and economic meltdown is reflected by big numbers, the loss of almost two trillion dollars by the banking system, the loss of various trillions more in the mortgage and stock markets, and the rise in unemployment of between 50 and 70 million persons worldwide in those years. An obvious question is whether we can identify the causes of the great fall, and it is clear that there is now a much better understanding, although certainly there will long be intense debates on this question. This is not surprising but not especially encouraging, for as we know explaining the Great Depression of 1929–1933 continues to be a holy grail of economists, as one prominent central banker of our day has phrased it.

Inevitably, financial disasters lead to an outpouring of publications, but in this essay we emphasize that financial and economic historians should pay special attention to the official reports which include the most detailed investigations. This is particularly pertinent to evaluate the extent to which current banking and financial reforms around the world can be considered adequate responses to this human and economic tragedy. This is so because every large financial crisis in the modern era has marked fundamental changes in the international monetary, financial, and political regimes. That the global financial crisis of 2008/2009 has revealed and accentuated notable contradictions within modern capitalism can be found in many realms of the contemporary capitalist economy. The crisis of the euro in 2012-2014, the Greek crisis which has followed, and the recent financial upheavals in Chinese financial markets in 2015 all speak to the instability of finance in the twenty-first century. Crises will continue to explode in unexpected fashion and it is important to understand where they come from and what are their implications. As this essay suggests, in order to understand the causes and consequences of financial catastrophes, it is indispensable to take into account global history in the long run.

Primary sources

Aldrich, N. W. and National Monetary Commission. Interviews on the banking and currency systems of England, Scotland, France, Germany, Switzerland, and Italy. Accessed at http://fraser.stlouisfed.org/docs/historical/nmc/nmc_405_1910.pdf

Bagehot, W. (1858) The Monetary Crisis of 1857. National Review. Accessed at http://oll.libertyfund.org/title/2260/212971 on 2013-08-08

Baxter, D. (1874) The Recent Progress of National Debts. *Journal of the Statistical Society.* (36), pp.1-20.

Financial Services Authority (United Kingdom). (2009) The Turner Report, A Regulatory Response to the Global Banking Crisis, pp. 16, 19, 20, 22.

Giffen, R. (1904) The Liquidations of 1873-76. In Giffen, R., Economic Inquiries and Studies. London, pp.98-120.

House of Common, Committee of Public Accounts. (2010) Maintaining financial stability across the United Kingdom's banking system, Twelfth Report of Session 2009–10, published on 9 February 2010.

Hyde, C. (1878) On the Debts of Sovereign and Quasi-Sovereign States Owing by Foreign Countries. *Journal of the Statistical Society.* (41), pp. 249-347.

Parliamentary Papers. (1875) Loans to Foreign States, (Reports from Committees), vol. XI, London.

Treasury, H.M. (2009) Reforming Financial Markets. London.

United States Congress House. Committee on Banking and Currency. (1912) Money Trust Investigation: Investigation of Financial and Monetary Conditions in the United States Under House Resolutions Nos. 429 and 504. Accessed at http://fraser.stlouisfed.org/publication/?pid=80

United States Congress House. (1894) Hearings before the Committee on Banking and Currency, regarding systems of banking in the States and Territories, 1893-1894. Accessed at http://fraser.stlouisfed.org/docs/historical/house/1894hr_hearingsbankingcurrency.pdf

United States, Department of the Treasury. (2009) *Financial Regulatory Reform*, June 17: TG-175 -(US Dept of the Treasury). Accessed at http://www.financialstability.gov/docs/regs/FinalReport_web.pdf

United States. Congress. Senate. Committee on Banking and Currency (1932-1933), Stock Exchange Practices. Hearings before the Committee on Banking and Currency Pursuant to S.Res. 84 and S.Res. 56 and S.Res. 97. Accessed at https://fraser.stlouisfed.org/title/?id=87

United States. Congress. Senate. Committee on Finance, (1931-1932) Sale of Foreign Bonds or Securities in the United States. Hearings before the Committee on Finance, United States Senate, Seventy-second Congress, first session, pursuant to S. Res. 19 a resolution authorizing the Finance committee of the Senate to investigate the sale, flotation, and allocation by banks, banking institutions, corporations, or individuals of foreign bonds or securities in the United States. Accessed at https://fraser.stlouisfed.org/title/?id=398

References

Bordo, M. D. and Rockoff, H. (1996) "The Gold Standard as a 'Good Housekeeping Seal of Approval'. " *Journal of Economic History*. 56 (2), pp.389- 428.

Bordo, M. D. and Schwartz, A. (1984) (Eds.). *A Retrospective on the Classical Gold Standard, 1821-1931*. University of Chicago Press, Chicago.

Bouvier, J. (1973) *Deux Scandales de Panamá*. Gallimard, Paris.

Cassis, Y. (2006*) Capitals of Capital: A History of International Financial Centres, 1780-2005*. Cambridge University Press, Cambridge.

Das, S. (2005) *Credit Derivatives, CDO's and Structured Credit Products.* Wiley Finance, New York.

Dehesa de la, G. (2010) *La primera gran crisis financiera del siglo XXI: orígenes, detonantes, efectos, respuestas y remedios.* Alianza Editorial, Madrid.

Eichengreen, B. (1995) *Golden Fetters. The Gold Standard and the Great Depression 1919-1939.* Oxford, New York.

Flandreau, M. and Flores, J. (2009) Bonds and Brands: Intermediaries and Reputation in Sovereign Debt Markets: 1820–1830. *Journal of Economic History.* 69 (646), pp. 646-684.

Flandreau, M. (2012) "The Vanishing Banker ". *Financial History Review.* 19(1), pp.1-20.

Haldane, A.G. (2009) "Rethinking the financial Network " speech at the Financial Student Association meeting, Amsterdam, April 2009. Accessed at www.bankofengland.co.uk/publications/speeches/2009/speech386.pdf

Marichal, C. (1989) *A Century of Debt Crises in Latin America, 1820-1930.* Princeton University Press, Princenton.

Martín Aceña, P. (2013) *Las crisis financieras en la España contemporánea, 1850-2012.* Crítica, Barcelona.

Millmow, A. (2010) The origins of Keynesian macroeconomic management in interwar Australia 1929–39. Australian National University, Canberra.

Moro, A., Nuño, G. and Tedde, P. (2013) "A Twin Crisis with Multiple Banks of Issue Spain in the 1860s ". European Central Bank, Working paper. Series, no. 1561.

Musson, A. E. (1959) "The Great Depression in Britain, 1873-1896 ". *Journal of Economic History.* XIX (2), pp.199-228.

O'Rourke, K. (2009-2010) A Tale of Two Depressions. Vox (website CEPR).

Sánchez Albornoz, N. (1968) *España, hace un siglo: una economía dual.* Ediciones Península, Barcelona.

Saul, S.B. (1969) *The Myth of the Great Depression.* Macmillan, London.

Ideas towards a new international financial architecture?

Tarullo, D.K. (2008) Banking on Basel: The Future of International Financial Regulation. Peterson Institute for International Economics, Washington, D.C.

Vizcarra, C. (2009) Guano Credible Commitments and Sovereign Debt Repayment in Nineteenth Century Peru. *Journal of Economic History*. 69 (2), pp.358-387.

Walton Newbold, J. T. (1932) The Beginnings of the World Crisis, 1873-1896. *Economic History*. 2 (7), pp.425-441.

Wynne, W. (1951) State Insolvency and Foreign Bondholders: Selected Case Histories of Governmental Foreign.

CHAPTER 3
New financial governance model for the new global economy of the 21st century

Constantine E. Passaris

The mission and mandate of economic governance and its accompanying institutional architecture requires a realignment in order to conform to the realities of the new global economy of the 21st century. Two recent economic events, one foundational and the other cataclysmic, have precipitated the need for a new vision and a new direction for financial governance. These two defining milestones are: (1) the emergence of the new economy and (2) the aftermath of the financial crisis of 2008.

The new global economy of the 21st century is composed of a trilogy of interactive forces that include globalization, trade liberalization and the information technology and communications revolution. Globalization has melted national borders and redefined economic policy. Free trade has enhanced economic integration and extended the economic architecture. The information and communications revolution has made geography and time irrelevant and enhanced the reach of economic parameters.

The global financial crisis of 2008 took everybody by surprise (Greenspan, 2008). Furthermore, the financial crisis had a more devastating effect than simply creating the most significant global economic crisis since the Great Depression of the 1930s. It revealed the structural fault lines on the contemporary economic landscape.

The advent of economic globalization, requires a new perspective and a renewal of governance principles. Furthermore, the institutional governance architecture and a country's economic policies should be adapted in order to conform to the realities of contemporary globalization. This is especially true of the economic landscape in the aftermath of the financial crisis of 2008. Globalization impacts on a country's domestic economic landscape and a global mindset must permeate a country's outward reach in terms of the formulation of its economic policies. In a sense, global economic integration results in diminished national and domestic autonomy. This is further accentuated by the existence of multinational and transnational corporations in the private sector that have embraced the benefits of economic globalization for a very long time.

The modern rules of economic engagement require the adoption of governance principles of fiscal propriety, enhancing competitive advantage, renewing the economic infrastructure, achieving full employment, embracing the tools of the information and communications technology revolution, reformatting tax policies, revising the regulatory mechanism and promoting a stable economic environment for foreign investment. All of this to underline that enhanced competition on a global scale and the formulation of its domestic and international economic policies require new governance structures and directions.

All of the above suggest that the contemporary economic landscape is redefining the scope and substance of economic governance. In some cases it has increased the responsibilities of national governments, in other cases it has modified or renewed them. In some cases the existing economic governance institutions and architectures require a refit and renewal and in other cases a modern economic governance institutional architecture needs to be built from the ground up. The management of these new or renewed governance institutions should also reflect the forces of economic globalization as well as economic integration and interdependence. This should allow governments to confront the modern economic challenges and take advantage of the contemporary economic opportunities.

In consequence, the institutional architecture of economic governance requires modernization as well as transitional and transformational change. This is particularly true since the existing economic governance architecture was designed for the old economy and has proved ineffective and inadequate for the new economy.

The aftermath of the financial crisis has precipitated a more interventionist role for government and has laid the foundations for new institutional and regulatory structures that will impact on the financial landscape of the 21st century. This paper explores the future architectural governance landscape for the financial industry and the scope and substance of regulatory initiatives and mechanisms that should be designed in order to avert a future financial crisis.

2. Economic globalization

The new global economy of the 21st century has transformed the economic, social, educational and political landscape in a profound and indelible manner. The new economy is composed of a trilogy of interactive forces that include globalization, trade liberalization and the information technology and communications revolution. Globalization has melted national borders and redefined economic policy. Free trade has enhanced economic integration and extended the economic architecture. The information and communications revolution has made geography and time irrelevant and enhanced the reach of economic parameters. Furthermore, the new economy is built on a culture of innovation. Indeed, the signature mark of the new global economy is new ideas, new technologies and new initiatives (Passaris, 2006).

The advent of the new economy has resulted in the fundamental restructuring of economic society. The role of innovation as a catalyst that drives the engine of economic growth has become a fundamental postulate of the new global economy. Furthermore, the pivotal role of a country's human resources and the unique economic value of its human capital endowment which is reflected in the educational attainment and technical skills of its population is an essential prerequisite for empowering the new economy and facilitating the integration of labour in the knowledge based industries. The knowledge based economy is fuelled by technology, human capital and research and development. In short, the fuel of the new economy is technology and its currency is human capital. The product of the new economy is knowledge and its market is the virtual marketplace of the internet (Passaris, 2011).
Economic globalization is not simply a theoretical, qualitative or conceptual construct. The extent of globalization can be determined by the growth of

foreign direct investment (FDI), the increase in international trade and the volume of transactions in international financial markets. Also the global outreach and economic integration beyond national borders impacts on numerous economic activities. More specifically, statistical data on the increase in yearly flows of FDI and merchandise trade in relation to gross domestic product, the rate of growth in the stock of FDI, the increase in international financial flows and the international mobility of labour (United Nations, 2000).

Multinational and transnational private sector corporations have emerged as a catalyst for globalization. There are also significant qualitative aspects to globalization that should be noted as well. The transformation of the composition of trade from finished products to intermediate and sub-components is a case in point. Another example is the global reach of new financial products is derivatives and hedge funds.

Indeed, the full impact of economic globalization should be considered in the context of its quantitative and qualitative dimension. There is no denying that the observed acceleration in the pace of economic globalization can be attributed to technological advances and innovations in information technologies and communications, trade liberalization, the growth in incomes and consumption and productivity growth.

Globalization has enhanced the fluidity and mobility of financial capital and foreign direct investment. The same is true for immigrant receiving countries with respect to the international mobility of labour, especially highly educated and skilled labour. Economic globalization, accompanied by trade liberalization, has accentuated the global competition for export markets. Clearly national economic policies have been influenced by both of those domestic and international forces and events.

The combination of trade liberalization and economic globalization have created global markets with the full significance of that concept. The international integration of production and distribution, enhanced trade activity, global investment and capital flows have defined the modern economic landscape and impacted on the scope and substance of economic governance. In the absence of a truly global framework for economic governance, countries have formed regional economic governance frameworks, associations and trading blocks that are defined by geographical proximity.

Globalization has created limitations and reduced the degrees of freedom for governments with respect to economic governance domestically as well as the operational features of the domestic market mechanism. This is especially true in the context of the financial quagmire faced by several countries including some European Union countries such as Greece, Portugal and Ireland. There is no denying that the formulation and implementation of domestic and international economic policies requires renewal and realignment with respect to the contemporary realities of the new global economy. The increase in economic interdependence or conversely the multilateral economic dependence of countries is the wave of the future. No doubt this generates a new environment where national governments are required to manage their respective economies with a diminished level of economic autonomy and sovereignty. One of the most challenging features of the new globalized economic system is the degree of asymmetry that was introduced as a result of economic globalization.

It is worth noting that the process of economic outreach in the context of the new global economy can create tensions for the domestic governance system. The scope of international influences diminishes the economic autonomy of the national governance system and creates the momentum for establishing a multilateral forum or a global governance regime, institution and protocol for international engagement. Global governance institutions can resolve problems and disputes in a multilateral context. There is no denying that the contemporary forces of economic globalization require governance institutions that are more inclusive, resilient, focused, rules based and serve as a neutral referee of national economic policies. In short, global economic governance regimes are an essential requirement in the modern economic environment of globalization. A more arduous next step is the development of global public policies and providing global public goods.

3. The 2008 financial crisis

The financial crisis of 2008 unfolded with record speed into a devastating economic crisis of global proportions. Indeed, the recent financial crisis had a more devastating effect than simply creating the most significant economic crisis since the Great Depression of the 1930s. It rocked the very epicentre of the economics profession. More specifically it revealed the fault lines on the economic landscape and particularly with respect to financial governance.

A prescription to reform the financial sector must necessarily commence with an incisive examination and analysis of the economic fault lines that triggered the financial crisis of 2008. Indeed, it was the financial crisis which in turn fuelled the prolonged economic recession that followed. At the outset, it should be stated that the financial crisis of 2008 was a made in America financial crisis. The epicentre of the recent financial crisis was the sub-prime mortgage crisis that unfolded during 2007 and 2008. Despite the fact that the eye of the financial storm was the asset backed securities collateralized with sub-prime mortgages, it was the US housing market that influenced in a profound and indelible manner the economic outcome and should take the blame as being the principal cause of the financial crisis. Indeed, the contextual narrative for the 2008 financial crisis starts with the abrupt collapse of the US housing market that started in 2006.

The perfect financial storm was created by the adverse alignment of a combination of political, economic and financial factors. These factors included political pressure in the US to increase home ownership for low and medium income earners, the advent of economic globalization and the global contagion effect, the introduction of new financial products such as derivatives and hedge funds that carried a significant level of risk, the process of de-regulation that allowed large investment banks to carry excessive leverage and the existence of a large global supply of investment funds seeking investment grade bonds. All of this created unsustainable mortgage lending practices and a vulnerable financial governance institutional architecture. In short, the financial crisis reflected a systemic failure of the US housing market in particular and the global financial industry in general. More precisely, the recent financial crisis created an implosion of the financial industry with global consequences (Schwartz, 2009).

A more meticulous analytical examination of the financial crisis of 2008 will set the stage for correcting the economic fault lines that have developed. The contextual narrative starts with the abrupt collapse in 2006 of the housing boom which had started in the 1990s. Clearly a contributing factor to the recent financial crisis was the creeping de-regulation that took place during the two decades prior to the financial crisis. The derivative market was allowed to self-regulate starting in 1998. This in turn created an enhanced use of credit default swaps in order to hedge against credit risk. In 2004, the US Securities and Exchange Commission relaxed the net capital rule which opened a window of economic opportunity for investment banks and other non-bank financial institutions to increase their level of debt. By way of maximizing this financial opportunity some commercial banks shifted a major portion of their assets and liabilities off the balance sheet to a more leveraged position. In effect, as a direct consequence of this de-regulation, large investment banks significantly increased their leverage ratio.

It is worth noting that there is a disconnect of economic intent and purpose that can culminate in a dysfunctional relationship between mortgage holders on the one hand and mortgage brokers on the other. Indeed, the financial incentives for mortgage brokers and mortgage holders are divergent rather than compatible. More specifically, mortgage brokers are the beneficiaries of a commission for issuing the mortgage. On the other hand, mortgage holders receive interest payments directly from the homeowner. In consequence, the mortgage broker has a vested interest to make the terms of the mortgage as easy and attractive to the prospective homeowner without due diligence to the homeowner's ability to meet their financial obligations in the future.

The increase in the supply of credit during the period immediately preceding the financial crisis facilitated the promotion of less stringent financial requirements associated with new mortgages. Indeed, this is the context for the emergence of sub-prime mortgages which are defined as mortgages issued to a homeowner without a strong credit worthiness and consequently carry a greater risk of default in comparison to holders of prime mortgages.

Ideas towards a new international financial architecture?

Another emerging economic fault line prior to the financial crisis was reflected in the fact that the pricing of complex derivatives was not congruent with the systematic risk associated with them. In consequence, the financial markets did not accurately measure the risk contained in financial products such as collateralized debt obligations and mortgage backed securities. Finally, the period prior to the financial crisis witnessed political pressure in the US to increase the supply of mortgages to low and moderate households. The abrupt collapse of the housing boom in 2007 created a high default rate and an increase in foreclosures which in turn generated serious liquidity challenges not only for major banks but for several large financial firms that had a significant investment in mortgage backed securities and other forms of collateralized debt obligations.

By 2008, the serious economic challenges of the US housing market had contaminated the global financial market. In addition, many financial institutions attempted to safeguard their liquidity by recalling outstanding loans and raising the bar with respect to new loans. All in all, a full-fledged and worldwide decrease in the supply of credit developed. The economic impact of the failure of several major US financial institutions with a large exposure to subprime mortgages confronted the financial markets around the world.

Greenspan put it more succinctly during his testimony before the Committee of Government Oversight and Reform of the U.S. Congress:

> "The evidence strongly suggests that without the excess demand from securitizers, subprime mortgage originations (undeniably the original source of crisis) would have been far smaller and defaults accordingly far fewer. But subprime mortgages pooled and sold as securities became subject to explosive demand from investors around the world. These mortgage backed securities being 'subprime' were originally offered at what appeared to be exceptionally high risk-adjusted market interest rates. But with U.S. home prices still rising, delinquency and foreclosure rates were deceptively modest. Losses were minimal... The consequent surge in global demand for U.S. subprime securities by

banks, hedge, and pension funds supported by unrealistically positive rating designations by credit agencies was, in my judgment, the core of the problem. Demand became so aggressive that too many securitizers and lenders believed they were able to create and sell mortgage backed securities so quickly that they never put their shareholders' capital at risk and hence did not have the incentive to evaluate the credit quality of what they were selling... It was the failure to properly price such risky assets that precipitated the crisis" (Greenspan, 2008, pp. 2-3).

The capital markets were in a downward tailspin. By 2009, the exporting of problematic securitized financial instruments, conveniently but most certainly in appropriately rated triple A by the credit rating agencies, brought about a freeze in global markets with global repercussions. The mechanics of the operation involved packaging mortgage products that financial institutions would not want on their own books and selling them globally at prices that were significantly higher than what would have been recorded in their books by carrying the mortgages in the traditional banking manner. This process gave birth to the global demand for sub-prime mortgages.

During the course of the better part of 2008 and in the early months of 2009 stock markets around the world incurred significant losses which were driven by fears of bank insolvency, a sharp decline in credit availability and a plummeting investor confidence. Countries around the world were confronted with a weak level of economic activity, international trade declined and credit shrank. The blame for all of this was pointed at credit rating agencies and investors that failed to account for the risk involved with mortgage related financial products.

The financial crisis of 2008 has precipitated the need to redesign the financial architecture in a manner that is congruent with the structural and transformational change that was brought about as a result of the emergence of the new global economy of the 21st century. The magnitude of the economic devastation was recorded in the collapse of some leading financial institutions, the bailout of banks by national governments, the significant spike in unemployment, the creation of stimulus packages by national governments to spur economic growth despite considerable public debt and the downward spiral of the stock markets. The financial crisis led to business bankruptcies, the loss of personal wealth and a prolonged downturn in economic activity. All of this created a resonance and a *déjà vu* of the Great Depression of the 1930s.

Considering this scenario, the advent of what has become known as the Great Recession resulted in the resurgence of the economic presence and involvement of governments in the economy and particularly in the financial sector. The corrective action that was taken by governments and central banks can be summarized as three pronged. First, a massive fiscal stimulus; Second, a purposeful expansionary monetary policy; Third, institutional bailouts that supported economic activity and helped maintain existing jobs.

The emergence of shadow banks on the financial landscape during the latter part of the 20th century consisting of investment banks and hedge funds precipitated a two-tiered financial infrastructure for governments and policy makers. This was particularly the case as shadow banks began to play an increasingly important role in financial transactions. Despite the fact that they assumed commercial banking roles, nevertheless, they escaped the supervisory and regulatory role of commercial banks. They became a major source of credit in the US economy. Furthermore, the period preceding the financial crisis witnessed a deviation from the norm of prudent credit management. In consequence, shadow banks as well as commercial banks amassed huge debt burdens without an appropriate financial cushion that could have absorbed the potential risk of large loan defaults or risky mortgage-backed securities. In short, the decades preceding the recent financial crisis witnessed the elevation of the shadow banking system to rival the traditional commercial banking sector and assume an equally important role on the financial landscape. In consequence the implosion of the shadow banking system resulted in significant and widespread economic damage.

There is no denying that the financial crisis of 2008 precipitated an urgent need for greater government involvement and the introduction of enhanced regulation in the financial sector. Prior to that there was a minimalistic overview of the financial sector. This had started in the USA during the Reagan administration with the process of a gradual relaxation of regulations. This redesigned *laissez-faire* approach culminated with the endorsement by the former Federal Reserve chairman's prediction that the markets would self-regulate because it was in their best interest to do so. In this regard, it is worth noting the remarks of Greenspan during his testimony before the Committee of Government Oversight and Reform of the U.S. Congress, when he stated "We are in the midst of a once-in-a century credit tsunami. Central banks and governments are being required to take unprecedented measures.... those of us who have looked to the self-interest of lending institutions to protect shareholder's equity, myself included, are in a state of shocked disbelief" (Greenspan, 2008, p.1).

All of this set the stage for the harshest repudiation of the modern laissez-faire system that had been re-introduced during the two decades prior to the recent financial crisis. In consequence, the financial sector can no longer take for granted the governments' passive non-interference as the future norm. On the contrary, governments have already taken the first steps towards a more pronounced presence in economic decision making and the formulation of economic policy. On the contemporary landscape, governments have assumed a leadership role, providing direction and have embraced a more provocative role as an economic referee and regulator. More specifically, this will take form and substance as governments assume a direct role in the financial sector and influence the process of structural change through enhanced regulation. Governments are no longer prepared to sit on the bleachers and watch the spectator sport of the economy unfold. There is no denying that the financial crisis has ushered in a new era of government intervention. Indeed, the presence of government in the economy and its role as an enforcer and referee on the financial playing field is likely to accentuate rather than abate. The rules of the game have changed and governments are in the process of unveiling a new set of rules for the financial sector in the foreseeable future. This will also require a new institutional architecture for financial governance to implement the new guidelines and regulations in an effective and efficient manner. In addition, we can anticipate a long list of new guidelines and regulations to be implemented that will curtail the degrees of freedom previously enjoyed by the financial sector. In short, the process for financial reform and cleansing will be long and arduous.

Ideas towards a new international financial architecture?

In Chinese, the word crisis is composed of two characters - one represents danger and the other opportunity. Furthermore, a Chinese proverb reads "a crisis is an opportunity riding the dangerous wind". There is no denying that the global financial crisis of 2008 has precipitated an awakening for the deficiencies in economics. Indeed, the recent cataclysmic financial and economic crisis may turn out to be the catalyst for redesigning our economic mission, realigning the scope and substance of economic governance and creating an institutional architecture that is congruent with the new global economy of the 21st century.

4. Economic governance

There is no denying that civil society has raised the bar and placed higher standards and expectations on the performance of economic governance. In the past, economic governance was shrouded in mystery, mystique and secrecy. These were the traditional operational features for the conduct of economic governance. The preparation and public disclosure of government budgets was a case in point. In the contemporary phase there is a tendency to consult with the public and become increasingly more transparent in the process and performance of a government's economic responsibilities. Furthermore, the formulation and dissemination of public policy has been structurally altered in its scope and outreach as a result of the advent of the technology enabled social media.

The future evolution of economic governance in the 21st century will be shaped by two recent economic events. First, the emergence of the new global economy and second the consequences of the financial crisis of 2008. At the outset, the scope and substance of public policy should be re-examined for the purpose of modernizing its reach and effectiveness. The forces shaping the direction of economic governance in the 21st century will also require a forensic evaluation of the accompanying institutional architecture. This new economic environment will require the renewal of existing economic institutions as well as the birth of new institutions. The reason being that the modern version of our economic institutions should be adept, nimble and equipped with the tools to deal with contemporary issues that are multifaceted in their genetic composition inasmuch as they intertwine economic, social and environmental issues simultaneously. In consequence, the economic governance institutions of the 21st century should have the capacity to develop public policy and implement informed solutions in a manner that is holistic and comprehensive. In effect, recognizing that contemporary challenges and future opportunities will be embedded in economic, social and environmental dimensions.

Economic governance can take different forms and shapes. A simple, direct and operational definition of economic governance is the multidimensional aspects of direction and policy that impact on the economy including the machinery and institutional architecture for the delivery of economic governance initiatives. In this regard, a conventional approach to economic governance includes the traditional private and public sectors, household, financial institutions and labour organizations. More specifically, it is directed to all aspects of economic engagement including production, distribution, consumption and investment of resources. In short, economic governance refers to the formulation and implementation of policies, the institutional economic architecture and the administration and management of the economic landscape.

Economic governance is an area of study that analyses how economic governance institutions affect the decisions of economic agents, the design and implementation of public policies and the interaction between the public and private economic spheres. One strand examines the ways in which institutions (understood as formal and informal rules, norms and values) affect economic outcomes through their effects on market structures, collective action outcomes, principal-agent problems, credibility and accountability of public policy and quality of regulation. The other tends to examine bottom-up processes leading to emergence of norms, rules and social networks that function as privately-ordered economic governance institutions (Dixit, 2008).

It should be underlined that economic governance impacts upon individual and collective behaviour and standards. In consequence, the organizational structure must promote the principles of effective and efficient economic governance in compliance with the legal, statutory and regulatory frameworks. Governance institutions including the machinery of government,

Ideas towards a new international financial architecture?

the economic and financial markets as well as government agencies, boards and commissions form the institutional landscape. They are mandated to formulate and implement principles, norms, rules and decision-making protocols that impact upon the economic behaviour of individuals and groups. It goes without saying that the critical analysis of economic governance as well as the design of new organizational structures must include both the governance institutions as well as the institutional environment. Clearly, the specific nature and scope of government intervention in the economy should be aligned with the desired public policy objectives, the formulation of enlightened public policy initiatives and the creation of the most effective and efficient governance institutions.

Good economic governance is not a static concept. It should evolve in order to accommodate the structural changes on the economic landscape. Clearly it is a concept that is not only time sensitive but also responsive to societal permeations. In this regard Dixit points out that "different governance institutions are optimal for different societies, for different kinds of economic activity, and at different times. Changes in underlying technologies of production, exchange and communication change the relative merits of different methods of governance" (Dixit, 2008, p.673).

A couple of decades prior to the financial crisis of 2008, economic governance had developed a marked tendency to rely on the free market mechanism. This translated into a diminished presence for government in the economy. Some examples of this devolution include enhanced privatization, strategies for deregulation and an emphasis on marketization. There was a discernable trend towards privatizing public sector activities, the exploration of different forms of contractual arrangements for public sector activities and generally the extension of market instruments within the public sector. Indeed, the public sector became more entrepreneurial in its mission and mandate. This retrenchment resulted in a sharp decline in government interventions as well as a more restricted, limited and targeted reliance of government interventions. This retraction was especially discernible in the regulatory enforcement by government in the financial industry. It meant a retraction from an influential presence in the organizing and the controlling of production activities to a more peripheral role in the form of a facilitator and catalyst for private sector activities and initiatives. In some cases it evolved to take the form of private and public partnerships.

There are several reasons for the retreat of the public sector from its previous level of economic engagement and involvement. These include, declining tax revenues, an increase in the public debt, public displeasure with the government's management of the economic agenda, the restructuring of government organizations, a decentralization of government operations, the belt tightening and reduction in government expenditures particularly with respect to social programs and the privatization of government activities. It is worth noting that along with the downsizing and downloading of government economic initiatives and an increased reliance on the market mechanism, the public sector institutional architecture has been neglected and allowed to atrophy to the point that it has reached a minimalistic existence. There is no denying that this weakness in the structural foundation for the formulation and implementation of economic public policy has had a deleterious effect on economic governance. The redirection of influence and leadership on the economic landscape has favoured the market mechanism and the private sector. All of this has generated an adverse effect on macroeconomic stabilization efforts and the role of the public sector in economic governance.

The application of Keynesian economics during the second half of the 20th century promoted the complementary role of the private and public sector in economic governance. The entry point for government influence and involvement in economic decision making is the acknowledgement that the free enterprise system does not result, in all instances, in achieving the desired economic objectives. In consequence, government is required to provide a supportive role to the private sector. It should be noted that both the public and private sectors do not stand alone but in reality will complement and reinforce each other. In other words, they provide a complementary mission for economic governance. For example, the advent of globalization was accompanied by the removal of many government restrictions regarding international financial flows and the international ownership of financial institutions and assets. Regrettably, this was achieved without the introduction of the necessary government regulatory architecture and mechanism. In large measure, this resulted in the financial crisis of

2008. In short, it is not a matter of simply shifting responsibilities for economic actions from government to the market and *vice versa*. There is an additional pre-requisite for installing an adequate supporting structure and architecture.

In the modern context, the economic role of government within the framework of a mixed economy has evolved to embrace the following economic functions: a legislated, legal and regulatory framework that is conducive to the protection of property rights, intellectual property and the enforcement of contracts; an agent for investing in physical and human capital infrastructure that permits the private sector to accomplish its mission and contribute to economic growth and development; the role of an overseer and referee with respect to the private sector through economic regulations that promote fair competition and that prevent concentration of economic power with the social addendum of a regulatory outreach in the form of human rights codes that protect the rights of individuals and groups; to provide all those public goods that are not produced by the private sector; to provide collective social security systems that cover basic risks; to promote macroeconomic policies such as monetary and fiscal policies that support a vibrant private sector and contribute to the long term economic goals of sustainable economic growth; and to intervene in order to correct market outcomes that contradict social goals such as the redistribution of wealth.

The pursuit of an effective economic governance model in the contemporary context requires a re-examination of the scope and substance of public policy for the purpose of modernizing its thrust and effectiveness. Public policy has a long tradition of separating and compartmentalizing between two foundational arms of public policy; economic policy and social policy. This has resulted in a vacuum with regard to the development of synergies and the creation of a cohesive and holistic approach for good governance. The traditional approach was to formulate economic policy and social policy on two different tracks. However, the financial constraints faced by governments in the 1990s resulted in prioritizing economic policy above social policy.

Public policy can no longer be segmented and compartmentalized in this manner. We need to recognize the interdependent nature of those two policy variables. In addition, the modern construct of public policy requires the incorporation of a third dimension which has considerable contemporary currency; that of environmental policy. Furthermore, the modern context requires elevating the mission of public policy to a completely different formulaic structure as well as embracing a three dimensional context for formulating public policy. One that embraces a more holistic and comprehensive mission than anything we have inherited in the recent past. By that I mean the recognition of the complementarity and inter-independence between economic policy, social policy and environmental policy in the 21st century.

Increasingly we will need to build the new economic institutions with the purpose of becoming more proactive and incorporating a longer term horizon in their decision making mandate. This in contrast to the previous genre that was propelled by the electoral cycle which was more suited to a short term and reactive mode. This may take the form of restructuring existing institutions through renewal or institutional innovation or building new ones from the ground up. In addition, technological advances in information and communications have provided a degree of public scrutiny that is unprecedented. They have raised the bar on the interchange between civil society and public institutions. There is no denying that public expectations of government performance are at a higher standard than at any time in the past. The invasive nature of modern technology has resulted in a public demand for government disclosure regarding their vision, policies, strategies, performance and actions.

Furthermore, the modern institutional architecture of economic governance should have a global mindset. The reason being that the dividing line between the national domestic context and the international linkages is blurred at best, and fluid on most economic issues. This does not negate the need for domestic institutions but simply recognizes and acknowledges that their efficacy in responding to national issues can be constrained. Furthermore, a global mindset embraces the prevailing axiom of internationalization and creates a positive environment for taking advantage of international opportunities. Global economic interdependence is a fact of life in the 21st century and our institutions need to adapt and evolve to embrace it rather than ignore its existence. The economic linkages associated with internationalization in the context of the new global economy can emerge as contentious and controversial. More specifically, countries may endorse the process of trade liberalization while at the same time recognizing the existence of irritants such as the linkages between an enhanced trade outreach and labour regulations, environmental standards, or direct and hidden subsidies. In this regard, there is a need to invent a modern mechanism, an effective framework and a purposeful capacity for resolving trade disputes.

All of this requires redefining the role, functions and modern economic mission of government. Clearly, business as usual is not an option. There is a need for conceptualizing a new structural framework along with a modern institutional architecture. The structural changes on the economic landscape require a transformational mandate for government. Furthermore, the institutional architecture should be modernized in order to ensure the formulation of enlightened public policy, its strategic implementation as well as an effective and efficient machinery for economic governance that is congruent with the realities of the 21st century.

Good governance has become the gold standard for measuring a government's competence and accomplishments on the economic, democratic and political landscape in the 21st century. What exactly is good governance? Good governance does not have a simple and straightforward definition. The concept of good governance is in many respects multi-layered and multidimensional. In fact, we could say that good governance has many different faces. When these faces are combined in an appropriate manner they form the portrait of good governance. There is no denying that contemporary civil society is placing a higher premium on ethical, efficient and effective governance than at any time in the past. My list of what constitutes the contemporary principles of good governance includes ten interactive and complementary characteristics: leadership, vision, strategy, accountability, transparency, inclusiveness, participation, equality, consensus building and efficiency.

Leadership is the art of providing direction towards achieving predetermined objectives. It is not finding out which way the crowd is going and moving to the front to lead it. Leadership is about making the right choices for the

64

common good that are in the best long-term interest of the citizenry. Vision requires a thoughtful, purposeful and articulate expression of what can be rather than what is. Strategy is the road map of how to get there. Accountability is perhaps the most important ingredient of good governance. It is both a mindset and a goal. The spirit and practice of accountability involves a commitment to announce and defend the actions, policies and legislation of the government so that they can be held up to public scrutiny. In many respects accountability is the very essence of a country's democratic institutions.

Transparency in governance does not mean denying privacy and confidentiality. It does mean however, that the process of decision-making is clear, widely known and has earned the public trust. Furthermore, transparency requires that the decisions taken and their implementation are done in a manner that is consistent, predictable and follows established rules, regulations and guidelines. All of this by way of underlining the importance for governments to practice openness and accessibility.

The inclusiveness characteristic of good governance acknowledges that political, social and economic success is contingent upon all the stakeholders in civil society feeling a part of the mainstream without having to contend with overt or covert barriers of exclusion. This requires a governance mindset and an institutional framework that will promote inclusiveness in every aspect of our daily lives. Participation is the cornerstone for the successful operation of democratic institutions and good governance. The eminent Greek philosopher Aristotle pointed this out in the fourth century B.C. by saying, "If liberty and equality, as is thought by some are chiefly to be found in democracy, they will be best attained when all persons alike share in the government to the utmost" (Barnes 1984, p.IV.1291b34). Furthermore, a prerequisite for participatory democracy is an institutional framework, an impartial legal system and an inspiring human rights code.

Equality of opportunity is a fundamental condition of good governance. This is essential in any society, which is characterized by diversity. It is reflected in our collective commitment to pursue gender equality between men and women, promote the acceptance of religious diversity, celebrate our multicultural population profile. All of this without disenfranchising persons with disabilities, the aboriginal population, visible minorities and those who are marginalized because of their social condition.

Good governance promotes consensus building. This process allows different ideas and varied perspectives to formulate future objectives. Consensus building encourages all citizens to work in harmony rather than in collusion with each other. An efficient, effective and responsive government contributes to good governance. A form of government where waste, mismanagement and inefficiency are not tolerated.

On the economic and political landscape, the pursuit of good governance has become the signature mark of the 21st century. It empowers our democratic institutions to respond to the direction set by civil society. It also ensures that our economic, environmental, cultural and social resources are protected and passed on to future generations. There is no denying the significant impact of the technology enabled social media on the modern parameters of good governance. In consequence, the modern institutional architecture must conform to the contemporary standards set by civil society for good governance. In effect, they must embrace and reflect the modern principles of good governance.

5. Financial Innovations and financial reforms: the need for a financial commission

The process of de-regulation that swept through the US economy immediately prior to the financial crisis of 2008, precipitated the global financial tsunami and the economic crisis that engulfed the international community of nations. The economic fault lines that were revealed were primarily due to an economic governance structure and the accompanying regulatory framework that was designed for the old economy and was not subjected to the required re-calibration and renewal dictated by the structural changes that accompanied the emergence of the new global economy of the 21st century. More specifically, it fell short of the financial innovation, the emergence and the growing importance of the shadow banking system, the development of new financial products, derivatives and off balance sheet financing. Furthermore, the legislative infrastructure remained unchanged and the machinery for enforcing existing regulation was weakened for certain segments of the financial system.

On the financial landscape a two-tiered institutional system emerged. On the one hand, financial institutions that formed the shadow banking system were not subjected to the same regulations as the commercial depository banks, allowing them to carry larger debt obligations in comparison to their capital base or financial cushion. On the other hand, the financial innovation that took place consisted of the development of financial products that were designed to meet specific client objectives. Some specific examples of innovative financial instruments linked to the 2008 financial crisis are: the adjustable-rate mortgage; the packaging of sub-prime mortgages into mortgage backed securities or collateralized debt obligations for scale to investors, a type of securitization; and a form of credit insurance that has become known as credit default swaps. The financial sector made extensive use of these innovative financial instruments during the years leading up to the recent financial crisis. It goes without saying that these financial vehicles differ in terms of the degree of complexity and the level of ease with which they can be valued on the books of financial institutions. All of these instruments – off balance sheet instruments, the derivatives and the shadow banking system that emerged – were clearly designed to circumvent the existing set of rules and regulations.

The development of new and innovative financial products facilitated the process of circumventing regulations. For example, the practice of off-balance-sheet financing that impacts on the leverage or capital cushion reported by the banks. Furthermore, the new financial products were more complex and more difficult to value. Investors were guided by the re-assurance of the international bond rating agencies and the bank regulators that used complicated mathematical models to conclude that these financial products carried a lower risk than what the financial crisis determined was their real level of risk. In short, the financial gatekeepers including the auditors, analysts, boards of directors and politicians failed to do their duty and exercise due diligence. All in all and in hindsight, it turned out to be a major abdication of integrity and responsibility.

Ideas towards a new international financial architecture?

The two decades prior to the financial crisis of 2008 were marked by extending the parameters of *laissez faire* and the introduction of a steady stream of de-regulation initiatives directed towards the financial sector. The aftermath of the recent financial crisis has led to the rediscovery of Keynesian economics and a more influential role for government in the economy. Already there are signs of a significantly different perspective and orientation in the management of the financial industry. More specifically, we have started to witness a more pervasive and pronounced role for government intervention in the financial sector. The next two decades will witness the re-engineering of the financial governance architecture, the re-calibration of the financial governance machinery, the introduction of more stringent regulations, guidelines, systems and directives and a host of structural reforms aimed at ensuring the stability of the financial sector and promoting economic growth .

There is no denying that in the aftermath of the financial crisis, the prolonged economic downturn and the jobless recovery the financial landscape can anticipate a profound shake up. The scope and substance of the changing structural landscape on a national scale will be directly related to the magnitude of the economic adversity experienced by individual countries subsequent to the global financial crisis. Furthermore, the financial crisis has underlined that in the context of the new economy with its global outreach, globalization has meant that future financial crises and economic recessions can no longer be neatly confined to an individual country or even region. Henceforth, they are going to be most pronouncedly global in scope and impact. We are therefore on the cusp of defining a new relationship and a new modus operandi between the government and the financial sector and the international community of nations. In one respect the structural changes to the financial governance infrastructure that are required are going to be symmetrical to the fault lines that have emerged as a consequence of the financial crisis.

The new global economy of the 21st century has been empowered by the electronic capacity and connectivity of the digital age. This is especially true of the electronic capacity that has served as a catalyst for the speed and outreach of economic transactions in the contemporary financial landscape. It is worth noting that the advantages of the modern financial transmission process have also created distinct disadvantages. Foremost among the adverse effects of the digital connectivity is the capacity for fraud, the blurring of the jurisdictional boundaries and national borders as well as diluting the effectiveness of domestic regulatory agencies. Indeed, this is one area where an international financial governance architecture is urgently needed to serve as a regulatory, monitoring and overseeing institution with a mandate to promote global financial stability.

In the ensuing decades, the most pronounced change for the financial sector will be the influential and pervasive presence of government as a regulator, supervisor, referee and decision maker. It is anticipated that a slew of stringent regulations will emerge in the next few decades. The list of new regulatory initiatives will contain proposals for enhancing consumer protection from unfair, abusive or deceptive financial practices, creating adequate bank financial cushions and capital requirements, introducing expanded regulations for the shadow banking system, regulating institutions that perform similar functions as banks with the same rules and regulations that are applied to banks, setting limits and ceilings for executive pay, restricting the leverage that financial institutions can assume, ensuring that all institutions engaged in financial transactions have the necessary capital to support their financial commitment, containing the spread of exotic financial products, regulating credit derivatives and require that they are traded within the parameters of well-capitalized exchanges in order to contain and limit exposure and risk.

In my opinion, the re-engineering and the re-calibration of the financial sector should take place at two distinct levels. At the micro level or the business operational level the emphasis should be on drafting stringent financial regulations with the purpose of enhancing consumer protection and advancing the financial stability of individual firms. This will also simultaneously strengthen the financial system in general. More specifically, the micro level regulations will require a higher standard of accountability with respect to the quality and transparency of each financial corporations' capital base. This may also take the form of introducing specific leverage ratios. On the other hand, the macro level or at the national scope of engagement, new initiatives will trigger economic policies that will enhance the financial stability and minimize the costs to the overall economic system.

69

Ideas towards a new international financial architecture?

These will also require designing a new financial governance architecture in order to implement the new financial directives.

The post financial crisis reforms should have as their principal and foremost macro focus to enhance the role of national regulatory supervision. In consequence, a new set of institutional architecture, tools and systems will have to be designed and built. Keeping in mind the lessons of the recent financial crisis and how large financial corporations can adversely affect the stability of the entire global financial landscape. Regulations aimed at these financial institutions will be directed at preventing the contagion effect of insolvency in the global financial system and closing the window of opportunity for financial products that carry an excessive amount of risk such as hedge funds, private equity funds or other types of toxic financial products. In the first instance, the introduction of stringent regulations is directed at preventing the insolvency of individual financial corporations and at the same time serving as a buffer to immunize individual financial institutions from contaminating the entire financial system.

At the present time, most governments' are faced with a substantial deficit and a burdensome public debt as a consequence of the financial crisis and the prolonged economic recession that followed. The current financial restructuring efforts are contemplating the introduction of a bank levy. The purpose of the bank levy is designed to recover the bailout funds that were dispensed to support individual financial institutions during the recent financial crisis. They can also serve to create a capital reservoir and a financial safety net that will be earmarked for bailout funds for future financial crises. In effect, with the precarious condition of government finances at the present time and the significant burden of the public debt, governments are interested in having financial institutions contributing to a nest egg that can serve as a capital endowment fund in the event of a future financial crisis. Another proposal that is currently under consideration is a global tax on financial transactions in the form of a "Tobin tax" for the purpose of enhancing capital market stability. The theoretical intent of the proposed global tax is to raise the opportunity cost for high risk financial transactions and reduce the flow of speculative capital (McCulloch and Pacillo, 2011).

New financial governance model for the new global economy

The concept of a bank levy has resulted in polarizing the debate into two opposing camps on an international scale. It is not coincidental that the most ardent proponents of a bank levy are those countries that have suffered the most economic damage from the recent financial crisis and were forced to allocate a significant amount of public funds in the form of bailouts to individual financial firms. These countries include the U.K., US, France, Italy and Germany. On the other hand, Canada, escaped relatively unscathed the economic consequences of the financial crisis and is the most vociferous opponent to the bank levy. Furthermore, Canada is joined in its opposition chorus against a bank levy with such countries as Australia, Japan, China, Russia, Brazil and India.

In the contemporary globally interconnected new economy, individual countries are reluctant to impose additional costs to their financial institutions that will adversely affect their international competitiveness and profitability. In the final analysis, and in the absence of an omnibus global financial governance architecture, every country should select its institutional architecture and regulatory protocols that are responsive to domestic needs and economic priorities. Undoubtedly, this will include structural reforms that will correct for the systemic failure of the financial system. In short, every country should set up its own regulatory institutional framework and guidelines that will correct the contemporary financial fault lines and promote the stability of their respective financial sector.

The pursuit of good economic governance will require the creation of a new agency whose principal mission and mandate would be to promote the integrity and the stability of the national financial system. There is no denying that the emergence of the contemporary economic governance fault lines requires an urgent and purposeful effort to redesign the domestic financial governance skyline. A new economic governance institution will enhance and complement the existing financial architecture. Indeed, the pursuit of good economic governance in light of the recent financial crisis will require the creation of a new national institution whose singular mission will be to promote the integrity, stability and economic potential of the financial sector. This institution will have as an overarching mandate to promote an economic and financial environment that is conducive to promoting full employment and sustaining economic growth and development within the parameters of the new global economy.

I am proposing the creation of a national Financial Commission that will serve as an early warning system in effect alerting us to the impending economic crises on the financial landscape. This Commission should create a financial firewall that will significantly reduce the probability of any future financial crises. The Commission should also be empowered to detect the vulnerable facade of the financial system and take appropriate action in order to correct and sustain the integrity of the financial industry and its accompanying governance infrastructure. The Commission should also develop a protocol for proactive interventions in order to arrest the convergence of systemic risk. The broad purpose of this institution would be to serve as an economic intelligence gathering and financial forecasting agency.

There is no denying that the mission and mandate of a Financial Commission is a daunting task. Nevertheless, it is an imperative machinery of institutional engineering that we need to put in place in order to come to grips with a new financial governance protocol that is congruent with the challenges and opportunities of the new global economy of the 21st century. I believe that if more stringent financial oversight and regulations were in place, over exposure to risky investments of the genre of sub-prime mortgages by large investment banks might have been prevented. This new institution must earn the respect and confidence of the financial industry as well as the general public.

The new national Financial Commission should be accountable, transparent and embrace the highest standards of efficiency and effectiveness. This new institution should be independent and at arm's length from government. The Commission should report to the national parliament and be governed by a board of directors that will include representatives of government, the private sector, professional experts as well as representatives from the public and private sector unions. The national Financial Commission should be capable of making long-term economic and financial decisions rather than focusing on the short-term electoral cycle. The undeniable benefit of a financial

Commission would be to protect and promote the integrity and stability of the financial sector in the decades ahead.

6. Conclusion

The mission and mandate of economic governance and its accompanying institutional architecture requires a realignment in order to conform to the realities of the new global economy of the 21st century. Two recent economic events, one foundational and the other cataclysmic, have precipitated the need for a new vision and a new direction for economic governance. They are: the emergence of the new global economy and the financial crisis of 2008.

Economic globalization has precipitated the need for a renewal of our governance principles, the institutional architecture and a country's economic policies in order to conform to the realities of the contemporary landscape. The modern rules of economic engagement require the adoption of governance principles of fiscal propriety, enhancing competitive advantage, renewing the economic infrastructure, achieving full employment, embracing the tools of the information and communications technology revolution, reformatting tax policies, revising the regulatory mechanism and promoting a stable economic and financial environment.

Good governance has become the gold standard on the economic and political landscape in the 21st century. My list of what constitutes the contemporary principles of good governance includes ten interactive and complementary characteristics: leadership, vision, strategy, accountability, transparency, inclusiveness, participation, equality, consensus building and efficiency.

An operational definition of economic governance is the multidimensional aspects of direction and policy that impact on the economy including the machinery and institutional architecture for the delivery of economic governance initiatives. The modern institutional architecture of economic governance should have a global mindset. It should reflect the complementarity and inter-independence between economic policy, social policy and environmental policy. Indeed, there is room for new economic institutions that are proactive and incorporate a longer term horizon in their decision making mandate.

The realities of the new global economy and the pursuit of financial stability require the re-engineering of our inherited economic institutions and the introduction of a new set of economic architecture that is more conducive to meeting the challenges and taking advantage of the opportunities of the 21st century.

The pursuit of good economic governance will require the creation of a new institution whose singular mission is to promote the integrity and stability of the financial sector. I propose the creation of a national Financial Commission that is at arm's length from government influence and direction and serves as a catalyst for sustaining financial stability.

References

Barnes, J ed. (1984) *The Complete Works of Aristotle: The Revised Oxford Translation,* Princeton University Press, Princeton, NJ.

Claessens, S. and Kose, M.A. (2010) "The Financial Crisis of 2008-09: Origins, Issues, and Prospects", *Journal of Asian Economics*, 21(3) pp. 239-241.

Dixit, A. (2008) "Economic Governance", in Durlauf S.N and Blume L.E eds, *The New Palgrave Dictionary of Economics,* 2nd ed., Palgrave Macmillan, New York.

Greenspan, A. (2008) Testimony before the Committee of Government Oversight and Reform, US Congress, October 23, 2008, available at http://www.federalreserve.gov/boarddocs/testimony/1998/19980923.htm (accessed September 2, 2015).

Ivashina, V. and Scharfstein, D. (2010) "Bank Lending During the Financial Crisis of 2008", *Journal of Financial Economics,* 97(3), pp. 319-338.

Gaffney, M. (2009) "Money, Credit & Crisis", *The American Journal of Economics and Sociology,* 68(4), pp. 983-1038.

McCulloch, N. and Pacillo, G. (2011) "The Tobin Tax: A Review of the Evidence", May 2011, available at http://www.ids.ac.uk/go/ids publication/the-tobin-tax-a-review-of-the-evidence (accessed Sept. 2, 2015).

Passaris, C. (2001) "Schumpeter's Legacy of Technological Innovation in the Context of the Twenty-first Century", in V. Orati and S.B. Dahiya eds, *Economic Theory in the Light of Schumpeter's Scientific Heritage*, Spellbound Publications, Rohtak, India, pp.1985–2009.

Passaris, C. (2003) *"Schumpeter and Globalization: Innovation and Entrepreneurship in the New Economy"*, Fifth Annual International Schumpeter Lecture, International Institute of Advanced Economic and Social Studies,Viterbo, Italy.

Passaris, C. (2006) "The Business of Globalization and the Globalization of Business", *Journal of Comparative International Management*, 9(1), pp.3–18.

Passaris, C. (2008) "Macroeconomic Policy in the New Global Economy of the Twenty first Century", Proceedings of the Society of Heterodox Economists Conference on Contemporary Issues for Heterodox Economics, Sydney, pp. 109–137.

Passaris, C. (2011) "Economic Governance and Full Employment" in M.Ugur and D. Sutherland eds, *Does Economic Governance Matter?* Edward Elgar Publishing, Cheltenham, UK, pp.168-183.

Rotman, J.L. (2008) *The Finance Crisis and Rescue*, University of Toronto Press, Toronto.

Schwartz, A.J. (2009) "Origins of the Financial market Crisis", *The Cato Journal*, 29(1), pp.19-24.

Stiglitz, J. (2010) *Freefall: America, free markets, and the Sinking of the World Economy*, W.W. Norton , New York.

United Nations. (2000) Globalization and Economic Governance, available: http://unpan1.un.org/intradoc/groups/public/documents/un/unpan000554.pdf (accessed on September 2, 2015).

Williamson, O. (2005) "The Economics of Governance", *American Economic Review*, 95(2), pp.1–18.

Ideas towards a new international financial architecture?

CHAPTER 4
Public debt is economic nonsense

Gerson P. Lima

1. Introduction

Public debt is a macroeconomic fact and not a simple company's accounting problem as the mainstream economists pretend. Accordingly, this paper describes a theorem based on the difference equation method to demonstrate that the public debt may have a theoretical equilibrium solution. However, this solution may be unattainable since monetary policy may preclude the convergence to equilibrium in the real world. In order to test the adherence of this theorem to the reality it is presented an experiment, the estimate of the US federal tax revenue in a non-mainstream aggregate supply and demand approach. Statistical results obtained do not suggest rejecting the hypothesis that it may be expected a negative combined effect of the public debt and interest expenditure on the tax revenue. Therefore, the main conclusion is that monetary policy creates a positive feedback process that leads the public debt to follow an explosive trend to infinity. Economic, financial and social consequences of such a public debt trend are not different from what has been reported on economics and finance the world around.

Public debt has been a widespread problem for mainstream economists have no dependable procedure to deal with it and prevent its economic and social negative consequences. They are convinced that stabilizing the public debt ratio to GDP is the right thing to do and create sophisticated accounting methods to calculate the primary surplus that supposedly provides the targeted public debt/GDP ratio stability. Testing hypotheses against reality and the feasibility and consequences of such a primary surplus were until recently not considered in the mainstream monetarist approach. Some progress has been done since the failure of mainstream models to deal with the crises they create, and especially after Krugman's post at The New York

Ideas towards a new international financial architecture?

Times (Krugman, 2010). Many mainstream economists are considering the idea that actually the public debt may follow an explosive trend. However, mainstream economists cannot provide a solution for the problem since instead of searching into the public debt performance they keep doing the same accounting exercise, looking for a primary surplus that under convenient assumptions would stabilize the ratio public debt/GDP.

The paper is organised as follows. Section 2 brings a critical appreciation of the mainstream methodology applied to the public debt. Section 3 shows the estimate of the US GDP, stressing the effects of the monetary policy on the tax base. Section 4 presents the estimate of the US federal tax revenue both as a reduced equation in a simultaneous equations model and as a function of GDP. The return coefficients of the fiscal and the monetary policies on the US tax receipts are remarked. Section 5 develops the theorem of the public debt time trend and discusses the probability of attaining the necessary condition for debt equilibrium. Finally, Section 6 offers some conclusions.

2. The failure of the mainstream approach to the public debt time trend

Governments are neither profit seeking companies nor common consumers; they are social institutions that sometimes behave as irresponsible consumers. The right lecture of the economics' paradigm by governments seems to be "governments shall never spend more than their earnings". This does not mean that governments should save and harm society; this means that governments can raise their earnings to increase social expenditures and people's income. Governments can do that at will as their sources of earnings are peculiar: they are legally empowered to collect taxes and to print money. Notwithstanding, congresses of democratic countries transferred the power of money printing to private central bankers who imposed their paradigm: governments cannot print money. Who has the power of printing money rules the economy; so, mainstream economics created the monetary policy to justify the public debt. After decades this arrangement led to many financial crises, but despite not eliminating crises all mainstream proposals have been turning around the same: governments should save to pay the interest on their public debts.

Public debt is economic nonsense

Mainstream monetarist economics dismissed the supply and demand theory thus adopting the convenient methodology of "models", a methodology that allows mainstream economists to create convenient models focused on results previously established, based on appropriate assumptions and using suitable mathematical methods. Accordingly, in the case of public debt the mainstream monetarist approach is essentially accounting and hence the result systematically obtained is that there is a primary surplus that provides a condition for public debt stability. The mainstream proposal is not to ask if in the real world the public debt actually or potentially may converge to an equilibrium level, but to calculate the primary surplus that supposedly assures debt stability, a necessary condition for monetary policy to exist.

The primary surplus condition must be fulfilled by the fiscal policy; it is not a duty of the creators of the public debt. This mandatory primary surplus shall be delivered the next year or in the long run. "The standard debt sustainability assessment frameworks used by international organisations like the European Commission is based on an analysis of debt and debt service dynamics derived from projections of a number of indicators over a medium to long-term horizon" (Veld *et al.*, 2012, p.3). Therefore, the stability of the public debt is assured sometime after monetarists provided the "right" projections.

Given the goal of the model, that is, the stable ratio debt/GDP that may be attained through the right economic fiscal policy, three basic ad hoc assumptions are necessary to the monetarist models: 1) at any point in time the previous public debt is "given", despite the fact that the public debt is a dynamic economic phenomenon, 2) public debt is not affected by the monetary policy; it is a fiscal policy concern and, crucially, 3) GDP and tax revenue are independent from previous public debts and primary surpluses. "Their method was to dismiss the problem from the *corpus* of Economics not by solving it but by not mentioning it", (Keynes, 1936, p.364). Illustrating, Veld and others propose the following model (Veld & O, 2012, p. 3):

$$\frac{B_t}{Y_t} - \frac{B_{t-1}}{Y_{t-1}} = \frac{PD_t}{Y_t} + \left\{ \frac{B_{t-1}}{Y_{t-1}} * (r_t - g_t) \right\} + \frac{SF_t}{Y_t}$$

where B/Y is the public debt ratio to GDP, PD is the primary deficit, r is the interest rate, g is GDP growth rate and SF/Y is stock-flow adjustment (a kind of fix-all device?). Debt is a stock, hence this monetarist model is a difference equation, but in the mainstream literature it was traditionally not developed as such. Notwithstanding, monetarists realise that this equation bears a time trend for the term in parenthesis is said to provide a "snow ball" effect on the debt ratio. Mainstream monetarists' conclusion is that the condition for the debt ratio not to follow an explosive trend is that g>r for the "snow ball" effect becomes negative.

However, monetary policy failure in recovering economies after the 2007 crisis obliged mainstream economists to admit that the monetary policy alone is incapable of restoring the economic activity and some of them manifested concern and doubts about their methods. They changed their ideas about the multiplier and realized that primary surpluses may cause more deficit and more unemployment (Krugman, 2010; Nautet and Meensel, 2011; Cherif and Hasanov, 2012; Gechert, 2013; Semmler, 2013). One remarkable work was done by Escolano (2010) for it is based and developed using difference equations to prepare the International Monetary Fund's Practical Guide to Public Debt Dynamics. However, it is just one more impressive mathematical work that looks for the same as ever, the primary surplus that stabilize the public debt ratio. In Escolano words: "Given an initial debt ratio (d_0), and a target debt ratio (d^*_N) to be achieved in N periods, the constant primary balance (p^*) that reaches the target debt ratio if maintained constant during periods t = 1,..., N is..." (Escolano, 2010, p.5).

Especially worth is the statement by the International Monetary Fund:

> "This chapter examines the effects of fiscal consolidation –
> tax hikes and government spending cuts – on economic
> activity. Based on a historical analysis of fiscal consolidation
> in advanced economies, and on simulations of the IMF's
> Global Integrated Monetary and Fiscal Model (GIMF), it
> finds that fiscal consolidation typically reduces output and
> raises unemployment *in the short term*" (IMF, 2010, Chapter
> 3, p. 112, emphasis added).

Public debt is economic nonsense

IMF and others recognise the problem but try to find mitigating situations, for instance talking short and long run, weak economic environment or normal times (Cherif and Hasanov, 2012), low and high debt ratios (Cecchetti, Mohanty and Zampolli, 2011), and anything else that can be used to produce the desired end.

Even mainstream economists can no longer deny that primary surplus decreases GDP thus reducing tax revenue and increasing the public deficit and debt. Despite evidences, countries ruled by central banks' monetary policy keep running primary surpluses and producing negative total results. Accordingly, these countries' public debts may follow explosive trends (Cherif and Hasanov, 2012; Boussard, 2012). Why primary surplus does not stabilize the public debt ratio? A hypothesis is that the interest expenditure is the most important individual item in the public outlays and deficit and may grow more than the tax revenue, thus creating a rising public deficit. For instance, the figure nearby shows that in United States the interest expenditure accounted for more than half of the federal government deficits in the period 1960-2007, second period of President Clinton aside. During this period 1960-2007 the US federal tax revenue increased yearly at the rate of 7.76% while the interest expenditure rose at 8.36% and the federal public deficit expanded at 6.52%. Therefore, if the intention is to answer to the question above it seems that the first thing to do is to discard monetarist assumptions and method and search into the possible positive feedback hitting the public debt through the interest expenditure.

INTEREST EXPENDITURE ON THE US FEDERAL PUBLIC DEBT (% OF TOTAL DEFICIT)

ALL PERIOD 1946-2013
AVERAGE = 59,0%

SUPER LOW DEFICITS CLINTON SECOND PERIOD

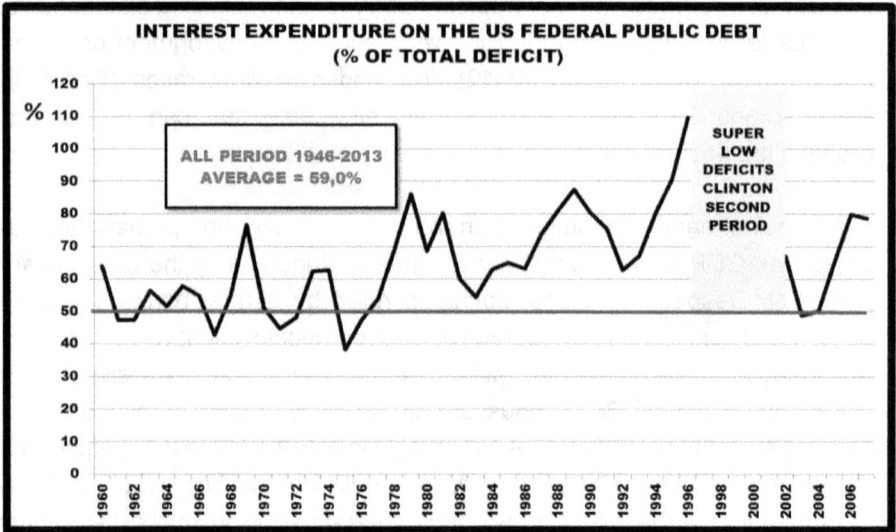

3. The US GDP estimate

The estimate of the US GDP obtained in Lima (2015) is:

$$GDPe = -277.807 + 6.36696*FE + 15.5759*ER - 0.40728*DP + 3.92613*INT \quad (1)$$

In this equation **GDPe** is the theoretical equilibrium series[1] of the US GDP in US$ billions, **FE** is the US Federal Government fiscal expenses (fiscal policy) in US$ billions, **ER** is the exchange rate (foreign sector relations policy) in US dollars needed to buy a foreign currencies basket, **DP** is the federal public debt hold by the public and the Federal Reserve in US$ billions, and **INT** is the interest expenditure on the gross US federal public debt in US$ billions. Statistical tests indicated that the federal minimum wage (income distribution policy) was never significant (full description of all variables in the Appendix).

---

[1] The theoretical series of an endogenous variable is the series of values that it *would* reach *if* at each point in time all explanatory variables stop varying time enough for their full effects to come about, a condition that is never fulfilled in the real world. Actually, there is no equilibrium between supply and demand for in the real world production takes time (more in Lima, 2015).

Public debt is economic nonsense

Both **DP** and **INT** represent the monetary policy in this context; as expected, **DP** has negative sign and **INT** the positive sign for it is rent transferred to some people who spend the least and save the most. The credit supply thus increases and the aggregate demand expands. But it is not the total interest rent that goes to final products demand. Part of the rent is used to by real estate and financial assets in transactions that only change property but do not create real wealth. Moreover, credit is not free money like government fiscal expenditures produce but interest bearing money; borrowers will somehow take money somewhere to pay the due interest, some demand is thus cut. Furthermore, the flow of interest rent to Treasury bonds' holders is perennial and is almost always increasing, thus creating an ever growing stock of financial capital and credit supply. Meanwhile borrowers' income available to pay instalments expands slower than the credit supply; credit demand grows slower than credit supply. Thus, probably the aggregate demand expansion caused by interest expenditure is restricted.

The monetary policy effect looks undefined for the public hold debt DP reduces the GDP while the interest expenditure INT does the opposite and INT is partially a function of DP. But it is possible to estimate the combined effect of DP and INT by omitting DP in the GDP equation. This omission imparts a bias to INT such that INT carries the effect of DP and is associated here with the monetary policy applied to the public debt or simply monetary policy. Alternatively, this bias may be introduced without distorting the other coefficients by replacing the **DP** variable in the **GDPe** equation above by its function of **INT** (1960-2007):

$$DP = -181.112 + 11.012*INT$$

It is therefore obtained GDPo, an abridged version of the US GDP that produces the same estimate of the GDP as shown in the figure nearby:

$$GDPo = -204.044 + 6.36696*FE + 15.5759*ER - 0.5588*INT$$

This means that if the public debt is allowed to vary INT becomes a measure of the monetary policy and, ceteris paribus the other exogenous explanatory variables, INT bears a negative sign. The combined effect of public debt and its interest rent produces a negative coefficient (−0.5588) and thus the conclusion is that the monetary policy, ceteris paribus the fiscal policy FE and the exchange rate ER, imposed a negative effect on the GDP and on what depends on the GDP.

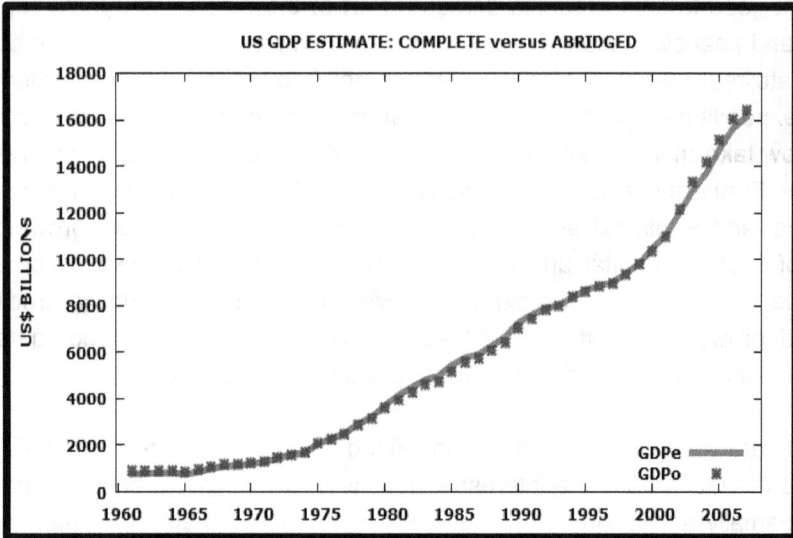

Sources of raw data in the Appendix.

The past history of the US economic policy mix may be associated with the time performance of the importance of each **GDPo** explanatory variable calculated by its elasticities as shown in the figure nearby. This survey seems to be dependable information for the design of future policy mixes.

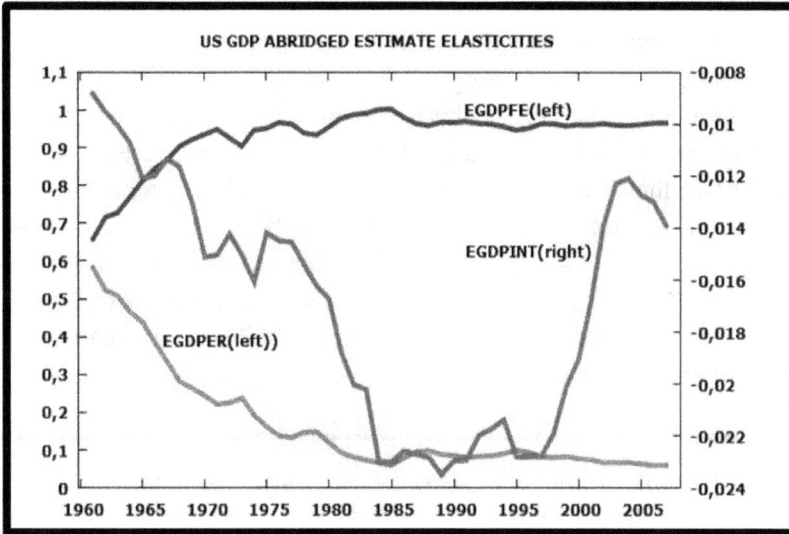

US GDP ABRIDGED ESTIMATE ELASTICITIES

Sources of raw data in the Appendix.

This figure shows that the most important variable in the US GDP formation during the period 1960-2007 was the fiscal expenditure for it expanded the aggregate demand without touching the aggregate supply in such a way that its elasticity EGDPFE was always positive and the greatest one. On the foreign side, devaluation of the US dollar also created more GDP for the shift to the right it caused to aggregate demand more than compensated the contraction that the exchange rate imparted to aggregate supply. However, the elasticity EGDPER dropped significantly, suggesting that despite the US dollar devaluation the contribution of American exports to the US GDP reduced expressively. The importance of the monetary policy was relatively low and unstable but more public debt continuously reduced GDP for its elasticity EGDPINT was always negative. Therefore, it may be expected that monetary policy also reduced tax revenue in that period.

4. The US tax receipts estimate

The next step is the estimate of the theoretical equilibrium series of the US federal tax revenue whose reduced equation proposed is:

$$T_t = a + D(L)FE_t + D(L)MW_t + D(L)DP_t + D(L)INT_t$$

where **D(L)** is a lag operator, **T** is the federal government current total receipts in US$ billions, and the exogenous variables explanatory set are the federal government fiscal expenditure **FE** in US$ billions, the income distribution policy measured by the US federal minimum wage **MW** in US$ dollars per hour, the Federal Government debt hold by the public and the Federal Reserve System **DP** in US$ billions, and the Federal Government interest expenditure **INT** in US$ billions. Statistical tests revealed that the exchange rate (foreign relations policy) did not influence tax revenue significantly. The estimate obtained for the period 1960-2007 is presented in the Gretl's report nearby.

ESTIMATE OF THE US FEDERAL TAX REVENUE, 1960-2007
Dependent variable: T

	Coefficient	Std. error	t-statistics	p-value	
const	-44.8262	15.5885	-2.8756	0.00637	***
FE_1	0.672873	0.128773	5.2253	<0.00001	***
FE_3	0.513895	0.17324	2.9664	0.00501	***
MW	39.8287	10.4706	3.8039	0.00047	***
DP	-0.957127	0.0395121	-24.2236	<0.00001	***
DP_1	0.899345	0.0439773	20.4502	<0.00001	***
INT_3	0.458746	0.140064	3.2753	0.00215	***

Média var. dependente	865.8853	Dep. var. std. error	726.7012
Soma resíd. quadrados	24001.23	Regression std. error	24.19496
R-quadrado	0.999033	Adjusted R-square	0.998891
F(6, 41)	7059.738	F p-value	3.84e-60
Durbin-Watson	1.739868	DW 1% (6,45): 1.065-1.643	

Sources of raw data at the Appendix.

Collecting coefficients for fiscal expenditures FE and public debt DP it is created the theoretical equilibrium reduced equation of the United States Federal Government tax receipts **Te** for the period 1960-2007:

Te = -44.8262 + 1.1868*FE + 39.8287*MW – 0.0578*DP + 0.45875*INT   (2)

The US tax revenue responded positively to the fiscal policy (**FE**) and to **MW**, the income distribution policy indicator. Monetary policy, given by the combination of **DP** and **INT**, also has a negative effect on the tax revenue. In fact, replacing **DP** in the **Te** equation by its equation above:

DP = -181.112 + 11.012*INT

It is obtained the abridged version of the US tax revenue theoretical equilibrium equation:

To = – 34.3679 + 1.1868*FE + 39.8287*MW – 0.1777*INT   (3)

The figure below shows that both equations (2) and (3) produce the same estimate of the US federal tax revenue series.

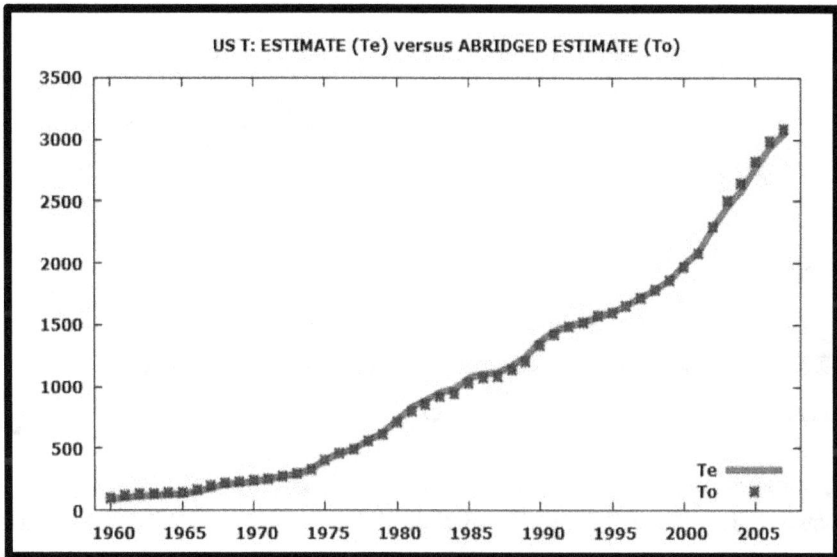

Sources of raw data in the Appendix.

The derivative of the tax receipts **T** in relation to the fiscal expenses **FE** (≈1.19) may be seen as the financial "return coefficient" of the social investment made through fiscal policy. Therefore, ceteris paribus **MW, ER, DP** and **INT** government fiscal expenditure cuts cause **GDP** and thus **T** to fall and therefore public debt **DP** and **INT** to grow. Accordingly, the "return coefficient" of the monetary policy is negative (- **0.1777**). This result allows for not rejecting the hypothesis that the monetary policy measured by the interest expenditure associated with the public debt may cause a negative effect on the tax revenue. The time performance of the importance of the monetary policy and the other economic policy instruments in the US tax revenue formation, calculated by their elasticities, is shown in the figure nearby.

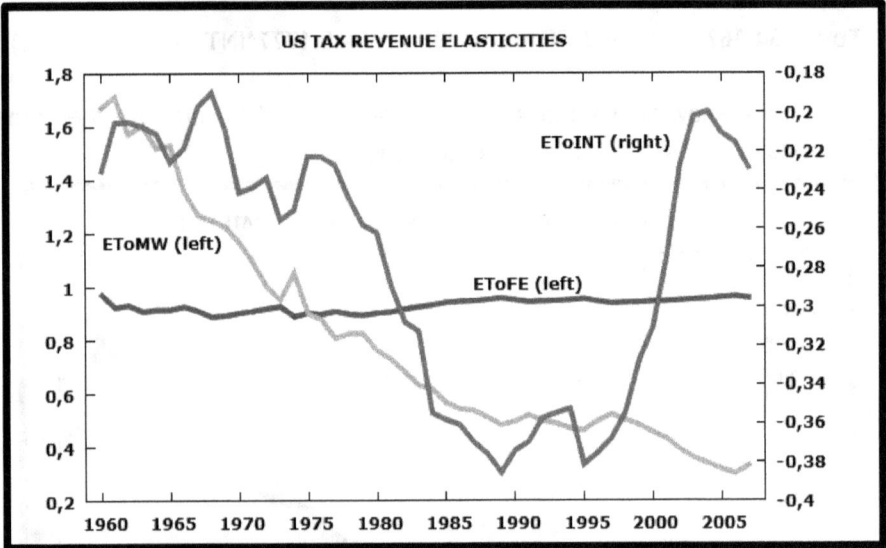

Sources of raw data in the Appendix.

The most important exogenous variable in the **To** formation was the fiscal policy for its elasticity **EToFE** besides stable was the highest one since 1975. The elasticity of **To** in relation to the minimum wage **EToMW** presents a fading performance, what is evidence that this instrument of income distribution policy despite its strong positive effect was neglected. On the negative side, the monetary policy as measured by merging **DP** and **INT** suggests that the positive effect to the tax revenue allowed by the credit supply was insufficient to offset the negative effect provided by the public debt itself. Actually, the monetary policy effect given by **EToINT** besides unstable is always negative and relevant. The conclusion is thus that this experiment does not allow for the rejection of the hypothesis that monetary policy may cause tax receipts losses.

Actually, the endogenous variable tax revenue is a function of another endogenous variable, the GDP as a measure of the tax base. The estimate of a relation between two or more endogenous variables requires that all exogenous variables of all endogenous variables but one be in the explanatory set of the dependent variable and that the endogenous variables be measured by their theoretical equilibrium series. The exogenous variable omitted will then be the only one that makes all endogenous variables vary thus revealing one relation among them; different exogenous variable omitted produces different slope coefficients (Lima, 2015).

Accordingly, in this experiment the estimate of the tax revenue **T** as a function of **GDP** was made using the theoretical equilibrium series, respectively **Te** (equation 2) and **GDPe** (equation 1) and the exogenous variable omitted is the fiscal expenditure **FE**. While the other variables are kept under the ceteris paribus condition, fiscal expenditure **FE** varies thus creating the line of points (Te, GDPe) in the orthogonal plan GDPe x Te. This line may be obtained by algebra, but in order to avoid mistakes it was run the regression presented in the Gretl's report below in which statistical tests are of course meaningless.

US FEDERAL TAX REVENUE as a function of GDP, 1961-2007

Dependent variable: Te

	Coefficient	Std. error	t-statistics	p-value	
const	6.95697	5.121e-012	1.35845E+12	<0.00001	***
GDPe	0.1864	0	2.13411E+14	<0.00001	***
MW	39.8287	2.3523e-012	1.6932E+13	<0.00001	***
ER	-2.90334	1.7762e-013	-1.63457E+13	<0.00001	***
DP	0.0181169	0	4.51458E+12	<0.00001	***
INT	-0.27308	0	-9.29123E+12	<0.00001	***

Dependent var. avg.	1095.627	Dep. var. std. error	852.8918
Square residuals sum.	8.36e-22	Regression std. error	4.52e-12
R-square	1.000000	Adjusted R-square	1.000000

Sources of raw data in the Appendix.

The "structural" US tax revenue equation thus obtained is:

Te = - 6.9570 + 0.1864*GDPe + 39.8287*MW –
$$2.90334\text{*ER} + 0.01812\text{*DP} - 0.2731\text{*INT}$$

Once again, merging DP and INT creates the abridged US tax revenue equation:

To = - 10.239 + 0.1864*GDPe + 39.8287*MW - 2.90334*ER - 0.07356*INT

This estimate adheres to the idea that GDP is a measure of tax base. However, it is not possible to apply the ceteris paribus condition to an endogenous explanatory variable for its variations are associated with variations in at least one of the exogenous variables that simultaneously produce variations in the dependent endogenous variable. This means that this equation is not a safe indicator of the tax burden and the relevance of the exogenous variables in the tax revenue formation. Actually, the analysis of the causes of endogenous economic events must be based on the theoretical equilibrium reduced equations of endogenous variables associated with such events. Nevertheless, empirical data suggests not discarding the idea that the interest expenditure combined with the public debt causes a negative effect on the tax revenue. The main conclusion is that this experiment does not allow for rejecting the hypothesis that monetary policy causes GDP and, consequently, tax revenue losses.

Therefore, it seems that there is a positive feedback to the public debt: more public debt leads to more interest expenditure and lower tax revenue that leads to larger deficit and to more public debt and so on. The next point is the demonstration that this feedback imparts an explosive trend to the public debt.

5. A theorem for the public debt time trend

This section presents a dynamic non-mainstream approach to the public debt demonstrating that it may follow an explosive trend, possibly as a natural economic fact. Suppose initially that there is neither money emission to pay the interest or the principal, nor public debt created by pure monetary policy.[2] So, once initiated the public debt levels result only from the accumulation of previous deficits. Therefore, the time performance of the public debt may be described by the following accounting-looking expression:

$$D = D_{-1} + FE + INT - T \tag{4}$$

where D is the public debt at the end of the current period, D_{-1} is the public debt at the end of the previous period, FE is the government's fiscal expenditure, INT is the government's expenditure on interest and T is the tax revenue. All values are nominal and not ratios to GDP. Defining the interest expenditure INT as the product of the exogenous variable interest rate r by the public debt at the end of the previous year D_{-1} it comes:

---

[2] A monetary policy is here said to be "pure" in the cases it refers to money supply or inflation control, quantitative easing and others; public deficit financed with Treasury bonds emission is not pure monetary policy but a condition for pure monetary policy to exist.

$$INT = r\, D_{-1} \tag{5}$$

Next, substituting INT in the accounting-looking expression (4) and rearranging one obtains:

$$D = (1 + r)\, D_{-1} + FE - T \tag{6}$$

The expression that describes the public debt is no longer an accounting-looking one; it is a linear difference equation since debt is a matter of economics. Accordingly, the tax receipts T is not given nor assumed nor predicted, but an endogenous variable, a straight function of the tax base measured by the GDP and the tax rate imposed by government. Given the experiment above, and especially the equation (3), it is expected that the combined effect of the public debt (D and r^*D_{-1}) over GDP and hence on the tax earnings T be negative. It may thus be assumed that there are evidences supporting the assumption that the tax receipts may be generically described by a function like:

$$T = \beta_0 + \beta_1\, FE + \beta_2\, INT + \beta_3\, OV \tag{7}$$

where β_1 is the return coefficient of the fiscal policy, or the measure of the return to the government of the social investment it made through fiscal expenditures FE, and it is expected to be positive. β_2 is the return coefficient of the monetary policy, or the measure of the return to the government of the public debt it made, and it is expected to be negative (equation 3). OV refers to other exogenous variables except D; for instance, in this US case OV contains only the federal minimum wage MW.

Replacing T given by equation (7) and INT, defined in (5), in the expression of the public debt (6), and rearranging it comes:

$$D - \{1 + r\,(1 - \beta_2)\}\, D_{-1} = -\{\beta_0 + (\beta_1 - 1)\, FE + \beta_3\, OV\} \tag{8}$$

This is a difference equation that describes the time behaviour and the possible theoretical equilibrium levels of the public debt. The theoretical equilibrium solution for this function is given by:

Public debt is economic nonsense

$$D^* = 1/\{r\,(1 - \beta_2)\}\,\{\beta_0 + (\beta_1 - 1)\,FE + \beta_3\,OV\} \tag{9}$$

This is a complex solution, stressing that the hypothetical equilibrium level of the public debt D^* depends on the monetary policy's exogenous variable interest rate r, on the coefficient of the monetary policy β_2, on the social investment return β_1, on the exogenous variable fiscal expenses FE, and on other exogenous variables OV. Under normal conditions the hypothetical equilibrium level of the public debt D^* is expected to be positive and not constant; the theoretical equilibrium status of the public debt is always moving. Complementing, the trend solution is expressed by:

$$D_{trend} = A\,[1 + r\,(1 - \beta_2)]^t \tag{10}$$

where A is a constant to be determined. The twofold condition for the public debt to be convergent to a theoretical equilibrium status is:

$$0 < \{1 + r\,(1 - \beta_2)\} < 1$$

Taking one of the inequalities:

$$\{1 + r\,(1 - \beta_2)\} > 0$$

and transposing terms one obtains the first condition for convergence:

$$r > -1/(1 - \beta_2) \text{ or } \beta_2 < (1/r)\,(1 + r)$$

This inequality may hold or not for alternative pairs of r and β_2. Particularly, if as expected from the experiment above β_2 is negative while r is positive, then any pair of simultaneous normal values of r and β_2 satisfies the first condition. Complementing, the second condition for convergence towards a stable public debt level is:

$$\{1 + r\,(1 - \beta_2)\} < 1, \text{ implying that } r\,(1 - \beta_2) < 0.$$

This inequality may hold only if the interest rate r and the term $(1 - \beta_2)$ have simultaneously opposite signs. This means that the public debt may converge towards a stable level only in one of two possibilities. In the first one the interest rate r is positive, and thus β_2 must be positive and greater than one, meaning that the tax receipts must be positively associated with the interest expenditure on public debt. The second possibility is that the public debt causes a so huge negative effect on the economic activity that the credit expansion allowed by the interest on the public debt cannot compensate it and hence the net effect of the monetary policy is a reduction of the tax receipts; that is, β_2 is negative. In this case (1 - β_2) is positive and thus equilibrium requires that the interest rate r upon the public debt be negative.

The conclusion is firstly that if as expected from the experiment above β_2 is negative while r is positive then no pair of simultaneous values of r and β_2 can satisfy the second condition. This means that the product {r (1 - β_2)} is always positive and that the partially autonomous trend component (10) leads public debt to infinity. Depending on the capacity of the public debt in creating tax revenue any public debt may carry an explosive trend. Secondly, data demonstrates that the US public debt was following an explosive trend until 2007. Thirdly, the debt trend (10) depends exclusively upon β_2, the effect of interests over the tax receipts, and r, the interest rate fixed by the central bank. Hence, primary surplus does not touch the public debt trend; if β_2 is negative primary surplus cannot provide stability to the public debt and hence to the debt ratio. All the same, privatisation does not touch public debt's trend but reduces the fiscal expenses and raises the implicit tax rate thus reducing GDP and tax revenue. Fourthly, dividing public debt by GDP changes nothing for GDP depends ultimately on natural resources and cannot grow to infinity.

If the US case can be generalized, once initiated public debt keeps always growing to infinity; it is out of the control of the mainstream monetarist economic policy. Falsifying this conclusion requires the proof that in dependable cases β_2 is positive, i.e. that an increase in the interest rent on the public debt normally expands tax revenue.

The general solution of the public debt time performance is given by the summation of theoretical equilibrium and trend solutions:

Public debt is economic nonsense

$$D_t = A \, [1 + r \, (1 - \beta_2)]^t + D^*$$

The value of the coefficient A is found associating the value of D_t to the point zero in the time series, hence obtaining: $D_{t=0} = A + D_0^*$ and thus $A = (D_{t=0} - D_0^*)$. Therefore, the complete equation that describes the time performance of the public debt is:

$$D_t = (D_{t=0} - D_0^*) \, [1 + r \, (1 - \beta_2)]^t + D^* \qquad\qquad (11)$$

The sign of the coefficient A gives the direction that D_t will follow. For instance, it may be expected that in case of debts normally A>0 for at each point in time the theoretical equilibrium of any debt should be lower than the actual one. In this US case the figure nearby shows that the coefficient A was positive as expected but growing, revealing that the distance between the present and theoretical equilibrium public debts increased, that is, in dollars the theoretical equilibrium was further and further away.

Both theoretical equilibrium D^* and interest rate r are not constants; they are time series that depend on economic policy decisions and performance and on other exogenous variables that are changing continuously. Equation (11) reveals the nature of the phenomenon but the trend slope and speed are also always changing. Hence, there is an equation (11) for each point in time that could trace out the future time behaviour of the public debt if economic policy and exogenous variables stop varying; actually, each point is not a single debt value but an equation. What matters is that always that the interest rate is positive and β_2 is negative the coefficient $[1 + r \, (1 - \beta_2)]$ will be greater than one and consequently the public debt D_t will follow an explosive trend towards infinity.

US Federal public held debt (1960-2007) – Coefficient A in equation (11)

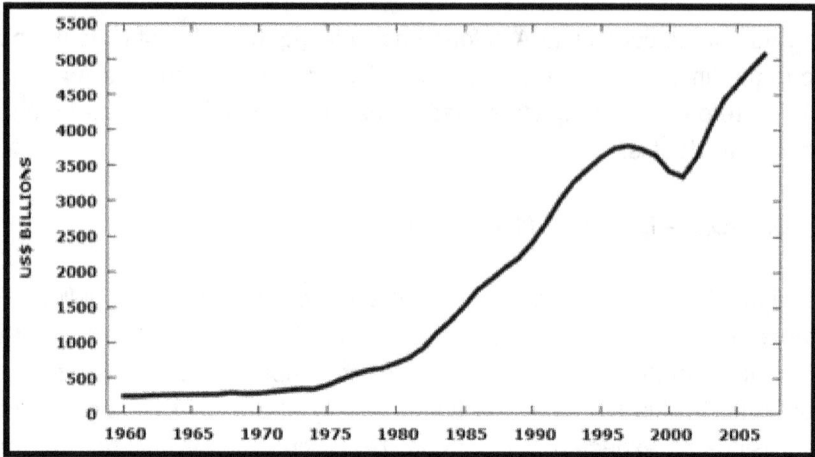

Sources of raw data in the Appendix.

About β_2, in a private investment project interest expenses push debt upwards and return on the financial capital invested pushes debt down. The return must be positive and greater than the expenditure on interest; a coefficient like β_2 must be positive. If so, then the private debt will follow a trend to zero; otherwise the debt will follow an explosive trend to infinity, the project will bankrupt and stockholders will lose their income and, partially or entirely, their wealth. The same principle applies to the public debt; money borrowed by government must generate tax revenue sufficient to pay the due interest. In the case β_2 is negative the primary surplus is systematically lower than the interest to be paid. Consequently, people may lose their income and, partially or entirely, their wealth. Of course, ethics oblige economists to disapprove economically unfeasible private investment projects, but the same principle has not been applied to the public investment that creates jobs and social wealth.

About interest rate, negative values mean money emission and money may be issued by private central banks or by governments directly. Central banks create money out of thin air when paying the interest rent on Treasury bonds they redeem. So, money that pays interest on Treasury bonds is unbacked money. This unbacked money is potentially inflationary especially of assets like for instance houses, directly or via credit; this unbacked money emission may be at the origin of financial crises. On the opposite direction, money created out of thin air by governments is backed money for it is issued to buy goods and services produced by people thus expanding GDP and employment. Of course in this case prices also rise but incomes rose first, people escalated the Maslow's Pyramid and that is fine.

About the theorem, are unfeasible the assumptions that there is no money emission neither to pay interests nor to amortize the debt, and that there is no pure monetary policy. This experiment refers to the case of public debt resulting only from the accumulation of previous governmental deficits but actually monetary policy may increase the public debt when asking Treasury to issue bonds to run the open market and reduce it by printing money to redeem Treasury bonds presented by the Treasury (seigniorage). These are casual autonomous events that cannot be anticipated neither in time nor in extension. Considering however that central banks are profit-seeking private business, the probability of bonds issuing is very much greater than money printing to reduce or avoid the public debt. Consequently, it seems that the probability of public debt explosions everywhere is not to be disregarded.

6. Conclusions

The mainstream approach to the public debt is the same one dedicated to the private companies and consumers; mainstream economists do not study public debt from a macroeconomic standpoint. Mainstream economists are convinced that there is always a feasible primary surplus that government can produce to stabilize the public debt ratio to GDP.

This study shows that the public debt may have an equilibrium level but suggests that the convergence to it looks improbable for it depends on how much the money borrowed by government can expand aggregate demand and thus increase tax receipts and pay interests. The estimate of the US federal tax revenue points to a positive effect of the interest rent on the US tax receipts that is insufficient to compensate the simultaneous negative effect of the public debt itself. Thus, considering that these variables are mutually dependent, the conclusion is that the combined result is negative. Therefore, at least in the period 1960-2007 the US public held debt was

Ideas towards a new international financial architecture?

following an explosive trend. The immediate consequence is that the unbacked money issued by central banks without auditing to pay interest on Treasury bonds followed the same trend to infinity.

The financial, economic and social crisis that came next was predictable for the same explosive tendency applies, besides unbacked money emission, to everything else touched by public debt: interest rent to the few, private excessive savings, money supply excessive expansion, financial assets inflation, real estate prices inflation, financial crises, frauds, corruption, bail outs, monetary policy crises, income and wealth concentrations, food prices inflation, unemployment, and much more. The main conclusion is that preventing public debt explosive trend and avoiding its consequences is not an exclusive mainstream monetary concern. It is missing deeper non-mainstream studies of the monetary policy questioning its scientific validity for it is possible that it is one important root of the great economic and social problems real world people are facing.

References

Boussard, J., Castro, F. and Salto, M. (2012) Fiscal Multipliers and Public Debt Dynamics in Consolidations. *European Commission, European Economy*. Economic Papers 460 (July). Available at: http://ec.europa.eu/economy_finance/index_en.htm. [Accessed: 12/2/2015].

Cecchetti, S. G., Mohanty, M. and Zampolli, F. (2011) The real effects of debt. *BIS Monetary and Economic Department*. Working Paper 352 (September). Available at: http://www.bis.org/publ/work352.pdf. [Accessed: 22/2/2015].

Cherif, R. and Hasanov, F. (2012) Public Debt Dynamics: The Effects of Austerity, Inflation, and Growth Shocks. *International Monetary Fund, Institute for Capacity Development*. Working Paper 12/230 (September). At: https://www.imf.org/external/pubs/ft/wp/2012/wp12230.pdf. [Accessed: 2/3/2015].

Escolano, J. (2010) A Practical Guide to Public Debt Dynamics, Fiscal Sustainability, and Cyclical Adjustment of Budgetary Aggregates. *International Monetary Fund, Fiscal Affairs Department*. January. Available:

https://www.imf.org/external/pubs/cat/longres.aspx?sk=23498.0
[Accessed: 12/2/2015].

Gechert, S. and Mentges, F. (2013) What Drives Fiscal Multipliers? The Role of Private Wealth and Debt. *Macroeconomic Policy Institute,* Working Paper 124 (October). Available at:
http://www.boeckler.de/pdf/imk_wp_124_2013 [Accessed: 21/2/2015]

International Monetary Fund. (2010) *World Economic Outlook: Recovery, Risk, and Rebalancing.* Chapter 3 (pp. 112-43). Available at: http://www.imf.org/external/pubs/ft/weo/2010/02/. [Accessed: 3/3/2015].

Keynes, J. M. (1936) *The General Theory of Employment, Interest, and Money.* Harvest Harcourt Brace 1st edition, 1964.

Krugman, P. (2010) Self-Defeating Austerity. *The New York Times,* [online]. July 7th. Available at:
http://krugman.blogs.nytimes.com/2010/07/07/self-defeating-austerity [Accessed: 12/2/2015].

Lima, G. P. (2015) Supply and Demand Is Not a Neoclassical Concern. *Munich Personal RePEc Archive.* Available at:
http://mpra.ub.uni-muenchen.de/63135 [Accessed: 3/3/2015].

Nautet, M. and Van Meensel, L. (2011) "Economic impact of the public debt." *Economic Review, National Bank of Belgium*, September. Available from: http://www.nbb.be/doc/ts/publications/EconomicReview/2011/ecorevII2011_H1.pdf [Accessed: 12/2/2015].

Semmler, W. and Semmler, A. (2013) The Macroeconomics of Fiscal Austerity in Europe. *Macroeconomic Policy Institute*, Working Paper 122 (July 2nd) http://www.boeckler.de/pdf/p_imk_wp_122_2013 [Accessed: 15/2/2015].

Veld, J., Pagano, A., Ratto, M., Roeger, W. and Sekely, I. P. (2012) Sovereign debt sustainability scenarios based on an estimated model for Spain. *European Commission, European Economy.* Economic Papers, Working Paper 466 (November). Available from:
http://ec.europa.eu/economy_finance/publications/economic_paper/2012/ec p466_en.htm [Accessed: 18/3/2015].

Appendix

Variables: definitions and sources
Data are current values

T - Federal government; current total receipts, US$ billions, White House, Office of Management and Budget, Historical Tables, 2014, Tables 1.4. http://www.whitehouse.gov/omb/budget/Historicals

FE - Federal Government, Fiscal Expenditure, estimated by subtracting Net interest expenditure from Total outlays, US$ billions, White House, Office of Management and Budget, Historical Tables, 2014, Tables 1.4 and 3.1. http://www.whitehouse.gov/omb/budget/Historicals

ER - Exchange rate, average exchange rate in US dollars needed to buy a foreign currencies basket weighted by the corresponding US exports. Original data: OECD. Sample: Austria, Belgium, Canada, China, France, Germany, Ireland, Italy, Japan, Mexico, Netherlands, Switzerland and United Kingdom. http://stats.oecd.org/Index.aspx?DataSetCode=SNA_TABLE4

MW - Federal minimum wage, US$ per hour, U.S. Department of Labor. http://www.dol.gov/whd/minwage/chart.htm

DP - Federal Government debt hold by the Federal Reserve System and the public, US$ billions, White House, Office of Management and Budget, Historical Tables, Table 7.1.
http://www.whitehouse.gov/omb/budget/Historicals

INT – Federal Government interest expenditure, US$ billion, Federal Reserve System, Data Download Program.
http://www.federalreserve.gov/datadownload/Choose.aspx?rel=Z1

PART II
Rethinking the international financial architecture

Ideas towards a new international financial architecture?

CHAPTER 5

Re-engineering the economic processes: "money", wealth, currencies, market forces and cash/banking

Tim Knight

1. Introduction

> "The composition of this book has been for the author a long
> struggle of escape, and so must the reading of it be for most
> readers if the author's assault upon them is to be successful
> – a struggle of escape from habitual modes of thought and
> expression. The ideas which are here expressed so
> laboriously are extremely simple and should be obvious.
> The difficulty lies, not in the new ideas, but in escaping from
> the old ones, which ramify ... into every corner of our minds"
> (John Maynard Keynes).

There is a general consensus at present that "radical things must be done" with the basic macro-economic, finance and banking processes, but great controversy as to what those "radical things" could or should be. Unfortunately, because of limited public attention spans when compared to the perceived complexity of the issues, propositions are typically presented using the current hotchpotch of *administrative* processes as the frame of reference, and it is often difficult to distinguish form from substance through the fog of terminology and inter-dependencies. How many of the general public really understand the underlying relationships between inflation, exchange rates, interest rates, "money", "money" supply, quantitative easing, credit and debt? Indeed, how many accountants, macro-economists, central bankers and politicians could genuinely claim to be able to articulate their understanding to the general public, or even to understand these concepts and relationships in the first place?

Ideas towards a new international financial architecture?

However, this paper argues that the *underlying* concepts and relationships themselves are *not* complex. The perception that they *are* complex arises mainly from the perverse and spurious complexity of many of the current *administrative* processes which most people, by default, use as the frame of reference for their understanding. Too many people are suffering from "bureaucratic alienation"; give up trying to understand, and simply "go with the flow". They presume that the "experts" know what they are doing, and have the community's best interests at heart, when all the evidence suggests that most "experts" are renowned (and remunerated) not so much for their fundamental insights and goodwill, but for their expertise in the use (*and/or abuse*) of the current *administrative* processes. At best, the "experts" have a conflict of interest in commenting on radical analysis and proposals for reform.

As depicted in the following diagrams, all process-development uses a paradigm (of the fundamentals) as the frame of reference for analysis (1), design (2), and migration (3).

Process re-engineering differs from conventional process-development as follows:

1. As illustrated in Figure 1, conventional process-development typically uses a paradigm *supposedly* based on the underlying fundamentals, but *actually* based on *current processes*. Over time, conventional process-development can lose sight of the underlying fundamentals, and can result in false assumptions and an incoherent network of processes each accommodating incoherent inter-dependencies.

Re-engineering the economic processes

Figure 1: Conventional Process Development

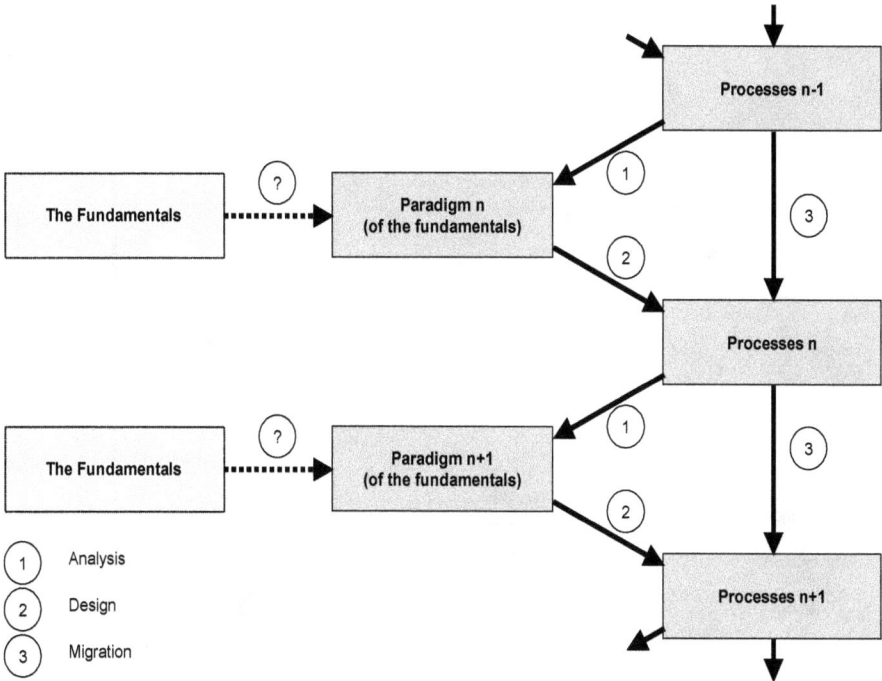

2. As illustrated in Figure 2, process re-engineering uses a paradigm based on *a more radical analysis of the nature of the issues under consideration*. It attempts to address and resolve those issues more directly "at source" through re-engineered processes aligned directly to the underlying fundamentals. Successful process re-engineering typically leads not only to a more rational, accurate, flexible and sophisticated resolution of the fundamental issues and requirements, but invariably also to much simpler and more transparent processes.

Figure 2: Process Re-Engineering

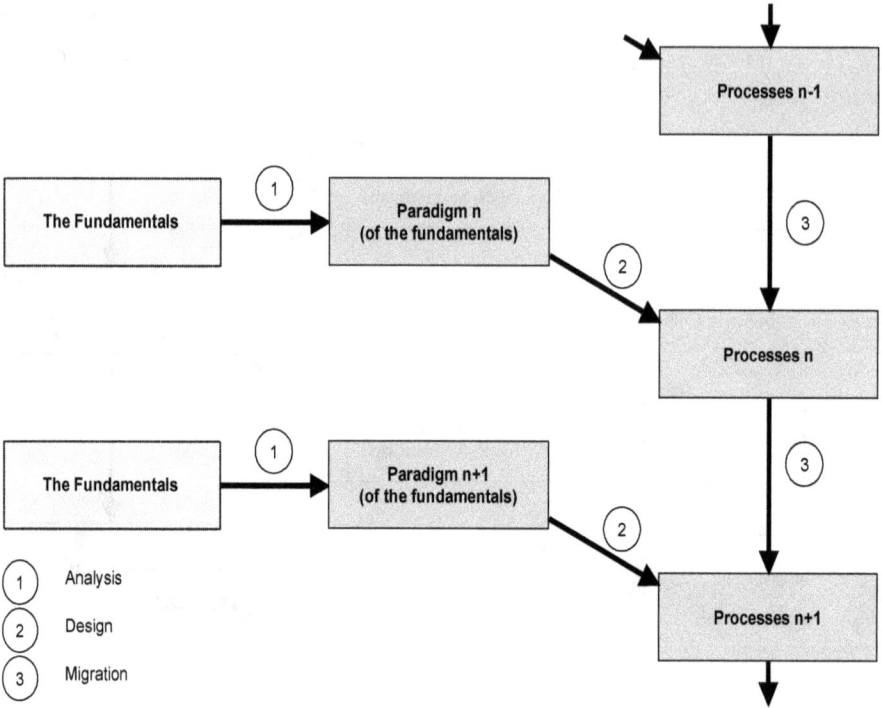

The requirement for simple transparent processes in a liberal democracy should not be underestimated. If liberal democracy is to survive and prosper, and if we citizens are to survive and prosper in liberal democratic regimes, it is essential that social and macro-economic justice is not only done, but is seen and *understood* to have been done. Without a solid base of coherent insight and understanding amongst the general population, the policy debate in a democracy will always be limited to what a politician can get into a sound-bite. With coherently re-engineered processes, we can hope to dispel "bureaucratic alienation", raise the integrity of proposals and debate, and build the sense of one-nation community essential to the success of democracy. Thus, by working from radical analysis through to definition of administrative processes more closely aligned to the fundamentals, process re-engineering techniques can introduce new insights into the macro-economic and political debates, and thereby facilitate an escape from the policy and process inheritance, and from Keynes's "habitual modes of thought and expression".

2. "Money"

Perhaps the least coherent aspect of Keynes's "habitual modes of thought and expression" in macro-economics is the all-pervasive and ill-considered use of the expression "money". Unfortunately, the concepts "enclosed" by that expression dominate the paradigm (supposedly of the underlying fundamentals) on which conventional macro-economic wisdom and conventional process-development is based. However, using a process re-engineering approach, we must not start with the expression "money" as a given, and then ask what that expression means, or ought to mean. That would lock us into the "habitual modes of thought and expression" from which we are (potentially) trying to escape. Accountants, macro-economists, central bankers and politicians cannot agree on a *macro-economic* distinction (i.e. as opposed to a legal, administrative or slang distinction) between "money" wealth and non- "money" wealth. The reason may well be because they are all fools or knaves (or even both). However, a much more likely reason is that there is simply no such macro-economically-significant distinction there to be made.

Experts in any and every field have a tendency to use "woolly" expressions and concepts to cover gaps in their insight and understanding, and to then obfuscate in a patronising manner about the meaning of those expressions in order to disguise those gaps. Early clinicians used the expression "the humours" as part of their conventional wisdom, and many such clinicians built reputations and fortunes on their claimed insight into the nature of "the humours". The clinician community re-enforced and built on each other's theories out of mutual self-interest. We now know that they were all talking complete codswallop. Many may well have been fools or knaves (or even both), but most were well-intentioned people groping their way forward in the manner of the partially-sighted leading the blind. They used such expressions in the absence of more fundamental insights, and gained the confidence of their patients with a form of smoke and mirrors. Similarly, early physicists used the expression "the ether" as the presumed carrier of light, and explored many theories about the nature of "the ether". We now know that light does not need a carrier in that sense, so we now know that their quest was doomed from the start.

The "habitual modes of thought and expression" with regard to the expression "money" include many variations on the following "woolly concepts":

- A slang synonym for "cash in your pocket".
- A slang synonym for "wealth".
- A store of "intermediate" wealth (intermediate between income and outgoings).
- A means of payment (for income and outgoings).
- A unit of measure of value.
- A slang synonym for "buying/employing power".
- A slang synonym for "propensity to buy/employ".

However, using a process re-engineering approach:

We will ignore the first two woolly concepts altogether for the rest of this paper (other than remaining on our guard against using the expression as such).

We will defer consideration of the last two woolly concepts until much later in this paper, when we will look at "real" economic activity (i.e. production, consumption, trade and employment, as opposed to finance and book-keeping).

That leaves us with the middle three woolly concepts; the ones used in most conventional (and unconventional, orthodox and heterodox, incremental and radical) macro-economic textbooks:

- A store of "intermediate" wealth (intermediate between income and outgoings).
- A means of payment (for income and outgoings).
- A unit of measure of value.

However, using a process re-engineering approach, this paper argues that the use of the expression "money" to enclose these three woolly concepts obfuscates and conflates two radically-distinct concepts, and that, if we wish to facilitate integrity of thought and expression, we must *reserve two radically-distinct expressions* for those two radically-distinct concepts, and we must consider those two radically-distinct concepts in isolation *before* considering policy options (potentially to try to link them). More specifically, in this paper, and as illustrated in Figure 3, the expression "Economics" is reserved to encompass the top-level concept of *"Production, Consumption, Trade and Employment"*, and the first level of analysis within that top-level concept qualifies the following two radically-distinct sub-concepts:

a. The expression "wealth" is reserved *solely* to encompass the concept of "value"; value which could be recorded as a line-item in a balance sheet in the form of an "asset" or a "liability" ("money" or non-"money" without distinction).

b. The expression "currency" is reserved *solely* to encompass the concept of a "unit of measure of value" (such as the US dollar, the GB pound, the Euro, the Yen, etc.). Units of measure are merely figures of speech. They cannot in themselves possess the characteristic of value, and their sole role in a balance sheet is in the *enumeration* of the value of wealth ("money" and non- "money" without distinction).

Figure 3: The proposed macro-economic paradigm – wealth and currencies

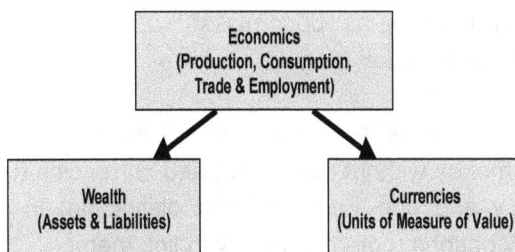

Indeed, in this paper, the expression "money" is reserved solely to encompass an "administrative subset" of wealth, and the *distinction* between "money wealth" and "non-money wealth" is deferred to a (much) lower level of analysis.

Ideas towards a new international financial architecture?

Of course, much of the literature acknowledges a minor and incidental distinction between money-wealth and currencies (with expressions such as "money things" for a subset of what this paper reserves the expression "wealth", and "monies of account" for what this paper reserves the expression "currencies"). However, even the literature which *does* acknowledge the distinction then immediately obfuscates and conflates that distinction.

In contrast, this paper insists that the distinction is *fundamental* and must be considered as such. Indeed, it argues that, contrary to conventional wisdom, whenever there was a relationship between some form of money wealth (as defined in this paper) and a currency (as defined in this paper):

> 1. The value associated with the given currency was *always* the *exogenous* factor (i.e. the externally-determined "given" factor in the relationship; determined on a rolling "macro-economically-incidental" basis by millions of naive economic agents agreeing millions of prices each day).

> 2. The value of the given item of money wealth was *always* the *endogenous* factor (i.e. the "managed" factor in the relationship; determined by willful policy).

In particular, the Bretton Woods agreement should be seen not as an attempt to anchor the value associated with the US dollar (a currency) to the "market" value of some form of gold money wealth, but as an (ultimately futile) attempt to rig the "market" value of gold (money and non-money without distinction) by acting as "bottomless" "supplier" and "demander" at a rigged price in a rigged market for gold.

Thus, this paper analyses the two radically-distinct concepts of wealth (money and non-money without distinction) and currencies (units of measure of value – money and non-money without distinction) in isolation *before* considering policy options (potentially to try to link them).

Re-engineering the economic processes

1 Wealth (money and non-money without distinction)

This paper analyses from first principles the concept of wealth (as defined in this paper), and argues that the sole worthwhile *macro-economic* distinction (i.e. as opposed to legal, administrative or slang distinction) between different types of wealth is *not* the distinction between money wealth and non-money Wealth, but the distinction between *owned-wealth* (money or non-money without distinction) and *owed-wealth* (money or non-money without distinction).

More specifically, and as depicted in Figure 4:

The expression "wealth" is reserved *solely* to encompass the concept of *value*; value which could be recorded as a line-item in a balance sheet in the form of an *asset* or a *liability* (money or non-money without distinction).

The expression *owned-wealth* (money and non-money without distinction) is reserved *solely* for anything which appears in precisely *one* balance sheet. Each such item is therefore a "net-equals-gross" increment to Keynes's "wealth of nations".

The expression *owed-wealth* (money and non-money without distinction) is reserved *solely* for anything which appears in precisely *two* balance sheets: once as an asset; and once as an equal and opposite liability. For every item of owed-wealth, there is a borrower and a lender within the same macro-economic system (and indeed, "within" the same currency). Each such item is therefore a "zero-sum" increment to Keynes's "wealth of nations". Indeed, owed-wealth is simply a zero-sum book-keeping exercise which keeps the score on where we are in our non-barter trading and employment activity. Those who have sold more than they have bought accumulate a net-positive balance, and those who have bought more than they have sold accumulate a net-negative balance. The aggregate (of course) is zero. Buyers/employers and sellers/employees then use the cash/banking processes merely to "intermediate" that owed-wealth. The aggregate (of course) remains zero.

111

Ideas towards a new international financial architecture?

The expression *net-wealth* (money and non-money distinction) is reserved *solely* for the sum of owned-wealth and owed-wealth; for each economic agent, and in aggregate. Because aggregate owed-wealth is zero-sum, aggregate net-wealth is equal to aggregate owned-wealth.

Figure 4: The proposed macro-economic paradigm – owed-wealth and owned-wealth

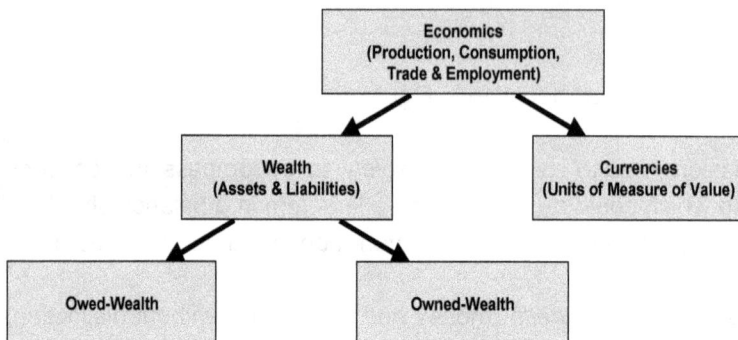

As a further level of analysis, and as depicted in Figure 5, this paper proposes the following three definitions of three different types of Owed-Wealth:

1. *Nominal* owed-wealth (money and non-money without distinction) can be characterised as follows:
    a. Ongoing cash-flows are determined by ad-hoc and/or scheduled fiat.
    b. Ongoing values are determined by fiat.
    c. E.g. cash, bank accounts, credit accounts, loan accounts, hire-purchase accounts, mortgage accounts and trading debts.

2. *Securitized* owed-wealth (money and non-money without distinction) can be characterised as follows:
    a. Ongoing cash-flows are determined by scheduled fiat.
    b. Ongoing values are determined by the market.
    c. E.g. GB Gilts, US Treasuries, and other state, commercial and mortgage-backed bonds.

112

3. *Equity* owed-wealth (money and non-money without distinction) can be characterised as follows:
   a. Ongoing cash-flows are determined by the debtor.
   b. Ongoing values are determined by the market.
   c. E.g. stocks and shares.

Figure 5: The proposed paradigm – de-construction of owed-wealth

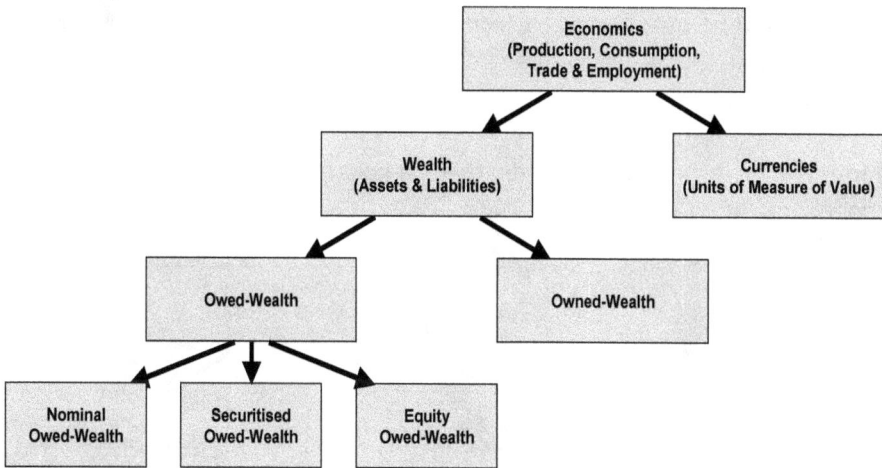

As a further level of analysis, and as depicted in Figure 6, this paper proposes the following definitions of three different types of "money" as sub-sets of owned-wealth and owed-wealth:

> The expression *precious cash* is reserved *solely* for the wealth "evidenced" by each "monetary token" "transacted" at the free-market value of its constituent commodities or as a collector's item (and *irrespective* of its "face" value). Each such item is **owned-wealth**; owned-wealth which appears solely as an asset in the balance sheet of the owner.

> The expression *non-precious cash* is reserved *solely* for the wealth

"evidenced" by each "monetary token" "transacted" at a "face" value *higher* than the free-market value of its constituent commodities or as a collector's item. Each such item is **owed-wealth**; owed-wealth which appears as an asset in the balance sheet of the bearer and which appears (or *ought* to appear) as an equal and opposite liability in the balance sheet of the issuer (typically as part of the M0 part of a national debt).

The expression *non-cash money* is reserved *solely* for wealth "associated with" a bank "current" account. Each such item is **owed-wealth**; owed-wealth which appears as an asset in one balance sheet and as an equal and opposite liability in another balance sheet.

Figure 6: The proposed paradigm – de-construction of money and non-money wealth

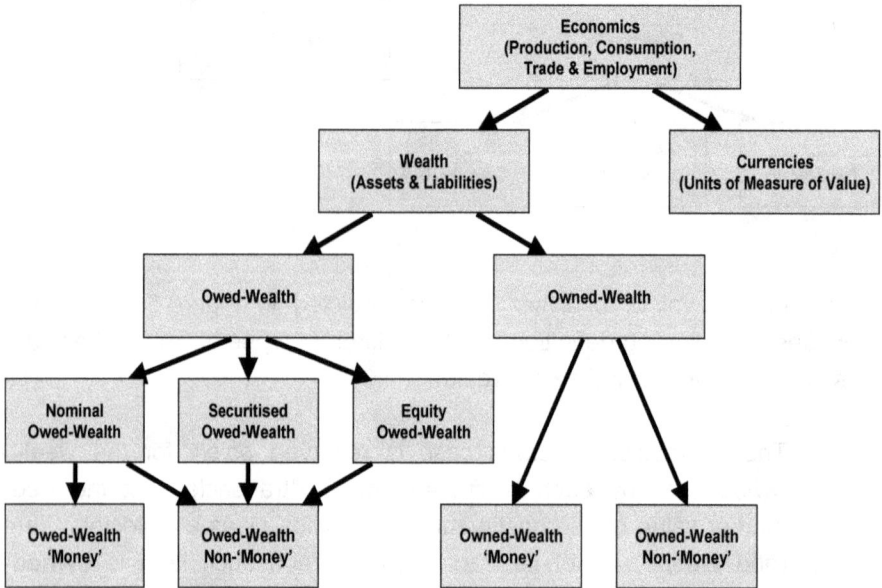

Re-engineering the economic processes

However, this paper argues that:

1. The *distinctions* between money wealth and non-money wealth, are (or *ought* to be) *purely-administrative/micro-economic* distinctions; of interest only to students of the history of routine commercial and financial administration.

2. The *distinctions* between nominal owed-wealth, securitised owed-wealth and equity owed-wealth are (or *ought* to be) *purely-administrative/micro-economic* distinctions; of interest only to students of the history of routine commercial and financial administration.

Thus, the paradigms depicted in Figures 5 and 6 above should be seen not as *purely-fundamental macro-economic paradigms*, but as *conflated macro-economic plus administrative paradigms*. Indeed, if we wish to establish a basis for re-engineering of the basic macro-economic, finance and banking processes, we must "back-off" to the *purely-fundamental macro-economic paradigm* depicted in Figure 4, and re-depicted here in Figure 7, in which:

1. The *distinction* between wealth (money and non-money without distinction) and currencies is recognised as *fundamental* (and *is* therefore represented).

2. The *distinction* between owned-wealth (money and non-money without distinction) and owed-wealth (money and non-money without distinction) is recognised as *fundamental* (and *is* therefore represented).

3. The *distinction* between nominal owned-wealth, securitised owed-wealth and equity owned-wealth is considered to be a *purely-administrative/micro-economic* distinction, and is therefore *irrelevant* in a macro-economic paradigm (and is therefore *not* represented).

4. The *distinction* between money owned-wealth and non-money owned-wealth is considered to be a *purely-administrative/micro-economic* distinction, and is therefore *irrelevant* in a macro-

Ideas towards a new international financial architecture?

economic paradigm (and is therefore *not* represented).

5. The *distinction* between money nominal owed-wealth and non-money nominal owed-wealth is considered to be a *purely-administrative/micro-economic* distinction, and is therefore *irrelevant* in a macro-economic paradigm (and is therefore *not* represented).

Figure 7: The proposed "necessary and sufficient" fundamental macro-economic paradigm

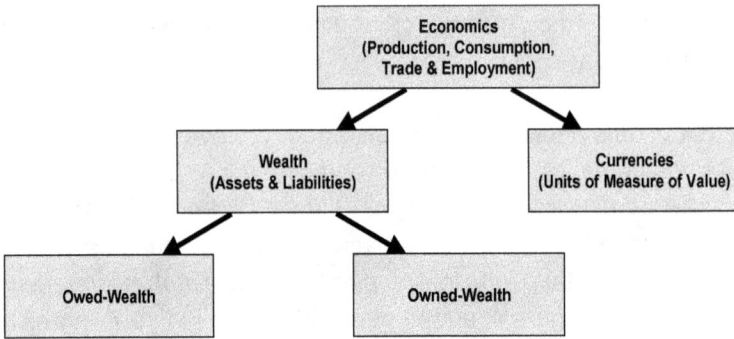

Finally, if the "atomic units" of economic *status* (as reported in balance sheets) are owned-wealth and owed-wealth (as above), then the "atomic units" of economic *activity* (as summarised in profit and loss reports and cash flow reports) are:

- Production/consumption transactions.
- Trade/employment transactions.
- Owed-wealth-rotation transactions.

More specifically:

Production/consumption transactions (as defined in this paper) require no "finance" (i.e. owed-wealth is not affected).

1. Trade/employment transactions (as defined in this paper) are "self-financing" (i.e. the buyer/employer effectively "borrows" from the seller/employee at the point of trade/employment; as recorded in

116

payables/receivables accounts).

2. Owed-wealth-rotation transactions (as defined in this paper) are "self-financing". They are simply zero-sum closed-circles of zero-sum double-entry postings by which the cash/banking processes are used to "intermediate" nominal owed-wealth.

Thus, accountants, macro-economists, central bankers and politicians should ignore all concepts, expressions and aggregates associated with distinctions between different types of wealth other than the distinction between owned-wealth and owed-wealth. Instead, they should recognise that the sole key factor determining ongoing economic activity is *the net propensity to buy/employ for production/consumption,* that that propensity is pro-cyclical and destabilising, and that economic stability is possible *only* with communal initiatives to 'swim against the market tide'.

3. Currencies (units of measure of value)

This paper analyses from first principles the concept of "currencies" as units of measure of value (as defined in this paper). It argues that inflation/deflation in the value associated with each currency is (or *ought* to be) a *purely-administrative* factor. *By default,* macro-economic factors whose value is determined by fiat *ought* to be inflation-linked passively. This passive inflation-linking should include currency-conversion rates (conventionally called currency- "exchange" rates), owed-wealth (or base interest rates), and scheduled payments. This passive inflation-linking would establish the zero-sum network of owed-wealth as a *global, macro-economically-neutral, level-value* frame of reference for "real" macro-economic activity (i.e. production, consumption, trade and employment, as opposed to finance and book-keeping). The macro-economic issues currently associated with inflation and exchange-rate instability should be seen as self-inflicted wounds caused by willful variations from that default. Thus, accountants, macro-economists, central bankers and politicians should promote that default through global and state institutions from the IMF downwards, should abandon "monetary" policy altogether, and should confine macro-economic policy exclusively to fiscal policy.

4. Market forces

This paper argues that "market forces" are actually a compound of three radically-distinct *perfectly-rational* factors:

a. In considering *supply-chain production/consumption* of owned-wealth, economic agents are *price-takers*. There is no feedback into market prices. If the de-facto market price is above/below the equilibrium level, net production/consumption will be positive/negative. The perfectly-rational but sub-optimal aggregate result is *inadvertent supply-chain investment/disinvestment in owned-wealth* (i.e. investment in market opportunity, productive capacity and stocks which, with the benefit of hindsight, the economic agent would not have made).

b. In considering *deliberate supply-chain investment/disinvestment* in owned-wealth, economic agents become *price-makers* as they attempt to increase/decrease their investment and prices to what they judge to be a revised equilibrium level. The perfectly-rational but sub-optimal *aggregate* result is *business-cycles of supply-chain investment/disinvestment in owned-wealth.*

c. In considering *speculative investment/disinvestment* in owned-wealth, equity owed-wealth or securitised owed-wealth, economic agents become *bubble-makers* as they attempt to increase/decrease their de-facto investment purely to take advantage of anticipated increases/decreases in market prices. The perfectly-rational but sub-optimal *aggregate* result is *de-stabilising self-fulfilling expectations,* which can be moderated *only* by "communal" initiatives to "swim against the market-sentiment tide".

The conclusion is that the (supposedly) self-optimising influence of "market forces" arises not from the interplay between "supply" and "demand" in the context of some form of "market", but from the interplay between production and consumption of owned-wealth within the context of a supply-chain. That interplay between production and consumption results not in stable-equilibrium investment and prices, but in *business cycles around* stable-equilibrium investment and prices. However, even for production and consumption of owned-wealth within the context of a supply-chain, the optimising influence of "market forces" is overlaid by long-run booms and busts created by the last of the above radically-distinct influences; speculative investment/disinvestment.

For *owed-wealth*, there is no such thing as production/consumption or a supply-chain. Owed-wealth is simply a zero-sum book-keeping exercise. Thus, the market prices of equity and securitised owed-wealth are dominated by the last of the above radically-distinct influences; speculative investment/disinvestment.

De-stabilising self-fulfilling expectations are exacerbated by excessive leverage, derivatives and other financial engineering, and can be moderated *solely* by communal initiatives to "swim against the market-sentiment tide ". In the interest of economic stability, the central banking system (including the global and state banks and regulators from the IMF downwards) should moderate conservatively the level of such financial engineering on behalf of creditors (rather than allowing politicians, bankers, corporate executives, and financial professionals free reign in their own self-serving interests). In doing so, they should follow the precautionary principle in regulating financial innovation (i.e. financial innovation should be 'prohibited unless specifically approved', as opposed to 'permitted unless specifically prohibited').

5. Solvency and liquidity of financial institutions

This paper argues that state and global banks and regulators *already* in effect acts as *implicit* guarantor for every non-equity owed-wealth liability of every financial institution and state (too big in aggregate to be allowed to fail), and that that role should be made *explicit.* The central banking system should act as borrower/lender of *first/default* recourse for banks and states (i.e. as opposed to borrower/lender of *last* recourse in current conventional wisdom).

This would eliminate (the need for) inter-bank debt, and would eliminate liquidity as a macro-economic factor. In order to moderate the risk implicit in such a guarantee, the central banking system (including the global and state banks and regulators from the IMF downwards) should require a transparently-conservative valuation of every asset of every financial institution and state, and of every asset offered by a debtor as security for each Owed-Wealth liability. In particular, in order to remove the perverse incentives and conflicts of interest in the current valuation and auditing standards and processes, the central banking system (including the global and state banks and regulators from the IMF downwards) should itself commission all of those valuation and auditing standards and processes conservatively on behalf of creditors (rather than allowing politicians, bankers, corporate executives, and financial professionals free reign in their own self-serving interests).

Again, in doing so, they should follow the precautionary principle (i.e. financial innovation should be "prohibited unless specifically approved", as opposed to "permitted unless specifically prohibited"). Indeed, the vast majority of financial innovation (including securitised owed-wealth such as GB Gilts, US Treasuries, and other state, commercial and mortgage-backed bonds) should be outlawed in favour of simple inflation-linked current-accounting. Thus, in turn, accountants, macro-economists, central bankers and politicians should abandon all concepts and aggregates associated with the expressions "money", "printing money", "quantitative easing", "Enronomics", "pyramid schemes", "toxic waste", etc., etc., etc..

Final considerations

In the Introduction of this chapter, we begged a temporary "suspension of disbelief" with regard to the content, and a sympathetic acceptance of a style of analysis and exposition which varies from standard academic practice. Our research has organized the analysis and arguments in heavily structured text to highlight the heavily structured nature of that analysis and argument, to using underlining and boldfacing to highlight key points within that structure, to using capitalisation for expressions which he pleads to reserve for highly-specific definition (e.g. the expressions "wealth" and "currencies"), and to using repetition of key points as a foundation for further analysis and argument. This method is aimed to aid assimilation by his readers (think of the concept of herding cats) in order to build the exposition as if it were being presented in person to a business audience, and to using such special formatting as a substitute for visual aids, voice modulation, eye contact and body language. Although aware that the academic world is very different from the business world, we have found it impossible to convey the full import and precision of his analysis and argument in writing without such special formatting.

As for so many issues, the devil is in the detail. A major part of our argument is that the detail of the macro-economic fundamentals *is* heavily structured (please excuse the emphasis), and therefore so must the exposition be if it is to explore, differentiate and pin down those fundamentals. Therefore, to analyse heavily structured detail with "stream of consciousness" text is like asking Newton to explain differential calculus in "plain English".

Indeed, without that heavily structured "heavy lifting" "process engineering" approach, it is far too easy to fall into snake-oil concepts such as "printing money" "Enronomics", "pyramid schemes", "quantitative easing", etc., etc.

References

Keynes, J. M. (1930) *A Treatise on Money*

Keynes, J. M. (1936) *The General Theory of Employment, Interest and Money*, Macmillan, 1936.

Ho, L. S. (2000) "Towards a New International Monetary Order: The World Currency Unit and the Global Indexed Bond". *The World Economy*, 23: 939–950. doi: 10.1111/1467-9701.00310.

Xiaochuan, Z. (2009) "Reform the International Monetary System" (PDF). *BIS Review*. Bank of International Settlements. http://www.bis.org/review/r090402c.pdf Retrieved 2010-11-28.

Recommendations by the Commission of Experts of the President of the General Assembly on reforms of the international monetary and financial system, 20.3.2009. http://www.un.org/ga/president/63/letters/recommendationExperts200309.pdf

Reserve Accumulation and International Monetary Stability, 13.4.2010, http://www.imf.org/external/np/pp/eng/2010/041310.pdf

Ideas towards a new international financial architecture?

CHAPTER 6
Infrastructure without debt

Ellen Brown and Uli Kortsch

Over the next five years, the US budget for infrastructure faces a shortfall of $1.6 trillion. Current funding mechanisms such as the Highway Trust Fund are no longer sustainable or are nearly bankrupt. Meanwhile, we are in a prolonged era of national austerity and budget crisis, with a general perception that the deficit must be reduced, not increased. Yet the cost of inaction will be greater than not acting. In the words of Joseph Stiglitz, a policy of austerity is a suicide pact.

Congress needs new ways to fund the shortfall. This paper proposes that the US adopt an infrastructure funding mechanism that is based on a new round of Quantitative Easing. Three Options are discussed:

1. Funding through the Federal Reserve (similar to existing QE rounds);
2. Funding through the Treasury through the printing of US Notes (government-issued money); and
3. Funding through the Treasury by the minting of special coins.

The authors show that this approach has historical precedents and a current legislative enablement, and that it will not lead to hyper-inflation. As part of the funding process, a new control framework is also proposed to ensure a balanced and equitable distribution of benefit.

1.   The problem: the infrastructure crisis

In 2013, the American Society of Civil Engineers (ASCE) gave the national infrastructure an overall grade of D-plus. Some of the biggest problem areas were aviation, drinking-water supply, roads, transit and sewage treatment. Restoring it all to good working order will require an investment of $3.6

trillion by 2020, the ASCE concluded, and if the current level of spending continues, funds will fall short of that figure by $1.6 trillion (ASCE 2013).

Infrastructure challenges continued in 2014, ranging from water main failures to increased highway congestion to bridge disrepair. Faced with these challenges, lawmakers from both political parties are pressing for increased infrastructure funding (Wolfertz, 2015).

Senator Bernie Sanders (I-Vt.) plans to introduce a bill in the new session of Congress to authorize $1 trillion in spending over several years to rebuild the nation's roads and bridges and invest in other infrastructure modernization projects. Speaker of the House John Boehner said that figuring out how to fund the highway bill is an important priority for this year. Senate Republican Environment and Public Works Chairman James Inhofe said that "everything is on the table. "

The call for vast new investment comes in an era of national austerity, with a major source of infrastructure funding – the Highway Trust Fund – on the brink of bankruptcy. But lawmakers are realizing that the cost of action in this case is less than the cost of doing nothing. After a thorough analysis of statistics from dozens of countries forced to apply austerity plans by the World Bank and IMF, former World Bank chief economist Joseph Stiglitz called austerity plans a "suicide pact" (Moore, 2012).

The possibility explored in this paper is that infrastructure could be funded through a new round of "quantitative easing" – effectively just issuing the money. This could be done either through the Federal Reserve or through the Treasury directly, with an issue of US Notes or special coins. All three options will be discussed here.

Under current market conditions, direct money issuance can be done without causing price inflation. (Duncan, 2015) Prices go up when demand (money) exceeds supply (goods and services); and with mechanization and the availability of cheap labor in vast global markets today, supply (productivity) can keep up with demand for decades to come. To quote financial author Richard Duncan:

"Quantitative Easing has only been possible because it has occurred at a time when Globalization is driving down the price of labor and industrial goods. The combination of fiat money and Globalization creates a unique moment in history where the governments of the developed economies can print money on an aggressive scale without causing inflation.

They should take advantage of this once-in-history opportunity to borrow more in order to invest in new industries and technologies, to restructure their economies and to retrain and educate their workforce at the post-graduate level. If they do, they could not only end the global economic crisis, but also ensure that the standard of living in the developed world continues to improve, rather than sinking down to third world levels" (Duncan, 2015).

The focus in this paper is on the US economy and US legal structure, but the principles apply globally. Quantitative easing (QE) as a funding mechanism for infrastructure is currently being proposed for the EU (Meadway, 2015), and Britain and Japan are already using a similar approach to address their transportation infrastructure needs (Peterson, 2013). Historically, a functionally similar approach has also been taken by many other countries, including China, Korea, Canada, New Zealand, Australia, Argentina and Brazil (Brown, 2013).

2. The solution: a round of QE for infrastructure

The Federal Reserve ("Fed") and other central banks have been engaging in massive programs of quantitative easing to counter deflation (a drop in the money supply). Deflation means there is insufficient money in the circulating money supply to fuel growth and productivity. The problem with the current form of QE is that most of it stays on the balance sheets of banks without getting into the real economy. The solution is for governments to use their money-issuing power to fund their own budgets – starting, least controversially, with infrastructure.

125

Ideas towards a new international financial architecture?

With the political will to do it, this could quite easily be achieved. Nothing backs the US dollar today but "the full faith and credit of the United States". The United States could issue its own credit directly to fund its budget, just as the American colonists did with their paper scrip, and as Abraham Lincoln did with the US Notes or "greenbacks" issued in the Civil War.

Any serious discussion of this alternative has long been taboo among economists and politicians. But in a landmark speech on February 6, 2013, Adair Turner, chairman of Britain's Financial Services Authority, broke the taboo with a historic speech recommending that approach. Turner is considered one of the most influential financial policy makers in the world. His recommendation was supported by a 75-page paper explaining why handing out newly-created money to citizens and governments could solve economic woes globally and would not lead to hyperinflation (Kaletsky, 2013).

People and governments are suffering from a crippling debt overhang today. The problem stems from the manner in which money gets into the real economy. Except for the coins and dollar bills that make up only a very small portion of the money supply, the entire circulating (M2) money supply comes into existence as a debt to banks at interest. We actually have no "permanent" money. As Robert Hemphill of the Atlanta Federal Reserve observed in the 1930s:

> "We are completely dependent on the commercial banks.
> Someone has to borrow every dollar we have in circulation,
> cash or credit. If the banks create ample synthetic money,
> we are prosperous; if not, we starve."

In its spring 2014 Quarterly Bulletin, the Bank of England acknowledged that banks do not actually lend their deposits, as is commonly believed. Rather, they create deposits when they make loans (McLeay et al., 2014).

In the monetary system of the US, as in other OECD countries, the only money that is not borrowed from banks is the "base money" or "monetary base" created by the Treasury and the Federal Reserve (the Fed). The

Treasury creates only the tiny portion consisting of coins. All of the rest is created by the Fed, and most of it is electronic rather than paper.

Most base money does not enter the circulating money supply. It goes directly into the reserve accounts of private banks at the Fed. Except for the small amount of "vault cash" available for withdrawal from commercial banks, bank reserves do not leave the doors of the central bank. This includes the base money created on a computer screen through "quantitative easing" (QE), which now exceeds $3 trillion in the US.

That explains why QE has not driven the economy into hyperinflation, as critics have long predicted; and why it has also not created jobs, as was its purported mission. The Fed's QE money simply does not get into the circulating money supply.

According to Peter Stella, former head of the Central Banking and Monetary and Foreign Exchange Operations Divisions at the International Monetary Fund:

> "[I]n a modern monetary system – fiat money, floating exchange rate world – there is absolutely no correlation between bank reserves and lending. . . . *[B]anks do not lend 'reserves'*. . . .
>
> Whether commercial banks let the reserves they have acquired through QE sit 'idle' or lend them out in the internet bank market 10,000 times in one day among themselves, the aggregate reserves at the central bank at the end of that day will be the same" (Kaminska, 2012).

Banks do not lend their reserves to individuals or businesses, but they do lend them to each other. The reserves are what they need to clear checks between banks. Reserves move from one reserve account to another; but total money in bank reserve accounts remains unchanged, unless the Fed itself issues new money or extinguishes it.

Ideas towards a new international financial architecture?

The money in the bank accounts of individuals and businesses is a mere reflection of the base money that is the exclusive domain of banks. Banks borrow from the Fed and each other at near-zero rates, then lend this money into the real economy at 4% or 8% or 16%, depending on what the market will bear. As in a house of mirrors, the Fed's "base money" gets multiplied over and over whenever "bank credit" is deposited and relent; and it is this illusory house of mirrors that composes the bulk of M2, the "circulating money supply" available to the real economy.

The cost of this system to the economy and the government is the interest paid on money created by banks – money the government could be issuing itself. For infrastructure, on average, interest and bank fees compose fully 50% of the cost (Rogers, 2013).

Infrastructure is a public utility that could be funded interest-free with government-issued currency. As Thomas Edison famously observed in an interview reported in *The New York Times* in 1921:

> "If the Nation can issue a dollar bond it can issue a dollar bill. The element that makes the bond good makes the bill good also. The difference between the bond and the bill is that the bond lets the money broker collect twice the amount of the bond and an additional 20%. Whereas the currency, the honest sort provided by the Constitution pays nobody but those who contribute in some useful way. It is absurd to say our Country can issue bonds and cannot issue currency. Both are promises to pay, but one fattens the usurer and the other helps the People."

3. Historical precedents: from paper scrip to US notes

Government-issued paper money was first successfully used in the Western world by the American colonists. The colonists' paper scrip consisted of receipts from the government acknowledging goods and services delivered to the government. The receipts were negotiable instruments that were accepted in the payment of taxes, allowing them to retain their value. They circulated in the colonies as a form of money that did not require either gold (which was scarce) or going into debt to the Bank of England.

The best of these colonial models was in Benjamin Franklin's colony of Pennsylvania, where government-issued money got into the economy by way of loans issued by a publicly-owned bank. Except for an excise tax on liquor, the government was funded entirely without taxes. There was no government debt, and price inflation from increases in the money supply did not result (Rabushka, 2004).

In 1938, Dr. Richard A. Lester, an economist at Princeton University, wrote, "The price level during the 52 years prior to the American Revolution and while Pennsylvania was on a paper standard was more stable than the American price level has been during any succeeding fifty-year period. "

Benjamin Franklin has been called "the Father of Paper Money". He argued before the British Parliament that it was government-issued money that had allowed the colonies to escape the yoke of debt, to thrive and grow. King George, urged by the Bank of England, responded by forbidding all new issues of paper scrip. The colonial economy then sank into a depression, and the colonists rebelled. They won the revolution, but the power to create money was lost to a private banking monopoly modeled on that dominated by the Bank of England.

During the American Civil War, President Lincoln revived the colonial system of direct money issuance by issuing about $450 million in US Notes or "greenbacks". This money helped fund not only the North's victory in the war but an array of pivotal infrastructure projects, including a transcontinental railway system.

The Greenbacks were the first *federal* paper money put into circulation after the US became a nation. Earlier in the 19th century, paper money was issued by state and private banks, and their bank notes were just receipts. Like the seventeenth century goldsmiths' notes, they represented the bank's promise to pay later in "hard" currency (gold or silver).

Ideas towards a new international financial architecture?

Greenbacks, on the other hand, were legal tender in themselves. They did not have to be paid in some other form of money later. The Legal Tender Acts of 1861 and 1862 made all coins and currency issued by the U.S. Government "legal tender for all debts, public and private". Government-issued paper notes were made a legal substitute for gold and silver, even for the payment of pre-existing debts specifying gold. The reverse of the note issued in the 1860s stated:

> "This Note is Legal Tender for All Debts Public and Private Except Duties On Imports And Interest On The Public Debt; And Is Redeemable In Payment Of All Loans Made To The United States. "

United States Notes or greenbacks were issued from 1862 to 1971, making their issuance longer than for any other form of US paper money.

In *A Monetary History of the United States, 1867-1960* (Princeton University Press 1963), Milton Friedman and Anna Jacobson Schwarz wrote of this innovative funding mechanism:

> "The United States notes are the 'greenbacks' of Civil War fame. First issued to supplement tax and loan receipts in the financing of war expenditures, the total outstanding (in and outside the Treasury) reached a maximum of $449 million in January 1864. Under the terms of the act of April, 12, 1866, the amount outstanding was reduced to $356 million by the end of 1867 and was then legally fixed at that level until 1873-74, when additional amounts were issued that raised the total outstanding to $382 million. As part of the Resumption Act of 1875 the retirement of the greenbacks was linked to the increase in national bank notes – for every five dollar increase in national bank notes the Treasury retired four dollars in greenbacks – and was to cease when the amount outstanding fell to $300 million. However, further retirement was suspended by an act of May 31, 1878, which established as a permanent issue the amount then outstanding, $347 million, the level at which the total issue

of US notes stands today" (Friedman and Schwarz, 1963, p.24).

Friedman and Schwarz wrote that the decade following the Civil War was one of extraordinarily rapid growth:

"... [T]here is much direct evidence of a rapid rise in output from 1867, to 1879 ...

This was a period of great railroad expansion dramatized by the linking of the coasts by rail in 1869. The number of miles of track operated more than doubled from 1867 to 1879, a rate of expansion not matched subsequently. In New York State, for which figures are readily available, the number of ton miles of freight carried on railroads nearly quintupled and, for the first time since the figures began, exceeded the number of ton miles carried on canals and rivers...

An index of basic production compiled by Warren and Pearson nearly doubled from 1867 to 1879..." (Friedman and Schwarz, 1963, pp .34-35).

The National Bank Act of 1863 called for retirement of the Greenbacks after the war as a temporary war measure, and it prohibited states from creating state bank notes. National Bank Notes were to be issued instead, by a system of federally-chartered banks. The National Bank Act thus gave private bankers a legal monopoly over the right to issue the national paper currency. The Act chartered not one but a whole series of private banks, which were authorized to issue notes of public money bearing interest to the banks' private owners.

In 1870, the constitutionality of the greenbacks was challenged in the US Supreme Court. In *Hepburn v. Griswold*, the Court held that the Constitution prohibited the states from passing "any ... law impairing the obligation of contracts". To compel holders of contracts calling for payment in gold and silver to accept payment in "mere promises to pay dollars" was, said the

Court, an unconstitutional deprivation of property without due process of the law.

But that decision was reversed in 1871, with two new justices on the bench. The Legal Tender cases (*Knox v. Lee*, 79 U.S. 457, 20 L.Ed. 287; and *Juilliard v. Greenman*, 110 U.S. 421, 4 S.Ct. 122, 28 L.Ed. 204), found the Legal Tender Acts constitutional. The Court declared that Congress has the power "to coin money and regulate its value" with the objects of self-preservation and the achievement of a more perfect union, and that "no obligation of contract can extend to the defeat of legitimate government authority".

In 1972, the United States Treasury Department was asked to compute the amount of interest that would have been paid if the $450 million in Greenbacks issued by President Lincoln had been borrowed from the banks instead. According to the Treasury Department's calculations, in his short tenure Lincoln saved the government a total of $4 billion in interest, just by avoiding this $450 million loan.

Over the next century, the legislation governing US Notes was modified many times and numerous versions were issued by the Treasury. Existing US Notes remain valid currency in the United States; but since no US Notes have been issued since 1971, they are increasingly rare in circulation.

4. Countering the inflation objection

The argument long raised to silence proponents of government-issued money is that it would trigger hyperinflation. The principle taught in economics class is that when the quantity of money goes up, more money will be chasing fewer goods, driving prices up.

But as economist John Maynard Keynes observed, this principle overlooks the supply side of the equation. As long as workers are sitting idle and materials are available, increased "demand" will put workers to work creating more "supply". Supply will rise along with demand and prices will remain stable.

Infrastructure without debt

Today these additional workers may be in China or they may be robots. But the principle still holds: to get the increased supply needed to satisfy the demands of the economy, more money must first be injected into the economy. *Demand drives supply*. People must have money in their pockets before they can spend it, stimulating increased production.

Increased demand will drive up prices only when the economy hits full productive capacity. It is at that point, and not before, that taxes may need to be levied – not to fund the federal budget, but to prevent "overheating" and keep prices stable. Overheating in the current economy could be a long time coming, however, since according to a February 2012 NY Federal Reserve Staff Report, $4 trillion would need to be added to the money supply just to get it back to where it was in 2008 (Pozsar *et al.*, 2012).

In a May 2011 Forbes article titled "Money Growth Does Not Cause Inflation!" John Harvey argued that the rule taught in economics class is based on some invalid assumptions. The formula is:

$$MV = Py$$

When the velocity of money (V) and the quantity of goods sold (y) are constant, adding money (M) must drive up prices (P). However, says Harvey, V and y are not constant. The more money people have to spend (M), the more money that will change hands (V), and the more goods and services that will get sold (y) (Harvey, 2011).

Only when V and y reach their limits – only when demand is saturated and productivity is at full capacity – will consumer prices be driven up. And they are nowhere near their limits yet. The US output gap – the difference between actual output (y) and potential output – is currently estimated at about $1 trillion annually. That means the money supply could be increased by at least $1 trillion without driving up prices.

In 2012, the velocity of M1 – the coins, dollar bills and checkbook money composing the money supply used by most people today – was 7 (down from a high of 10 in 2007). That means M1 changed hands seven times during 2012 – from housewife to grocer to farmer, etc. Since each recipient owes taxes on this money, increasing M1 by one dollar increases the tax base by seven dollars.

Total tax revenue as a percentage of GDP in 2012 was 24.3% (OECD, 2013). Extrapolating from those figures, $1.00 changing hands seven times for goods and services on which taxes had to be paid could increase tax revenue to the government by $7.00 x 24.3% = $1.70. That means the government could actually get more back in taxes than it paid out. Even with some leakage in those figures and deductions for costs, all or most of the new money spent into the economy might be taxed back to the government at the existing tax levels, so that the money supply would increase little if at all.

There are also other ways to get money back into the Treasury so that there is no net increase in the money supply. They include closing tax loopholes, taxing the $21 trillion or more hidden in offshore tax havens (Tax Justice Network, 2012), and setting up a system of public banks that would return the interest on loans to the government. Net interest collected by U.S. banks in 2014 was $423 billion (down from a high of $725 billion in 2007) (FDIC, 2014).

Thus there are many ways to return new money spent into the economy back to the government. The same money could be spent and collected back year after year, without creating price inflation or hyperinflating the money supply.

What of the hyperinflations of history, including the oft-cited Weimar Republic and Zimbabwe disasters? Professor Michael Hudson, who has studied them extensively, writes:

> "Every hyperinflation in history has been caused by foreign debt service collapsing the exchange rate. The problem almost always has resulted from wartime foreign currency strains, not domestic spending. The dynamics of hyperinflation traced in such classics as Salomon Flink's The Reichsbank and Economic Germany (1931) have been confirmed by studies of the Chilean and other Third World

inflations. First the exchange rate plunges as economies pay for foreign military spending during the war, and then – in Germany's case – reparations after the war ends. These payments lead the exchange rate to fall, increasing the price in domestic currency of buying imports priced in hard currencies. This price rise for imported goods creates a price umbrella for domestic prices to follow suit. More domestic money is needed to finance economic activity at the higher price level. This German experience provides the classic example" (Hudson, 2012).

5. Infrastructure funding option No. 1: QE from the Central Bank

The term "quantitative easing" was invented by UK Professor Richard Werner in the 1990s. What he had in mind, however, was not the sort of policy engaged in by most central banks today. Werner was then advising the Japanese, who were caught in a spiral of "debt deflation" like the one the US and other countries are struggling with now. What he recommended was credit creation by the central bank for productive purposes in the physical economy. But the Bank of Japan simply directed its QE tool at the banks, pursuing the same policy central banks are engaging in today. Werner commented in 2012:

> "[A]ll QE is doing is to help banks increase the liquidity of their portfolios by getting rid of longer-dated and slightly less liquid assets and raising cash... Reserve expansion is a standard monetarist policy and required no new label" (Werner, 2012).

In the US today, QE is engaged in to bail out the banks and keep interest rates low on the federal debt. But in earlier decades, the Fed actually ventured into commercial banking. In 1934, Section 13(b) was added to the Federal Reserve Act, authorizing the Fed to "make credit available for the purpose of supplying working capital to established industrial and commercial businesses". This long-forgotten section was implemented and remained in effect for 24 years.

Ideas towards a new international financial architecture?

In a 2002 article on the Minneapolis Fed's website called "Lender of More Than Last Resort," David Fettig noted that 13(b) allowed Federal Reserve banks to make loans directly to any established businesses in their districts, and to share in loans with private lending institutions if the latter assumed 20 percent of the risk. No limitation was placed on the amount of a single loan (Fettig, 2002).

Fettig wrote that "the Fed was still less than 20 years old and many likely remembered the arguments put forth during the System's founding, when some advocated that the discount window should be open to all comers, not just member banks." In Australia, New Zealand, Canada, and other countries in the first half of the twentieth century, the central bank was assuming commercial as well as central bank functions.

Section 13(b) was eventually repealed, but the Federal Reserve Act retained enough vestiges of it in 2008 to allow the Fed to intervene to save a variety of non-bank entities from bankruptcy. The problem was that the tool was applied selectively. The recipients were major corporate players, not local businesses or local governments. Fettig wrote:

> "Section 13(b) may be a memory... but Section 13 paragraph 3... is alive and well in the Federal Reserve Act... [T]his amendment allows, 'in unusual and exigent circumstances', a Reserve bank to advance credit to individuals, partnerships and corporations that are not depository institutions."

In 2008, the Fed bailed out investment company Bear Stearns and insurer AIG, neither of which was a bank. Bear Stearns got almost $1 trillion in short-term loans, with interest rates as low as 0.5%. The Fed also made loans to other corporations, including GE, McDonald's, and Verizon.

In 2010, Section 13(3) was modified by the Dodd-Frank bill, which replaced the phrase "individuals, partnerships and corporations" with the vaguer phrase "any program or facility with broad-based eligibility". As explained in the notes to the bill:

"Only Broad-Based Facilities Permitted. Section 13(3) is modified to remove the authority to extend credit to specific individuals, partnerships and corporations. Instead, the Board may authorize credit under section 13(3) only under a program or facility with 'broad-based eligibility'."

Lending for infrastructure, either directly or to federal or state governments for the purpose of engaging in infrastructure, could qualify as an extension of credit with "broad-based eligibility" (Canova, 2014).

In 2009, President Obama proposed that the Fed lend directly to cities and states battered by the banking crisis. "Small businesses and state and local governments are having serious difficulty obtaining necessary financing from debt markets," Obama said. He proposed that the Fed buy municipal bonds to cut their rising borrowing costs.

The proposed municipal bond facility would have been based on the Fed program to buy commercial paper, which had almost single-handedly propped up the market for short-term corporate borrowing. Investors welcomed the muni bond proposal as a first step toward supporting the market. But then-Chairman Bernanke rejected the proposal.

Why? It was not because the Fed could not come up with the money. The collective budget deficit of the states for 2011 was projected at $140 billion, a small sum compared to those the Fed came up with to bail out the banks. According to data released in 2011, the central bank had provided roughly $3.3 trillion in liquidity and $9 trillion in short-term loans and other financial arrangements to banks, multinational corporations, and foreign financial institutions following the credit crisis of 2008. Later investigation pushed the sum up to $16 trillion or more.

Bernanke's reasoning in saying no to the muni bond facility was that he lacked the statutory tools. The Fed is limited by statute to buying municipal government debt with maturities of six months or less that is directly backed by tax or other assured revenue, a form of debt that makes up less than 2%

of the overall muni market. However, statutes can be changed by Congress; and they are changed routinely.

Chairman Bernanke said no to funding municipal bonds with QE in 2011, but his advice was quite a bit different when he was addressing the plight of the Japanese in 2002. In a now-famous speech made in Washington titled "Deflation: Making Sure 'It' Doesn't Happen Here," Dr Bernanke stated that the Fed would not be "out of ammunition " to counteract deflation just because the federal funds rate had fallen to 0 percent. Lowering interest rates was not the only way to get new money into the economy. He said, "the U.S. government has a technology, called a printing press (or, today, its electronic equivalent), that allows it to produce as many U.S. dollars as it wishes at essentially no cost".

Later in the speech he said, "A money-financed tax cut is essentially equivalent to Milton Friedman's famous 'helicopter drop' of money." Dropping money from helicopters was Professor Friedman's hypothetical cure for deflation. The "money-financed tax cut" recommended by Dr Bernanke was evidently one in which taxes would be replaced with money that was simply printed up by the government and spent into the economy. He added, "[I]n lieu of tax cuts, the government could increase spending on current goods and services *or even acquire existing real or financial assets*." The government could reflate the economy by printing money and buying hard assets with it – apparently including assets such as real estate and corporate stock.

This speech and its ramifications were discussed by Mark Blyth and Eric Lonergan in an article in the September/October 2014 issue of *Foreign Affairs* titled "Print Less But Transfer More: Why Central Banks Should Give Money Directly To The People." The authors wrote:

> "Bernanke argued that the Bank of Japan needed to act more aggressively and suggested it consider an unconventional approach: give Japanese households cash directly. Consumers could use the new windfalls to spend their way out of the recession, driving up demand and raising prices.

138

... The conservative economist Milton Friedman also saw the appeal of direct money transfers, which he likened to dropping cash out of a helicopter. Japan never tried using them, however, and the country's economy has never fully recovered. Between 1993 and 2003, Japan's annual growth rates averaged less than one percent.

... It's well past time, then, for U.S. policymakers – as well as their counterparts in other developed countries – to consider a version of Friedman's helicopter drops. In the short term, such cash transfers could jump-start the economy. Over the long term, they could reduce dependence on the banking system for growth and reverse the trend of rising inequality. The transfers wouldn't cause damaging inflation, and few doubt that they would work. The only real question is why no government has tried them" (Blyth and Lonergan, 2014).

6. Infrastructure funding option No. 2: an issue of US Notes

QE through the Federal Reserve is not the only way to get new debt-free money into the economy. The direct route to reflating the money supply would be to re-issue US Notes through the US Treasury.

Today, paper currencies are issued by national central banks; and in the US and most other countries, this money is lent rather than spent into the economy. It is not simply handed over to the government to spend on its budgetary needs. However, that has been done quite successfully in the past, not only in the US but in other countries including Japan, Korea, Argentina, Germany, Canada, Australia, New Zealand, and China (which is probably still doing it today) (Brown, 2013).

A small historical experiment that is of interest because it has been successfully extended over two centuries is in the island state of Guernsey. New Zealand researcher Kerry Bolton summarizes the Guernsey experience like this:

"Guernsey's banking system was prompted by dire need, the island being in serious financial trouble from the beginning of the 19th Century. Guernsey's town was undeveloped, the roads were cart-tracks, and there was no prospect for employment... [I]t was the need to upgrade the Public Market that prompted a committee to report back with a solution in 1816 to issue £6000 worth of States Notes. The committee also recommended that the States Notes be used not only for the new market, but also for Torteval Church, road construction, and other State expenses. The notes' issue was started in 1820, and was followed by other issues, until by 1837 £55,000 of the Notes were in circulation, debt-free and having created prosperity and development, which in turn stimulated visitors to the island" (Bolton, 2011).

It was all going well, says Bolton, until two local banks flooded Guernsey with their own notes to undermine the State Notes. The Island responded by agreeing to limit the issue of its own Notes. But with the outbreak of war in 1914, the State Notes were reinstated; and they continued to circulate alongside British Pounds Sterling thereafter. Despite that influx of new money, writes Bolton, "there has never been inflation, and the prosperity of the island continues as it has since 1820, operating on minimal taxation."

7. Funding alternative No. 3: a treasury issue of special coins

US Notes have been declared constitutional and have a long and respected history. But re-issuing them would require legislation; and in today's political climate, that could be difficult to achieve.

There is another approach to issuing new money that could be done by Congress or the President very quickly, without changing any laws. The "trillion dollar coin" was proposed in 2013 in response to the budget crisis created by the debt ceiling. News commentators considered it a joke. But the proposal was taken seriously by Paul Krugman and some other economists, as a way to circumvent a limitation on spending that had been artificially imposed by a faction of Congress (Krugman, 2013).

The proposed solution was for the President to order the issue of a one trillion dollar coin, pursuant to the authority of the Coinage Clause of the U.S. Constitution. Article 1, Section 8, Clause 5, provides: "The Congress shall have the power to coin money [and] regulate the value thereof..."

In the 19th century, coins and paper banknotes issued privately on the "fractional reserve" model composed roughly equal portions of the money supply. Today, coins are all that is left of the Treasury's money-creating power; and they compose only about $1 billion of a money supply exceeding $10 trillion. The vast majority of the rest is created by private banks when they make loans.

The idea of minting large denomination coins to solve economic problems was evidently first suggested by a chairman of the Coinage Subcommittee of the U.S. House of Representatives in the early 1980s. He pointed out that the government could pay off its entire debt with some billion-dollar coins. The Constitution gives Congress the power to coin money and regulate its value, and no limit is put on the value of the coins it creates. In *Web of Debt* (2007), Ellen Brown suggested that to solve the government's debt problems today these would need to be trillion dollar coins (Brown, 2007, 2012).

That option was largely curtailed by legislation initiated in 1982, in which Congress chose to impose limits on the amounts and denominations of most coins. The one exception was the platinum coin, which a special provision allowed to be minted in any amount for commemorative purposes (31 U.S. Code § 5112).

In 2013, Carlos Mucha, an attorney blogging under the pseudonym Beowulf, proposed issuing a platinum coin to capitalize on this loophole. At first it was just an amusing exercise. But with the endless gridlock in Congress over the debt ceiling, it got picked up by serious economists as a way to move forward. (Tate, 2013)

Ideas towards a new international financial architecture?

Philip Diehl, former head of the US Mint and co-author of the platinum coin law, confirmed that the coin would be legal tender:

> "In minting the $1 trillion platinum coin, the Treasury Secretary would be exercising authority which Congress has granted routinely for more than 220 years . . . under power expressly granted to Congress in the Constitution" (Article 1, Section 8) (Diehl, 2013).

Warren Mosler, one of the founders of Modern Monetary Theory (MMT), also reviewed the idea and concluded it would work operationally. The funds would simply be new balances at the Fed, circumventing the need for new Treasury securities (Mosler, 2011).

Prof. Randall Wray, another MMT advocate, explained that the coin would not circulate but would be deposited in the government's account at the Fed, so it could not inflate the circulating money supply. The budget would still need Congressional approval. To keep a lid on spending, Congress would just need to abide by some basic rules of economics. It could spend on goods and services up to full employment without creating price inflation (since supply and demand would rise together). After that, the government would need to tax – not to fund the budget, but to shrink the circulating money supply and avoid driving up prices with excess demand (Wray, 2013).

8. Monetary control functions

Predictably, the beneficiaries of any monetary policy will do what they can to maximize their income and other benefits from the policy. In the current fractional reserve banking system, these beneficiaries would include bankers, participants in the shadow banking system, and individuals or institutions in a position to obtain loans or other advantages from low interest rates or loose monetary policies. To forestall these skewed benefits, control functions are incorporated into the monetary system.

Infrastructure without debt

In the current fractional reserve banking system, control functions have gone through a period of significant tightening over the years since the Great Recession. The primary control function is exercised by the central bank (in the US, the Federal Reserve). In normal times, increasing or decreasing interest rates is considered sufficient to expand or contract the growth of the money supply. Because funds are created by deposit creation through the issuance of debt, increasing interest rates reduces the rate of credit creation and thus the money supply, and vice versa.

A major problem with this control mechanism is the long lead time – often up to two years – before the anticipated result is seen. Further controls are exercised through liquidity ratios determined by a combination of national central banks and the Bank for International Settlements, called "the Central Bank of central banks." In the United States, the lengthy Dodd-Frank Act has significantly increased macro-prudential oversight as well.

For the infrastructure funding mechanisms suggested here, new control functions will be needed. First and foremost, the beneficiaries, whether direct or indirect, need to be separated from the decision-making bodies. Direct beneficiaries to infrastructure funding would typically be construction companies, with local municipalities as secondary beneficiaries.

A commitment of local funds would also need to be incorporated into the overall structure, to limit the proverbial "bridge to nowhere" approach. These costs could take the form of mandatory participation by the municipality, interest on loans, and other general payment provisions. For example, a maximum of 80% of a particular infrastructure project might be funded by one of the funding mechanisms outlined here, with the rest coming from typical tax incomes or loans through bond issuance.

It is strongly recommended that infrastructure projects funded by quantitative easing or credit creation have an overhead limit, such as 5% of the overall project. It would also be prudent to limit the overall issuance of this type of funding to a certain percentage of the total GDP, such as 7% or 8% per year. In the US economy, with a total annual GDP of about $18 trillion, that would put the maximum per year at about $1 trillion to $1.5 trillion.

9. Conclusion

With the US infrastructure budget facing a shortfall over the next five years of $1.6 trillion, in a political climate that is opposed to increasing the federal debt, Congress needs to find new ways to fund the gap. The solution proposed here is for the US to adopt an infrastructure funding mechanism that is based on a new round of Quantitative Easing. Three Options are discussed:

1) Funding through the Federal Reserve (similar to existing QE rounds);
2) Funding through the Treasury through the printing of US Notes (government-issued money); and
3) Funding through the Treasury by the minting of special coins.

The authors show that this approach has historical precedents and a current legislative enablement, and that it will not lead to hyper-inflation. As part of the funding process, a new control framework is also proposed to ensure a balanced and equitable distribution of benefit.

References

31 U.S. Code § 5112 – "Denominations, Specifications, and Design of Coins", *Law.Cornell.Edu*.

American Society of Civil Engineers (ASCE). (2013) "2013 Report Card For America's Infrastructure", Infrastructurereportcard.org.

Blyth, M. and Lonergan, E. (2014) "Print Less But Transfer More: Why Central Banks Should Give Money Directly To The People," *Foreign Affairs*.

Bolton, K. (2011) "Breaking the Bondage of Interest, Part 3," *Counter-Current*.

Brown, E. (2013) *The Public Bank Solution*, Third Millennium, Baton Rouge.

Brown, E. (2007, 2012) *Web of Debt*, 3rd Millennium, Baton Rouge.

Canova, T. (2014) "The Bottom-Up Recovery: A New Deal in Banking and Public Finance" (Chapter 3), *Social Science Research Network*.

Diehl, P. (2013) "Former Head Of The US Mint Addresses Confusion Over The Platinum Coin Idea," *Pragmatic Capitalism*.

Duncan, R. (2015) "QE Is Debt Cancellation," *Richard Duncan Economics*.

FDIC. (2014) "Quarterly Banking Profile, Fourth Quarter 2014," *FDIC.gov*.

Fettig, D. (2002) "Lender of More Than Last Resort," *Minneapolisfed.org*.

Friedman, M. and Schwarz, A. (1963) *Monetary History of the United States*, 1867-1960, Princeton University Press.

Harvey, J. (2011) "Money Growth Does Not Cause Inflation!", *Forbes*.

Hudson, M. (2012) "Financial Predators v. Labor, Industry and Democracy," *Michael-Hudson.com*.

Johnson, A. (2013) "76% Of Americans Are Living Paycheck-To-Paycheck," *CNN Money*.

Kaletsky, A. (2013) "A Breakthrough Speech On Monetary Policy," *Reuters*.

Kaminska, I. (2012) "The Base Money Confusion," *FT Alphaville*.

Krugman, P. (2013) "Be Ready to Mint that Coin," *New York Times*.

McLeay, M. et al. (2014) "Money Creation in the Modern Economy," *Bank of England*, Quarterly Bulletin 2014 Q1.

Meadway, J. (2015) "The ECB's Quantitative Easing Program," *Neweconomics.org*.

Moore, M. (2012) "Stiglitz Says European Austerity Plans Are a 'Suicide Pact'", *UK Telegraph*.

Mosler, W. (2011) "Joe Firestone Post on Sidestepping the Debt Ceiling Issue with Coin Seigniorage," Moslereconomics.com.

OECD. (2013) "Taxation: Key Tables from OECD, 2013."

Peterson, E. (2013) "Is Quantitative Easing An Option For Infrastructure Financing?", Enotrans.org.

Pozsar, Z. et al. (2012) "Shadow Banking," *Federal Reserve Bank of New York*, Staff Report No. 458.

Rabushka, A. (2004) "Representation Without Taxation: The Colonial Roots of American Taxation, 1700-1754," pp.67-82, *Policy Review*, pp.67-82.

Rogers, P. (2013) "Delta Tunnels Plan's True Price Tag: As Much Is $67 Billion," *San Jose Mercury News*.

Tate, R. (2013) "Meet the Genius Behind the Trillion-Dollar Coin and the Plot to Breach the Debt Ceiling," Wired.com.

Tax Justice Network. (2012) "Revealed: Global Super-Rich Has at Least $21 Trillion Hidden in Secret Tax Havens, "*Taxjustice.Net*.

Werner, R. (2012) "Time For Green Quantitative Easing," *Policy News,* University of Southhampton Management School.

Wolfertz, O. (2015) "New Year, New Congress, New Hope for Infrastructure Investment," *Civil Engineering Blog & News Network.*

Wray, R. (2013) "Update on Trillion Dollar Coin: Not Inflationary–It Is a Duration Trade," Mikenormaneconomics.Blogspot.com.

CHAPTER 7
Globalization, international trade and international payments

Paul Davidson

1 Introduction

Keynes's *General Theory* explains that increases in spending on goods and services creates additional profit opportunities for business firms. It follows that the managers of these business firms would be encouraged to hire additional workers whenever additional profit opportunities exist. In the closed economy model of most textbooks where all transactions are among residents of the same national economy, it is implicitly assumed that the additional spending would come from domestic households, domestic business firms and/or federal, state or local governments to be spent to purchase the output produced by enterprises located in the domestic economy.

Once the analysis is placed into a globalized market system involving many separate nations things change somewhat. For example, spending by United States households, business firms, and/or government to purchase products produced in foreign nations (i.e., imports), creates profit opportunities and jobs in the foreign nation and not in the domestic economy. On the other hand, demand by foreigners for the products of domestically located business firms (i.e., exports) creates profits and jobs for workers in the domestic economy.

If, in any year, exports from the United States approximately equals the imports into the United States, then the foreign job creating effects of United States imports and domestic job creation in United States export industries will approximately offset each other. If, however, the United States imports significantly more than it exports to foreigners, then American spending on imports will support more profit opportunities and jobs in foreign nations than foreigner's spending on U.S. imports creates profit and job opportunities in the United States.. In this latter case, American factories' profits and jobs will be less than if either the total imports equaled the same level of exports or if all the United States excess demand for imports over exports had been diverted to a market demand for these same products produced by domestically located production facilities.

For example in 2008 the United States imported $709 billion more of goods and services from foreign nations than it exported to foreign markets. If that $709 billion that Americans spent for imports over exports had been spent in 2008 on goods and services produced in the United States, it would have a big stimulus impact to the American economy that was then suffering from what some people called the Great Recession. This $709 billion was equal to approximately 95 per cent of the amount of additional federal government spending and tax cuts provided for in the economic stimulus bill that President Obama signed in February 2009. This stimulus bill that was supposed to end the Great Recession and restore jobs to several million US workers who had lost their jobs in this Great Recession.

Similarly suppose the Chinese, Japanese and other trading partners who experience exports to the US greater than imports from the U.S. had spent their 2008 total dollar earnings derived from their selling goods and services to people in the United States on exports from the United States instead of savings $709 billion of their export earnings. This additional $709 billion spending on United States exports also would have been approximately 95 per cent equivalent to the effect of the US federal government stimulus bill enacted in 2008 to alleviate the effects of the Great Recession. Accordingly, if a nation spend more on imports than it receives in exports, then the net effect is to reduce total market demand for the output from domestic industries and therefore to contribute to the market force causing domestic unemployment while encouraging greater employment and profits abroad.

Since 1976, the United States has been consistently importing more than it has been exporting, thereby creating more profit opportunities and jobs in foreign nations than foreigners have been creating in the United States export industries. The result has been that the United States has acted as the major engine for stimulus and economic growth for the rest of the world's industries for more than three decades. The impressive economic growth rates displayed by countries like Japan in the 1980s and China and India in the early years of the 21st century owe that prosperity in large part to the United States increases in spending on exports from these nations.

A simple example will illustrate this situation. Let us assume that in any one year the United States spends $10 billion more on Chinese imports (say toys) and therefore $10 billion less on domestically produced toys. Assume that China does not increase spending on United States and therefore the trade deficit with China has increased by $10 billion. The effect is that this $10 billion spent on imports from China has created profits and jobs in the Chinese toy industry, while United States residents who have diverted their spending on domestically produced toys to foreign produced toys has, in essence, destroyed profits and jobs in the United States toy industry.

In this hypothetical example, China has earned $10 billion more dollars on its international trade payments account. It is further assumed that China did not spend this on buying $10 billion worth of more products from the United States. Instead, this hypothetical example has assumed China has "saved" $10 billion out of its international earnings. Since in the Keynes - Post Keynesian analysis "a penny saved is a penny that cannot be earned" by anyone else, then in this hypothetical example the $10 billion the Chinese saved is $10 billion that cannot be earned by businesses and workers located in the United States. Former Federal Reserve chairman, Ben Bernanke, spoke of this foreign nations' hoarding of earning from exports to the USA as a "glut of savings overseas".

When imports exceed exports for a nation, there is a deficit in the trade balance of that nation that economists call an "unfavorable balance of trade". In our hypothetical example of $10 billion that Chinese saved, this unfavorable balance of trade results in a deficit in the United States' balance of payments with the rest of the world as the United States pays out more for its imports than it receives in payments for its exports.

Any nation experiencing a deficit in its international balance of payments must finance this deficit by either (1) the deficit nation drawing down its previous savings on international earnings (these savings are called the nation's "foreign reserves") to pay for its excess of imports over exports, or (2) by the deficit nation borrowing funds from the foreigners in the rest of the world to pay for the difference between the value of imports and the value of exports.

Since the United States imports have exceed exports every year since 1974, the United States, for many years, has borrowed from foreigners in order to finance its excess of imports over exports. The result has been that the United States has moved from being the world's largest creditor nation to being the largest debtor nation in terms of debt owed to the rest of the world.

To continue with our previous illustrative example, we might ask what do the Chinese do with the $10 billion savings on its international earnings. Like all savers the Chinese look for liquid assets to move their saved (unused) international contractual settlement (purchasing) power to the future. For the most part the Chinese have used their international savings to purchase United States Treasury securities and other debt obligations of U.S.. Government sponsored corporations. This indicates that the Chinese believe the United States dollar is the safest harbor for storing their unused international contractual settlement power. This savings by the Chinese have led many classical theory "experts" to say that the Chinese have been financing the American consumer shopping spree and the resulting growth of United States international debt. These "experts" have warned that if nations such as China stops buying United States securities with their annual international savings out of earnings from exports to the United State, then American consumers could no longer afford to buy as many imports and they would have to reduce their purchases of Chinese made goods at retail outlets like Walmart.

If Americans did stop buying Chinese imports, just think how this will devastate the profits of Chinese firms and threaten the jobs of Chinese workers. The result could even cause political unrest in China. The Chinese Communist party enjoys popular support as long as it not only protects the nation from foreign enemies but also as long as it continues to support economic actions that result in substantial improvement in employment and living conditions for all Chinese citizens. If Chinese exports were to decline, then Chinese unemployment might increase and living standards decline. That could induce demonstrations and political unrest in China. In other words politically as well as economically it is unlikely to be in China's interest to stop financing Americans huge imports over exports from China.

If, in our simple illustration, suppose the Chinese did not use their international savings to buy United States Treasury bonds. Instead assume the Chinese spent the $10 billion on the products of American domestically located industries. The result would be that:

1) in China there would be more products from American producers, perhaps such as meat, corn and wheat. If more of these food products were available in China they would strongly embellish and improve the standard food diet of the average Chinese worker.

2) American businesses and their workers would earn more income and therefore not have to borrow from the Chinese to finance their large import purchases of Chinese goods.

The morale of this illustration is that if the Chinese bought goods from the United States instead of buying United States Treasury bonds, then \the Chinese government would make available goods that could improve Chinese real living standards while American workers would have more employment and enough income to afford all the Chinese imports they bought without having to go into debt to the Chinese.

This simple illustration suggests that one engine of growth that a nation might try is to expand its exports to the rest of the world. If successful such an export expansion led growth policy will result in increasing profits for domestic firms, creating jobs for domestic workers. Moreover, the nation becoming a creditor to other countries as it runs a favorable balance of trade. If, however, one country runs a favorable balance of trade, then other nation(s) must run an unfavorable balance of trade, resulting in a tendency to lose jobs and profits to the nation pursuing an export led growth policy. Thus, as Keynes noted, if each nation tries to stimulate its economy by running a favorable balance of trade to increase domestic profit opportunities and employment then this "may lead to a senseless international competition

151

Ideas towards a new international financial architecture?

for a favorable balance of trade which injures all alike" (Keynes, 1936).

Keynes and his Post Keynesian followers have developed a solution for preventing a competition among nations to stimulate their economy via attempting to maintain a favorable balance of trade. This solution will end persistent trade imbalances that cause the nation(s) with an unfavorable balance of trade to lose profit and job opportunities while incurring huge international debts. What is required is some form of an institutional arrangement that prevents any trade imbalance among nations to persist.

In contrast, the classical efficient market theory solution to this trade imbalance problem is that the debtor nation must reduce its imports relative to its exports. One way this can occur is to have a free market in currency exchanges to solve the problem. The classical theory maintains that if the Chinese currency (the renminbi) was traded in a free flexible foreign exchange market, and if the United States ran an unfavorable balance of trade with the Chinese then the demand for the Chinese currency would substantially increase in value relative to the US dollar. As a result, the retail dollar price in the United States of Chinese goods would rise. American consumers would find that Chinese goods were so expensive in terms of dollars that they could no longer afford to buy very much from the Chinese. The rise in the consumer price level would adversely affect the real income and living standards of the average employed American worker. Thus Chinese imports to the United States would decline significantly.

In China, on the other hand, with the appreciation of the Chinese currency relative to the dollar, the Chinese would experience a decline in the renminbi price of United States imports and therefore they would buy more imports from the United States[1] as their real income and living standard improved.

---

1. For technical reasons (known as when the Marshall-Lerner conditions are not applicable) that we need not discuss here, it is possible that even with a decline in the value of the United States dollar relative to the Chinese yuan, the value of the trade imbalance between China and the United States would not disappear and – in the worse-case scenario – the trade imbalance between China and the United States could actually worsen. We will ignore this possible real world complication in the following discussion to illustrate other possible deleterious effects of this classical theory solution to trade imbalances where free markets are suppose always to solve

If, however, the value of the US dollar declined relative to the Chinese currency, then as the retail dollar price of Chinese imports increases then the rate of inflation in the United States as measured by the consumer price index would rise as such imports are a significant portion of the American consumer budget.[2]

If the Federal Reserve believes that its primary obligation is to fight inflation, then the Federal Reserve's might ramp up its anti-inflationary policy and increase the domestic interest rate. A rise in interest rates in the United States would destroy some existing profit opportunities for American business firms and increase unemployment in the United States. The goal of the Federal Reserve's anti-inflation monetary policy would be to reduce the incomes of Americans sufficiently so American households reduce their purchases of all goods and services including imports from China as well as products from American factories. In other words, the Federal Reserve's policy would try to dampen economic activity globally. If the Federal Reserve's anti-inflation policy is successful, then the decline in market demand will act as a brake as Americans buy less goods (both domestically produced and imports) in the market. This reduction in imports would probably slow the appreciation of the yuan relative to the dollar and thereby have some impact on reducing the measured rate of inflation over time.

In this depressing scenario, as Americans buy fewer Chinese imports, profits and jobs in China's export industries would be reduced creating unemployment and potential political unrest in China. With lower incomes in China, the Chinese market demand for United States exports should decline resulting less profit opportunities in American export industries made possible by the ongoing devaluation of the dollar. Clearly such a possible scenario is neither good for the American or Chinese workers and business firms.

Classical theory avoids this possible unpleasant scenario by assuming that

---

any trade imbalance problem by devaluing the currency of the country experiencing an unfavorable balance of trade.
[2] If money wages of American workers did not increase, then the result of this classical theory solution would be to lower the standard of living of the average American worker until it approached the standard of living of Chinese workers.

with free efficient markets there will *always* be full employment of capital and labor in all trading nations no matter what changes occur in the exchange rate of currencies between nations. In other words, classical theory merely assumes away the possible unemployment problem that could occur in both America and China if the free market permits the United States dollar to be devalued relative to the renminbi in order to end the United States' unfavorable balance of trade. In the long run, classical theory asserts, as a matter of faith rather than as empirical evidence, there must always be full employment in all nations.[3]

Thus by loading the classical model with sufficient but unrealistic assumptions, classical theory resolves any potential trade deficit problem by merely invoking the magic of free markets for foreign exchange of currencies, in a world where the future is known – at least in the long run.

Some more pragmatic economists have noted that historically when exchange rate have been permitted to change relatively freely in the market the results have often been devastating for the nation. Consequently some experts have advocated a foreign exchange market where a market maker actually fixes the exchange rate at some pre-announced level. As a result, very often economic discussions on the requirements for a good international payments system have been limited to this question of the advantages and disadvantages of fixed vs. flexible exchange rates.

The facts of experience since the end of the Second World War, however, plus Keynes's revolutionary liquidity analysis indicates that more is required then merely deciding whether exchange rates should be fixed or freely flexible. A mechanism must be designed to adequately resolve any persistent trade and international payments imbalances that could occur whether the exchange rates are fixed or flexible. The mechanism should be designed not only to resolve these imbalance problems but also to simultaneously promotes global full employment – rather than just assume global full employment will always occur. Such a mechanism is embedded in the Keynes Plan for international trade and payment imbalances.

---

[3] And as footnote 2 indicates, mainstream economists assume away all possible economic problems.

2. The Bretton Woods solution

In 1944, as the Second World War was winding down, the victorious Allied nations organized a conference at Bretton Woods, New Hampshire. The purpose of this Bretton Woods conference was to design a post war international payments system. Keynes was the chief representative of the United Kingdom delegation. In contrast to the classical view of the desirability of free exchange rate markets, Keynes's position was that there is an incompatibility thesis in the classical theory approach to international trade and finance. Keynes argued that permitting free trade, flexible exchange rates and free capital mobility across international borders can be incompatible with the economic goal of global full employment and rapid economic growth.

Keynes offered an alternative analysis to the classical approach to the problem. This alternative was the "Keynes Plan" solution, an arrangement that would make international trade and financial flow arrangement compatible with global full employment and vigorous economic growth while, when necessary, permitting nations to introduce controls on any flow of capital funds that was being sent across national boundaries.

Keynes argued that the "main cause of failure" of any traditional international payments system – whether based on fixed or flexible exchange rates – was its inability to actively foster continuous global economic expansion whenever persistent trade payment imbalances occurred among trading nations. This failure, Keynes (1980) wrote,

> "...can be traced to a single characteristic. I ask close attention to this, because I shall argue that this provides a clue to the nature of any alternative which is to be successful.
>
> It is characteristic of a freely convertible international standard that it throws the main burden of adjustment on the country which is in the *debtor* position on the international balance of payments – that is, on the country which is (in this context) by hypothesis the *weaker* and above all the

> *smaller* in comparison with the other side of the scales which (for this purpose) is the rest of the world."

Keynes concluded that an essential improvement in designing any international payments system requires transferring the major *onus* of adjustment from the debtor to the creditor nation when any persistent international payments imbalance develops. This transfer of responsibility for ending persistent international imbalances to those nations that experience exports that exceed their imports and are therefore in the creditor position would, Keynes explained, substitute an expansionist, in place of a contractionist, pressure on world trade. To achieve a golden era of economic development Keynes recommended combining a fixed, but adjustable, exchange rate system with a mechanism for requiring the nation "enjoying" a favorable balance of trade to initiate most of the effort necessary to eliminate this trade imbalance, while "maintaining enough discipline in the debtor countries to prevent them from exploiting the new ease allowed them" (Keynes, 1980).

During the Second World War, millions of people had been killed or wounded. Industrial and residential centers in most of Europe lay in ruins. Europe was on the brink of famine as agricultural production had been disrupted by the war. Transportation infrastructure was in shambles. The war-torn capitalist nations in Europe did not have sufficient undamaged productive resources available to produce enough to feed their populations and much less to rebuild their economies.

he only major economic power in the world that was not significantly damaged by the war was the United States. European rebuilding would require the European nations to run huge import surpluses with the United States in order to meet their economic needs for recovery. The European nations had very little foreign reserves. (At the time the major foreign reserves were in the form of the asset gold that European war-devastated nations could readily sell to the United States for dollars that they could then use to buy imports from the only post-war nation that had enough productivity capacity to produce for exports – the United States.)

The European nations had insufficient foreign reserves to obtain the

156

necessary large volume of imports from the United States necessary to restore their economies. The only alternative, under a free market *laissez-faire* system, would be for Europeans to obtain an enormous volume of loans from the United States to finance the purchase of required United States exports needed to feed the European population and rebuild their economies. Private sector lenders in the United States, however, were mindful that German reparation payments to the victorious Allied nations after World War I were primarily financed by American private investors lending to Germany (the so-called Dawes Plan). Germany never repaid these Dawes plan loans. Given this history of nations defaulting on international debt repayments and the existing circumstances immediately after the Second World War, it was obvious that private lending facilities in the United States could not be expected to provide the loans necessary for European recovery after the war.

The Keynes Plan, presented at the 1944 Bretton Woods conference, would require the United States, as the obvious major creditor nation, to accept the major responsibility for curing the post war trade imbalance where a tremendous amount of goods from the United States would be necessary to feed the populations in Europe while simultaneously rebuilding the factories and infrastructure necessary to reestablish viable European economies.

Where were the Europeans going to get the finance to purchase all the necessary goods from the United States? Keynes estimated that the European nations might require in excess of $10 billion to purchase United States exports for such a post-war rebuilding of the European economies. The Keynes Plan had an operational system that would have the United States simply provide these funds to the Europeans. The United States representative to the Bretton Woods Conference, Harry Dexter White, stated that the US Congress would never provide the $10 billion that Keynes estimated was the minimum required funding. Instead, White argued, Congress might be willing to provide, at most, $3 billion as the United States contribution to solving this post war international financial problem for rebuilding European economies.

The United States delegation at the Bretton Woods conference was the most important participant. It was clear that nothing could be done unless the United States delegation agreed to any plan that was developed at the conference. White had the US delegation veto the Keynes Plan. Instead, White provided a plan that set up the International Monetary Fund (IMF) and what we now call the World Bank.

The White plan envisioned the International Monetary Fund (IMF) providing short-term loans to nations running unfavorable balances of trade. These loans were supposed to give the debtor nation time to rebuild its economic structure and then stop importing more than it was exporting. Then these debtor nations were to pay off their debt to the IMF by earnings from their exports exceeding their import purchases. Under the White Plan, the United States would subscribe a maximum of $3 billion as its contribution to the IMF lending facilities

The World Bank would borrow funds from the free market. These World Bank funds would then be used to provide long-term loans for rebuilding capital facilities and making capital improvements initially in the war-torn nations and later in the less developed countries. When the new facilities were in place, it was assumed that sufficiently more goods could be produced and sold profitably. Then the nation would use the new income earned from the new facilities to pay off the World Bank loans. This White plan suggested by the US delegation was basically the institutional arrangements adopted at the Bretton Woods Conference.

Under this White plan, international loans from the IMF or the World Bank were the only available sources for financing the huge volume of imports from the United States that the war-torn nations would require *immediately* after the Second World War. It turned out, however, that the IMF and World Bank together did not have sufficient funds to make loans of the magnitude needed by the European nations. But even if the IMF and the World Bank could have provided loans sufficient to meet the needs of the war torn nations, the result would have been a huge international indebtedness of these nations. Paying off this immense debt obligations would require the European population to accept the main burden of adjustment by them being willing to "tighten their belts".

This belt tightening statement is a euphemism to indicate that the debtor nations would have to dramatically reduce their consumption spending for imports and even goods produced domestically. Such a plan could be put into effect only by reducing the income of the residents of European nations so they will buy less output from both foreign and domestic enterprises in order to pay the annual debt servicing charges. This suggested no significant improvement in the standard of living of Europeans for years to come. The result would so depress Europeans as to possibly inducing political revolutions in most of Western Europe. Not inconsequentially, the "tighten your belt" policies also would have limited Europe as a possible large profitable market in the future for American exporters.

To avoid the possibility of many European nations facing a desperate electorate that might opt for a communist system when faced with the dismal future the White Plan offered, the United States, developed an alternative plan in the hope that Communism did not spread west from the Soviet Union to the democratic European nations. In 1948, President Truman recommended Congress accept the Marshall Plan. Despite White's argument that the United States. would not be willing to give more than $3 billion to solving this international payments problem, the Congress approved the Marshall Plan which provided $5 billion in foreign aid in 18 months and a total of $13 billion in four years. (Adjusted for inflation, this $13 billion sum is equivalent to approximately $160 billion in 2014 dollars.) The Marshall plan was essentially a four year *gift* of $13 billion worth of American exports to the war devastated nations. The Marshall Plan required no repayment by the recipients of these funds – and hence no "belt tightening".

The 1948 Marshall plan gifts gave the recipient nations a sufficient number of dollars to buy approximately 2 per cent of the total annual output (Gross Domestic Product) of the United States each year for four years. Despite Americans giving away 2 per cent of their national income per annum, there was no real sacrifice for American households associated with the Marshall Plan as the remaining income was significantly greater than pre-war levels. The United States standard of living during the first year of the Marshall Plan was still 25% larger than it had been in the last peacetime year of 1940. American household income continued to grow throughout the Marshall Plan period.

Ideas towards a new international financial architecture?

The Marshall Plan funds created profit opportunities for American firms and jobs for US workers. Full employment was readily sustained. Immediately after the war ended, despite government military spending being significantly reduced, which by itself might have created some post-war unemployment problems. Partially offsetting this reduction in government military spending was the Marshall plan funds spending that created significant increases in employment in United States export industries just as several million men and women were discharged from the United States armed forces and entered the United States civilian labor force looking for jobs.

For the first time in its history, the United States did not suffer from a severe recession due to a lack of spending immediately following the cessation of a major war and a reduction in military spending by the federal government. The United States and most of the rest of the world experienced an economic "free lunch" as both the potential debtor nations and the creditor nation experienced tremendous real economic gains resulting from the Marshall Plan and other foreign aid give-aways. Despite the growth in output from foreign factories, however, the United States maintained a surplus merchandise trade balance of exports over imports until the first oil price shock in 1973.

By 1958, however, although the United States still had an annual goods and services export surplus of over $5 billion, the post war United States potential international payments surplus was at an end. By that time United States governmental foreign and military aid exceeded $6 billion while there was a net private capital outflow of $1.6 billion from the United State that financed United States companies investing in productive facilities abroad This total of $7.6 outflow of funds offset the earnings of the $5 billion export surplus by $2.6 billion. In other words by 1958, the international payments account of the United States saw a net outflow of $2.6 billion despite export earnings exceeding spending on imports by $5 billion. The post war international payments surplus of the United States was at an end.

As the United States total international payments account swung into deficit in 1958 other nations began to experience international payments surpluses. These credit surplus nations did not spend their payments surpluses on additional imports from the United States. Instead the nations used a portion

160

of their annual dollar surpluses to purchase international liquid assets in the form of gold reserves from the United States. For example, in 1958, the United States sold over $2 billion in gold reserves to foreign central banks.

These trends accelerated in the 1960s, partly as a result of increased United States military and financial aid in response to the construction of the Berlin Wall in 1961 and later because of the U.S.'s increasing military involvement in Vietnam. At the same time, a rebuilt Europe and Japan became important producers of exports so that the rest of the world became less dependent on purchasing products solely from United States export industries.

Still the United States maintained a surplus merchandise trade balance of exports over imports until the first oil price shock in 1973. More than offsetting this merchandise trade surplus during most of the 1960s, however, were foreign and military aid dollar outflows to other nations plus net capital outflows from the United States that financed United States companies investing in facilities abroad. Consequently, during the 1960s, the United States experienced an annual unfavorable total balance of international payments.

The Bretton Woods system had no way of automatically forcing the emerging creditor nations experiencing a payments surplus to step in and accept the responsibility for resolving the persistent international payments imbalances – a creditor adjustment role that contributed so wonderfully to global economic growth. A creditor role that the United States had started playing in 1948 with the Marshall Plan. Instead during the 1960s the surplus nations continued to converted some portion of their annual dollar international payment receipt surpluses into demands on United States gold reserves to be stored as a liquid asset for savings that could be used anytime in the future to meet international payments. As surplus nations in the 1960s drained gold reserves from the United States, the seeds of the destruction of the Bretton Woods system and the golden age of economic development were being sown.

In 1971, President Richard Nixon closed the gold window. Nixon stated that the United States government would no longer sell gold to foreign nations who had earned dollars and wanted to use these dollars to buy gold from the

Ideas towards a new international financial architecture?

United States rather than buy produced goods and services from American business firms. Nixon's closing of the gold window had, in essence, indicated that the United States had unilaterally withdrawn from any Bretton Woods agreement. At that point of time, the last vestiges of Keynes's enlightened international monetary approach where the creditor nation accepts a large responsibility for correcting persistent trade imbalances was on its way to be forgotten.

3. Reforming the international payments system

The post Second World War global golden age of economic development required international institutions and United States government foreign aid policies that operated on principles inherent in the Keynes Plan where the creditor nation accepting the major responsibility for solving any persistent international payments imbalance. The formal Breton Woods agreement, however, did not require creditor nations to take such actions. Since Nixon's closing of the gold window in 1971, the onus has been on nations with deficits in their trade and international payments balances to solve their own international deficit payments problems. The result has been that since 1971 the international payments system often impedes rapid economic growth and even induces recession for many nations of the world.

Utilizing the ideas Keynes presented at Bretton Woods, it is possible to update the Keynes Plan for a 21st century international monetary payments scheme that would eliminate persistent unfavorable payments imbalances, promote global economic prosperity and still meet the political realities of today without bowing one's knee to efficient market advocates. For, as Keynes wrote:

> "to suppose [as the classical theory does] that there exists some smoothly functioning automatic [free market] mechanism of adjustment which preserves equilibrium if only we trust to methods of *laissez-faire* is a doctrinaire delusion which disregards the lessons of historical experience without having behind it the support of sound theory" (Keynes, 1980).

Globalization, international trade and international payments

Since the 1990s, there have been several international finance crises. In 1994 when the Mexican government was faced with difficulties in trying to service its international debt repayments, some pragmatic policy makers recognized that free markets do not provide a system that automatically prevents a crisis in the international payments sector. In some cases, instead of relying on the market to solve the problem, these pragmatists advocated the creation of some sort of *crisis manager* to stop international financial market liquidity hemorrhaging and to "bail-out" the international investors. In 1994, for example, United States Treasury Secretary Robert Rubin encouraged President Clinton to use American funds to lend to Mexico to solve its financial crisis and thereby save the wealth of international buyers of Mexican bonds. This solved the problem.

In other cases, when the solution was left to the free market severe economic problems developed. In 1997, for example, Thailand, Malaysia, and other East Asian nations experienced an international currency crisis that battered their economies. In 1998 the Russian debt default caused another international financial crisis that lead to the collapse of the Long Term Capital Management (LTCM) hedge fund which, except for quick action by pragmatists at the New York Federal Reserve Bank, could have induced a significant drop in American equity markets. (We should note that among the principals of LTCM was Nobel Prize economist winner Myron Scholes, who won his Nobel Prize for discovering the formula for "properly" pricing risk in an efficient financial market environment. Scholes formula, however, could not save LTCM from its after-the-fact recognized investment blunder into Russian bonds by not correctly pricing the risks involved in such an investment.)

At the time of the Russian debt default and the LTCM collapse, President Clinton called for a "new financial architecture" for international financial market transactions. The then International Monetary Fund Director Stanley Fischer (who in 2014 Obama appointed as Vice Chair of the Federal Reserve) recognized that the IMF did not have sufficient funds to stem the international financial crises that was occurring. Fisher suggested that the major nations of the world, the so called G7 nations, make a temporary arrangement where they would provide additional financing to help provide funds to any nation suffering from deficits in its international payments

Ideas towards a new international financial architecture?

imbalances until such nations could get their economic house in order.

Fisher's cry for a G7 temporary collaboration to provide funds to deficit nations is equivalent to recruiting a volunteer fire department to douse the flames after someone has cried fire in a crowded theater. Even if the fire is ultimately extinguished there will be a lot of innocent casualties. Moreover, every new currency fire would require the G7 voluntary fire department to pour more liquidity into the market to put out the flames. Clearly a more desirable goal would be to produce a permanent fire prevention system, and not to rely on organizing larger and larger volunteer fire fighting companies with each new currency crisis. In other words, crisis prevention rather than crisis management should be the policy goal.

President Clinton's clarion call for a new international financial architecture implicitly recognized the need for a permanent prevention institutional arrangement in the existing international payments system, Unfortunately, President Clinton's call was not taken up as the international community managed to muddle through the experience although some nations and its residents suffered severe economic pains.

Beginning in 2007 the global economic system again experienced a crisis of the international financial system – a crisis of much larger proportions than those in the 1990s. The US sub-prime mortgage derivatives problem created a contagious disease that caused havoc with banking systems in many other countries including Germany, the United Kingdom, France, Spain, Greece and others. The contagion caused the almost complete collapse of the Icelandic banking system and even the Swiss banking system – usually considered a paragon of financial stability – appeared for a while to be in severe economic trouble. The need for a "new international financial architecture" is clearly more urgent than ever.

In the 21st century interdependent global economy, a substantial degree of economic cooperation among trading nations is essential. The original Keynes Plan for reforming the international payments system called for the creation of a single Supranational Central Bank. Given the problems Europe has suffered despite it possessing a Supranational central bank suggests that perhaps an institutional arrangement that avoids such a Supranational

164

central bank may be more desirable in that it permits participating nations to still manage their own monetary policy in the way the government thinks is in the best interests of its residents.

4. The international monetary clearing union

An international financial architecture system to deal with persistent trade imbalances and any international financial crisis can be developed to operate under the same economic principles laid down by Keynes at Bretton Woods. But this system does not require the establishment of a supranational central bank of the world as Keynes suggested in his "Keynes Plan" at Bretton Woods. Instead, this new international payment system is aimed at obtaining a more acceptable international agreement (given today's political climate in most nations) that does not require any nation to surrender the nation's control of either its domestic banking system or the operation of its domestic monetary and fiscal policies to a supranational authority. Each nation will still be able to use monetary and fiscal policies to determine the domestic economic destiny that is best for its citizens as long as it does not detrimentally affect employment and income earning opportunities in other trading partner nations.

What is required is a closed, double-entry bookkeeping clearing institution to keep the international payments "score" among the various trading nations plus some mutually agreed upon rules to solve the problems of persistent trade and international payment imbalances. It will also require an international agreement and a method to prevent international financial market transactions that can cause a financial market crisis that would be disruptive to the stability of any nation's economy as well as a threat to the global economy.

The new international institution to be set up under this plan could be labeled the International Monetary Clearing Union (IMCU). The IMCU would require all international payments between nations whether for imports or financial funds crossing national borders to go through this International Monetary Clearing Union. Each nation's central bank will set up a deposit account with the IMCU. Then any payments of a resident entity in nation A made to a

Ideas towards a new international financial architecture?

resident entity in nation B will have to clear through each nation central bank deposit at the IMCU. A payment from a resident in A to a resident in B when cleared through the IMCU would appear as a credit for nation's B central bank account at the IMCU and as debit to nation's A central bank's account at the IMCU. Although this may seem to be a complicated process to the average layperson, it is merely an international version of how checks are cleared when a residents of one region of the United States, say California, pays other entities in another region, say New York. The checks clear thru the clearing house mechanism set up by the United States Federal Reserve. System

This IMCU is a 21st century variant of the Keynes Plan. To operate it would require at least seven technical proposals for dealing with all types of international financial problems that we have already indicated may occur. These technical proposals are presented in the Appendix to this chapter. At this point, rather than letting the exposition getting bogged down in technical details, it is more appropriate to indicate how and why this IMCU proposal works to end the possibility of persistent trade imbalances and, disruptive flows of financial funds across national borders. Simultaneously this IMCU would be encouraging global full employment and economic growth.

The object of this International Monetary Clearing Union is

(1) to prevent a lack of global effective market demand for the products of industry occurring due to liquidity problems whenever any nation(s) holds either excessive idle foreign reserves by saving (i.e., not spending on products) too much of its internationally earned income. In other words this IMCU would encourage sufficient spending globally to produce enough profit incentives in export industries of nations to help assure global full employment,

(2) to provide an automatic mechanism for placing a major burden of correcting international trade imbalances on the nation running persistent export surpluses,

(3) to provide each nation with the ability to monitor and, if desired, to control movements out of the nation of (a) flight financial funds, as

Globalization, international trade and international payments

well as money moved across national borders in order to avoid paying taxes on such funds, (b) of earnings from illegal activities leaving the nation, and (c) to prevent funds that cross borders to finance terrorist operations, and

(4) to expand the quantity of the liquid asset used in settling international contracts (the asset of ultimate redemption) as global capacity warrants while protecting the international purchasing power of this asset.

The IMCU system would have a built-in mechanism to encourage any nation that runs persistent trade surpluses of exports over imports to spend what is deemed (in advance) by agreement of the international community to be "excessive" credit balances (savings) of foreign liquid reserve assets that have been deposited in the nation's deposit account at the IMCU. These accumulated credits (saving out of international earned income) represent funds that the creditor nation could have used to buy the products of foreign industries but instead used to increase its foreign reserves in terms of its deposit at the IMCU. When a nation holds excessive credits in its deposit account at the IMCU, it would mean that these excess credits are creating unemployment problems and the lack of profitable opportunities for business enterprises somewhere in the global economy.

The Keynes principle involved in this situation is to recognize that if the creditor nation spends its excessive credits, this spending will increase profit opportunities and the hiring of workers around the globe and thereby promote global full employment. The Keynes solution would encourage the creditor nation to spend these excessive credits in three possible ways – all beneficial to the global economy. These three ways are:

(1) on the products (exports) of any other member nation of the IMCU,

(2) on new direct foreign investment projects in other IMCU member nations, and/or

(3) to provide foreign aid, similar to the Marshall Plan, to deficit IMCU members.

Ideas towards a new international financial architecture?

The credit nation is free to choose any combination of the above three ways to spend its excessive credit at the IMCU but it must spend its excessive credits.

If the creditor nation spends its excessive credits on imports from foreign producers, the result will be that the surplus nation's trade imbalance will be reduced while it is creating additional profits opportunities and labor hiring in other nations. This means more income for people and businesses in the nations previously experiencing unfavorable balances of trade and who were borrowing from foreigners to buy their excess of imports over exports. In essence this excess credit spending on imports gives the deficit nations the opportunity to work their way out of international debt by earning additional income by selling additional exports to their creditors.

Direct foreign investment spending requires the nation with excess credits in its account at the IMCU to build plant and equipment in the deficit nation, thereby immediately increasing profits, jobs and income in the construction industries in the deficit nation and then creating jobs opportunities in manning the new plant and equipment when construction is completed. If the nation receiving this direct foreign investment is a less developed country, then this foreign direct investment spending helps to build the facilities of this less developed country up to 21st century standards.

Foreign aid spending provides the deficit nation with a "gift" that it can use to reduce its debt obligations and/or buy additional products from foreign producers without going further into debt.

These three spending alternatives encourage the surplus nation to accept a major responsibility for correcting trade and international payments imbalances. Nevertheless this provision gives the trade surplus country considerable discretion in deciding how to accept the onus of adjustment in the way it believes is in its residents' best interests. It does not permit, however, the surplus nation to shift the burden to the deficit nation(s) by lending the deficit nation or nations more and therefore imposing on any deficit nation additional contractual debt repayments obligations independent of what the deficit nation can afford.

The important thing is to make sure that continual oversaving by the surplus nation in the form of international liquid reserves are not permitted to unleash depressionary economic forces on other nations and/or to build up of international debts so encumbering as to impoverish the global economy of the 21 century.

In the event that the surplus nation does not spend or give away the credits that are deemed "excessive" within a specified time, then the IMCU managers would confiscate (and redistribute to debtor members) the portion of credits deemed excessive. This last resort is the equivalent of a 100% taxes on a nation's liquidity holdings that the international community has already agreed are excessive. Since continual excessive liquidity holdings implies continuing and excessive unemployment in one or more nations running trade deficits, if the surplus nation does not spend its excessive surplus, then confiscating these excessive credits and providing them to debtor nations will not only benefit the debtors but improve the global employment rate and output. Of course the nation with excessive credits will recognize that these credits are subject to a 100 per cent tax if not spent. It is therefore highly unlikely that this confiscatory tax will ever have to be enforced.

Under either a fixed or a flexible rate system with each nation free to decide how much it will import, some nations will, at times, experience persistent trade deficits merely because their trading partners are not living up to their means – that is because other nations are continually saving (hoarding) a portion of their foreign export earnings rather than spending it on the products of foreign workers and enterprises. By so doing, these oversavers are creating a lack of global market demand for the products that global industries can produce.

Under the Keynes principle requiring creditor nations to spend excessive credits, deficit countries would no longer have to have to tighten the belts and reducing the income of their residents in an attempt to reduce imports and thereby reduce their payment imbalance because others are excessively oversaving. Instead, the system would seek to remedy the payment deficit by increasing opportunities for deficit nations to sell products profitably abroad and thereby work their way out of their otherwise

Ideas towards a new international financial architecture?

deteriorating debtor position.

As the 2007-8 global financial crisis deepened, some recognized that merely attempting to tinker with the existing system by perhaps upgrading the power of the IMF and the World Bank or encouraging the G-7 to again act as a volunteer fire department did not solve the international trade and financial payments problems. For years now the international system has been running into trouble while patches to the existing IMF and World Bank system were applied in a vain attempt to end these global trade and payments problems. The world lost a great opportunity in 1944 when the United States vetoed the Keynes Plan at Bretton Woods. Let us hope we do not squander this opportunity again.

When the 2009 Obama recovery plan took effect, whatever economic recovery that the American economy experienced again placed the United States as the engine of growth for China and many other less developed nations. It tend to aggravate the United States international payments imbalance problem as, after 2009, the United States began again to increase its imports by a greater amount than it's increasing volume of exports. If this result continues, then, under the existing international payments system, the result may be to create an atmosphere where many fear the status of the dollar as the most liquid safe harbor foreign reserve asset. Such fears can only roil global financial markets and plunge the global economy into further crisis and recession.

If this were to occur, it should be even more obvious that a reform of the international trade and payments system is necessary if we are not to further aggravate any global economic crisis. Hopefully, the leaders of the major nations will recognize the need to adopt some form of the Keynes Plan such as the IMCU if the global economy is ever to reinstate prosperous times for all the nations on earth.

5. The case for capital controls

Since the future is uncertain, at any moment of time some event (ephemeral or not) may occur which can make residents of a nation feel more uncertain about the prospects of their economy. Under a system of free exchange markets, residents of the nation that fear the future can remove their savings from the domestic banking system and transfer them to another nation's banking and financial system where they believe the latter is a safe harbor to store their savings. The funds used in any attempt to find a safe haven in another nation are called "flight capital". If enough people try at the same time to move their funds from the domestic economy to this presumed safe harbor, the effect is similar to a run on a domestic bank that causes the bank to collapse.

In the case of bank runs, a policy of insuring deposits is usually sufficient to stopping bank runs. Unfortunately, a cascade of flight capital fund movements out of a nation to a safe harbor in another nation cannot be stopped by merely insuring the deposits at domestic banks. Instead this flight of funds if large enough can bring about the collapse of the domestic economy, as more and more people stop buying domestically produced goods to increase their holdings of foreign liquid assets. This creates significant recessionary pressures on the domestic economy thereby making it more difficult for the government to undertake economic policies to stabilize the nation's economy and prevent it from falling into recession or depression.

Since under the IMCU proposal all movement of funds across borders must go through the nation's central bank deposit at the IMCU, any nation can, if it desires, monitor and stop any cross border financial fund movements by merely refusing to allow the cross border banking transactions to be processed though the central bank's deposit on the IMCU's books. In other words each nation can institute an effective policy to limit fund outflows from its country if, for any reason, the government deems it in the best interest of the nation's economy to prevent such fund outflows.

Thus, for example, if such a system was in place, the United States government could via a Security Exchange Commission ruling prohibit the creation of domestic financial asset markets – such as mortgage backed derivatives – that are organized by investment bankers but do not have a reliable market maker institution to insure orderliness and liquidity. Under this capital control provision, the American financial services industries would not have to fear loss of customers and profits to foreign financial services firms who do not follow SEC rules when the SEC prohibited certain financial market activities by American financial services firms. The flow of funds could occur only if the foreign financial service firms agreed to all the SEC rules required of domestic financial service firms. Thus the playing field would be level.

Finally, all movements of funds gained from illegal activities, or funds being moved from a country to another nation in order to avoid the domestic country's tax collector, or funds raised in one country that is being funneled to other countries to finance international terrorist activities must also flow through the nation's central bank to the IMCU. Consequently, each nation has the facility, if it wishes to monitor and if necessary stop such cross border money flow transactions from occurring. Clearly this is an important aspect of the IMCU plan for it permits each nation to assure its citizens that others cannot take advantage of the international trading system to avoid paying one's fair share of taxes, and to constrain the international financing of terrorist organizations, as well as to permit the government to undermine the profitability of any international illegal drug trade.

Appendix: The technical requirements for creating an IMCU to reform the international payments system

There are seven major technical provisions in this IMCU system proposal. They are:

1. The unit of account and ultimate reserve asset for international liquidity is the International Money Clearing Unit (IMCU). All IMCU's can be held *only* by the central banks of nations that abide by the rules of the clearing union system. IMCUs are not available to be held by the public.

2. Each nation's central bank or, in the case of a common currency (e.g., the

Euro) a currency union's central bank, is committed to guarantee one way convertibility from IMCU deposits at the clearing union to its domestic money to be used for the purchase of goods and services provided by domestic producers. Each central bank will set its own rules regarding making available foreign monies (through IMCU clearing transactions) to its own bankers and private sector residents.[4]

Since Central Banks agree to sell their own liabilities (one-way convertibility) against the IMCU only to other Central Bankers via the International Clearing Union while they simultaneously hold only IMCUs as liquid reserve assets for international financial transactions, there can be no draining of reserves from the international payments system. Ultimately, all major private international transactions clear between central banks' accounts in the books of the international clearing institution.

The guarantee of only one-way convertibility permits each nation to institute controls and regulations on international capital fund outflows if necessary. The primary economic function of these international capital flow controls and regulations is to prevent rapid changes in the bull-bear sentiment from overwhelming the market maker and inducing dramatic changes in international financial market price trends that can have devastating real consequences.

There is a spectrum of different capital controls available. At one end of the spectrum are controls that primarily impose administrative constraints either on a case-by-case basis or an expenditure category basis. Such controls may include administrative oversight and control of individual transactions for payments to foreign residents (or banks) often via oversight of international transactions by banks or their customers. Other capital controls

---

[4] Correspondent banking will have to operate through the International Clearing Agency, with each central bank regulating the international relations and operations of its domestic banking firms. Small scale smuggling of currency across borders, etc., can never be completely eliminated. But such movements are merely a flea on a dog's back – a minor, but not debilitating, irritation. If, however, most of the residents of a nation hold and use (in violation of legal tender laws) a foreign currency for domestic transactions and as a store of value, this is evidence of a lack of confidence in the government and its monetary authority. Unless confidence is restored, all attempts to restore economic prosperity will fail.

might include the imposition of taxes (or other opportunity costs) on *specific* international financial transactions, e.g., the 1960s United States Interest Equalization Tax.

Finally there can be many forms of monetary policy decisions undertaken to affect net international financial flows, e.g., raising the interest rate to slow capital outflows, raising bank reserve ratios, limiting the ability of banks to finance purchases of foreign securities, and regulating interbank activity. It has been argued that the 1997 East Asian currency contagion problem that almost brought down the global financial system was due to the interbank market that created the whirlpool of speculation. Mayer has stated that what was needed was "a system for identifying... and policing interbank lending" (Mayer, 1998) including banks' contingent liabilities resulting from dealing in derivatives. Recognizing the inability of economic models to correctly price risk in a non-ergodic economic system, Mayer stated: "The mathematical models of price movements and covariance underlying the construction of these [contingent] liabilities simply collapsed as actual prices departed so far from 'normal' probabilities". (Mayer 1998)

The IMF, as lender of last resort during the 1997 East Asian contagion crisis, imposed the same conditions on all nations requiring loans for international liquidity purposes. The resulting worsening of the situation should have taught us that in policy prescriptions one size does *not* fit all situations. Accordingly, the type of capital regulation a nation should choose from the spectrum of tools available at any time will differ depending on the specific circumstances involved. It would be presumptuous to attempt to catalog what capital regulations should be imposed for any nation under any given circumstances. Nevertheless, it should be stressed that regulating capital movements may be a necessary *but not a sufficient* condition for promoting global prosperity. Much more is required.

If any government objects to the idea that the IMCU proviso #2 provides governments with the ability to limit the free movement of "capital" funds, then this nation is free to join other nations of similar attitude in forming a currency union and thereby assuring a free flow of funds among the residents of the currency union.

3. Contracts between private individuals in different nations will continue to be denominated into whatever domestic currency permitted by local laws and agreed upon by the contracting parties. Contracts to be settled in terms of a foreign currency will therefore require some publically announced commitment from the central bank (through private sector bankers) of the availability of foreign funds to meet such private contractual obligations.

4. The exchange rate between the domestic currency and the IMCU is set initially by each nation or currency union's central bank – just as it would be if one instituted an international gold standard. Since private enterprises that are already engaged in trade have international contractual commitments that would span the changeover interval from the current system, then, as a practical matter, one would expect, but not demand, that the existing exchange rate structure (with perhaps minor modifications) would provide the basis for initial rate setting.

Proviso #7 *infra* indicate when and how this nominal exchange rate between the national currency and the IMCU would be changed in the future.

5. An overdraft system should be built into the clearing union rules. Overdrafts should make available short-term unused creditor balances at the Clearing House to finance the productive international transactions of others who need short-term credit. The terms will be determined by the *pro bono publico* clearing union managers.

6. A trigger mechanism to encourage any creditor nation to spend what is deemed (in advance) by agreement of the international community to be "excessive" credit balances accumulated by running current account surpluses. These excessive credits can be spent in three ways: (a) on the products of any other member of the clearing union, (b) on new direct foreign investment projects, and/or to provide unilateral transfers (foreign aid) to deficit members. Spending via (a) forces the surplus nation to make the adjustment directly by way of the trade balance on goods and services. Spending by way of permits adjustment directly by the capital account balance, while (b) provides adjustment by the capital accounts (without setting up a contractual debt that will require reverse current account flows in the future).

Ideas towards a new international financial architecture?

In the unlikely event that the surplus nation does not spend or give away these credits within a specified time, then the clearing agency would confiscate (and redistribute to debtor members) the portion of credits deemed excessive.[5] This last resort confiscatory action (a 100% taxes on excessive liquidity holdings) would make a payments adjustment via unilateral transfer payments in the current accounts.

In the absence of proviso #6, under any conventional system, whether it has fixed or flexible exchange rates and/or capital controls, there can ultimately be an international liquidity crisis (as any persistent current account deficit can deplete a nation's foreign reserves) that unleashes global depressionary forces. Thus, proviso #6 is necessary to assure that the international payments system will not have a built-in depressionary bias. Ultimately then it is in the self-interest of the surplus nation to accept this responsibility, for its actions will create conditions for global economic expansion some of which must redound to its own residents. Failure to act, on the other hand, will promote global depressionary forces which will have some negative impact on its own residents

7. A system to stabilize the long-term purchasing power of the IMCU (in terms of each member nation's domestically produced market basket of goods) can be developed. This requires a system of fixed exchange rates between the local currency and the IMCU that changes only to reflect permanent increases in efficiency wages[6]. This assures each central bank that its holdings of IMCUs as the nation's foreign reserves will never lose purchasing power in terms of foreign produced goods. If a foreign

---

[5] Whatever "excessive" credit balances that are redistributed shall be apportioned among the debtor nations (perhaps based on a formula which is inversely related to each debtor's per capita income and directly related to the size of its international debt) to be used to reduce debit balances at the clearing union.
[6] The efficiency wage is related to the money wage divided by the average product of labor; it is the unit labor cost modified by the profit mark-up in domestic money terms of domestically produced GNP. At the preliminary stage of this proposal, it would serve no useful purpose to decide whether the domestic market basket should include both tradeable and non-tradeable goods and services. (With the growth of tourism more and more non-tradeable goods become potentially tradeable.) I personally prefer the wider concept of the domestic market basket, but it is not obvious that any essential principle is lost if a tradeable only concept is used, or if some nations use the wider concept while others the narrower one.

government permits wage-price inflation to occur within its borders, then, the exchange rate between the local currency and the IMCU will be devalued to reflect the inflation in the local money price of the domestic produced goods and services. For example, if this rate of domestic inflation was 5 cent, the exchange rate would change so that each unit of IMCU could purchase 5 per cent more of the nation's currency.

If, on the other hand, increases in productivity lead to declining domestic production costs in terms of the domestic money, then the nation with this decline in efficiency wages [say of 5 per cent] would have the option of choosing either [a] to permit the IMCU to buy [up to 5 per cent] less units of domestic currency, thereby capturing all (or most of) the gains from productivity for its residents while maintaining the purchasing power of the IMCU, or [b] to keep the nominal exchange rate constant. In the latter case, the gain in productivity is shared with all trading partners. In exchange, the export industries in this productive nation will receive an increasing relative share of the world market.

By devaluing the exchange rate between local monies and the IMCU to offset the rate of domestic inflation, the IMCU's purchasing power is stabilized and inflation in one nation cannot be exported to another via the price of the first nation's exports.

By restricting use of IMCUs to Central Banks, private speculation regarding IMCUs as a hedge against inflation is avoided. Each nation's rate of inflation of the goods and services it produces is determined solely by (a) the local government's policy toward the level of domestic money wages and profit margins vis-a-vis productivity gains, i.e., the nation's efficiency wage. Each nation is therefore free to experiment with policies for stabilizing its efficiency wage to prevent inflation as long as these policies do not lead to a lack of global effective demand. Whether the nation is successful or not in preventing domestic goods price inflation, the IMCU will never lose its international purchasing power in terms of any domestic money. Moreover, the IMCU has the promise of gaining in purchasing power over time, if productivity grows more than money wages and each nation is willing to share any reduction in real production costs with its trading partners.

Ideas towards a new international financial architecture?

Proviso #7 produces a system designed to, at least, maintain the relative efficiency wage parities amongst nations. In such a system, the adjustability of nominal exchange rates will be primarily to offset changes in efficiency wages among trading partners. A beneficial effect that follows from this proviso is that it eliminates the possibility that a specific industry in any nation can be put at a competitive disadvantage (or secure a competitive advantage) against foreign producers solely because the nominal exchange rate changed independently of changes in efficiency wages and the real costs of production in each nation.

Consequently, nominal exchange rate variability can no longer create the problem of a loss of competitiveness due solely to the overvaluing of a currency as, for example, experienced by the industries in the American "rust belt" during the period 1982-85. Even if temporary, currency appreciation independent of changes in efficiency wages can have significant permanent real costs as domestic industries abandon export markets and lose domestic market business to foreign firms and the resultant existing excess plant and equipment is cast aside as too costly to maintain.

Proviso #7 also prevents any nation from engaging in a beggar-thy-neighbor, export-thy-unemployment policy by pursuing a real exchange rate devaluation that does not reflect changes in efficiency wages. Once the initial exchange rates are chosen and relative efficiency wages are locked in, reduction in real production costs which are associated with a relative decline in efficiency wages is the main factor justifying an adjustment in the real exchange rate.

References

Keynes, J. M. (1936) *General Theory of Employment, interest and Money*, Macmillan, London, pp. 338-339.

Keynes, J. M. (1980) *The Collected Writings of John Maynard Keynes*, 25, edited by D. Moggridge, Macmillan, London, pp. 21-22, 27, 176.

Mayer, M. (1998) "The Asian Disease: Plausible Diagnoses, Possible Remedies", Levy Institute Public Policy Brief No. 44, pp. 29-31.

CHAPTER 8
A new international financial architecture: The regional *versus* the global view?

Oscar Ugarteche[1]

1. Introduction

This paper is geared to show the limitations of the existing financial architecture and the emergence of what appears to be a new financial architecture with regional financial frameworks. It starts by making a brief history of the existing international financial system and its role in international financial regulations in order to show lack of proper global organisations by arguing the changes in the governance issues of existing international financial institutions given the massive shift in world economic power and follows with the problem of a country based reserve currency, proposing a new reserve currency that will have more stability than current highly indebted country based reserve currencies, and thus serve better as a store of value. It explores direct exchange rates versus indirect exchange rates and weighs its costs and benefits and revises the existing experiences, to finally suggest ways forward in the strengthening of international financial regulations through regional mechanisms. The proposal concerns complicating the existing international institutional set up by including the new strong regional elements that are already evolving while redesigning global instruments such as the SDR while downscaling the role of the IMF.

2. IMF: Some history and current obsolescence

The 1944 design of the IMF was drawn on the grounds of a need for international financial stability so that a 1930's-type crisis – deflation with

[1] Instituto de Investigaciones Económicas, UNAM, México. It was done with the support of UNAM-DGAPA, Proyecto IN309608-3, *Elementos para la integración financiera latinoamericana*. The author thanks Aline Magaña Zepeda for her invaluable assistance.

depression – would not repeat itself. That was the point of H.D. White's design of an economic stabilization fund in 1936 in the first place and of the discussion amongst all contributors to the Bretton Woods Conference later on in 1944. Keynes's contribution on the one hand was to imagine an international clearinghouse that would help to compensate deficit countries through increased expenditure of surplus countries. The monetary unit would be supranational – Bancor – and in one of the proposals for its confection, he suggested a basket of 30 commodities (Keynes, 1943). On the other hand, the White Plan defined the role of the IMF as a watchdog for all countries and a whistle-blower particularly for major economies going under in order to prevent a crisis like that produced by the fall of the New York Stock Exchange in 1929-30 and later in 1931 by the very significant Austrian Creditanstalt bankruptcy and the consequent systemic effects (Shubert, 1991).

The point of White's monetary fund was to produce an embedded financial architecture (Graph 1) with fast financial support for those countries having a run on their currencies, major unfinanced external deficits, and/or a banking crisis. (Bordo and Eichengreen, 1993) In the 1930s it was clear that major problems were produced partially by existing floating exchange rates of major economies applying beggar thy neighbour policies after the end of the gold standard.[2] Setting a gold-dollar standard in the mid-1930s stabilized the world economy and allowed for the recovery of world trade. This was formalized in 1944 in Bretton Woods and came to an end in 1971. That was the end of Bretton Woods I. This was not the end, however of the financial architecture built since the 1950s.

---

[2] http://www.ustreas.gov/offices/international-affairs/esf

Graph 1

The embedded International Financial Architecture

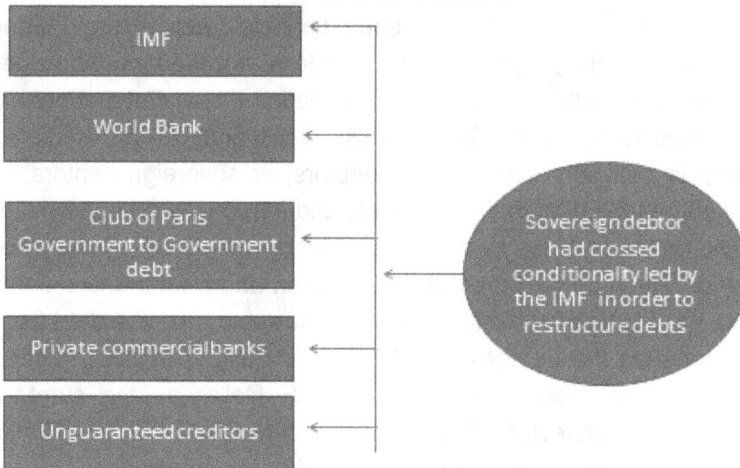

Source: Ugarteche, "The Embedded-Disembedded Financial Markets: A Variation", paper presented at the *International Conference: The Enduring Legacy of Karl Polanyi*, November 6-8, 2014, Concordia University, Montreal.

The IMF was designed as a State led multilateral institution composed of international agreements, to keep exchange rates stable but lost its track in the early 1970s after the collapse of the Bretton Woods fixed exchange system and ended up looking at emerging nations instead of looking at all of its constituency. It passed on the responsibility for major country emergency financing to central banks and treasuries of G7 countries. The G3, *library group*, formed in 1975 by French president Giscard d'Estaing with the United States and Britain, decided it would look after itself and later invited a further four countries – Italy, Canada, Japan, Germany – in order to constitute the G7 (Bayne, 1997). They would coordinate macroeconomic policies and look after themselves, making sure banks financed the rest of the world while the IMF supervised. It was the moment of the North-South divide, of the changed role of the IMF from major international economic problem overseer

Ideas towards a new international financial architecture?

into a North South agency (Ugarteche, 2009). It was the beginning of the privatisation of the international financial architecture and global governance. Not only was Bretton Woods dead, but the spirit in which it had been thought out, was annihilated. The 1970's were a new age for the Fund (Boughton, 2004). This was the start of Bretton Woods II.

The outcome was a new disembedded financial architecture (Graph 2) where it is credit rating agencies and investors, not lenders, who operate. Governments have little intervention in international financial matters except when it comes to rescuing critical banks. In the financial architecture, the relationship is between investors and debtors, or sovereign debtors, these are qualified by the credit rating agencies, and intermediated by investments banks who are somehow certified as safe by the Bank of International Settlements. When there are problems between an investor and a debtor, a distressed market agency (vulture fund) appears and buys the debt from the investor and sues the debtor in UFS courts, initially. The new architecture like the old is US based and uses the US Dollar as the currency of operations. This architecture does not cover the new OTC operations and the newer instruments such as derivatives and other innovations.

The 2008 crisis began to unfold after the signals of August 2007, namely a turn in the stock market trends and strong signs of bank over exposure with doubtful instruments in the US, but the IMF *Financial Stability Reports* (FSR) did not look that way. This was the case of IFIs that have a North South agency role. The FED has become the new lender of last resort so that the European Central Bank did a swap with them in late 2007 and the IMF kept very silent.

> "In December 2007 the ECB agreed with the Federal Reserve System a currency arrangement (swap line) in connection with their US dollar Term Auction Facility (TAF). Under this agreement, two operations with a maturity of one-month amounting to USD 10 billion each were initially conducted, subsequently renewed in January and expanded in mid-March to USD 15 billion each, while announcing that

Globalization, international trade and international payments

the USD funding operation would continue for as long as needed."[3]

Graph 2

The disembedded International Financial architecture

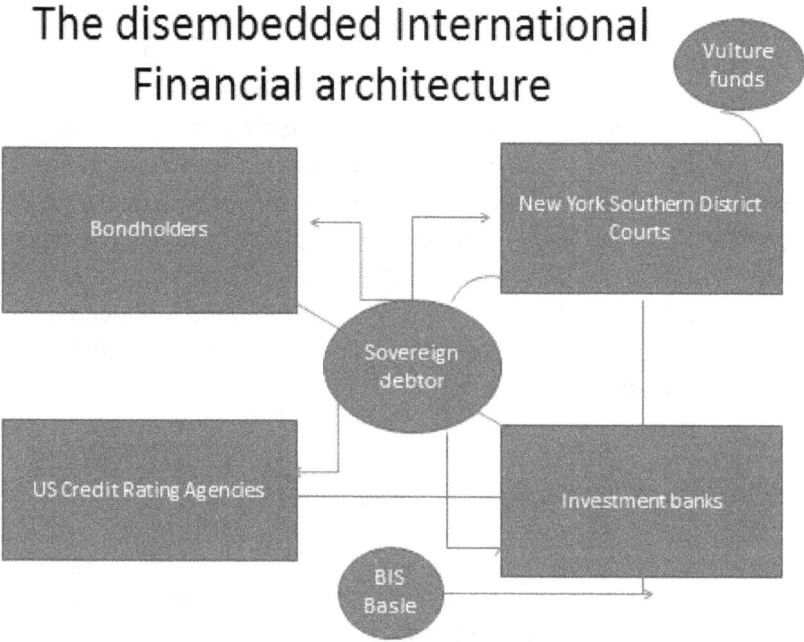

Source, *Ibid.*

The IMF did not blow the whistle and hence did not warn its members in order to prevent the crisis from unfolding, nor did it participate, nor was it even called in by the parties involved. The size of the problems they had to meet and the funds required were larger than those they had available. Previously, the Mexican rescue of 1995 was done by the US Treasury, not the IMF, for example.

---

[3] Liquidity, funding and solvency: Policy responses and lessons. Speech by José Manuel González-Páramo, Member of the Executive Board of the ECB, Universidad de Alcalá de Henares, Madrid, 16 January 2009
http://www.ecb.int/press/key/date/2009/html/sp090116.en.html

Ideas towards a new international financial architecture?

"In 1995 the (US) administration's aim was to solve Mexico's liquidity crisis in full. In fact, the administration stuck to this objective despite the strong opposition expressed by many in Congress. In fact, the U.S. executive took a notable political risk in rescuing Mexico when it decided to use the Exchange Stabilization Fund monies for an unprecedented amount" (Lustig, 1997).

The IMF is left as a scare crow that puts harsh conditions on the demand side pushing down wages and requiring the privatisation of public enterprises but the funds are provided elsewhere when it comes to leading economies. This is clear in the European cases of Ireland, Greece and Spain. By having the G7 limited the role of the IMF to that of guardian of its financial interests in the rest of the world, it has eroded its credibility and created a stigma around it. Having an IMF agreement has come to mean being near bankrupt.

3. The actors and the governance issue after the 1970s

Changes in the international economy have transformed the leading seven economies, as defined in 1975 by total size of GDP from creditors to major debtors with massive fiscal deficits. This of course means that the seven leaders of the world economy as defined in 1975 by the size of total GDP have suffered a sea change. This shift is currently nowhere reflected in the world institutional power structure, IFIs or in the international monetary system. Neither have the quotas changed significantly at the IMF nor has the composition of SDRs been modified to reflect this change. In principle, according to article XIII, 2, b) of the articles of agreement, international reserves must be kept in the currencies of the five leading economies, 50% in USD and 40% in the other four currencies, the balance in gold and local currency. This in modern language means international reserves must be kept 50% in USD and the balance in Euros, Pounds and Yen, These are the currencies that make up the SDR basket in proportions of 44% for the US Dollar, 35% the Euro, and 11% for the Yen and the Pound, respectively. Unfortunately these are deficit country/region currencies with a very low growth outlook in the next decade or more, therefore weak and uncertain

(Ugarteche, 2011). The instability between them can be observed for example in the relationship between the USD and the Euro which between February 2006 and February 2011 has observed wide swings, with a mean of 1.3712 dollars to the euro, a median of 1.3550 and a standard deviation of 0.0916, for the period in a range between 1.60 and 1.10 Dollars to the Euro.

What has emerged after 1990, the demise of the Soviet block and the start of globalisation as we know it (Ohmae, 1990), is a group of former leading nations (old G7) that are now the major world debtors facing the pressures from the new emerging nations in the international arena. These are highly indebted rich countries (HIRC), to use the World Bank categories that have sustained very high trade and fiscal deficits for more than a decade and accumulated major debts, while globally reversing credit flows. These are countries that have over consumed systematically and in some cases done so with a very lax domestic credit and exchange policies. The argument was that the consumer in the West was better off with cheaply manufactured goods from Asia, Central America and Africa. The fact that no nation can borrow indefinitely for consumption did not come to mind. Initially surplus countries bought US Treasury Bills and kept their reserves partly in those instruments, and then it extended to Japanese, British and European Government bonds and since 2011 reserves are also being held in Yuan. It was not very clear that buying Government bonds in large quantities was going to lead to over borrowing on the other side. The debt of the European periphery was not important during the decade. It was the overconsumption from Japan, the US and the larger European nations that were partially financed by growing international reserves around the developing world.

At the same time, the net reserves position switched. The table below shows the picture of the former G7 countries that hold roughly one-third the level of international reserves of the new leading emerging nations. (Table 1, column I) If Japan is removed, the group of leading nations holds one sixth the reserves of the seven largest emerging nations, most of which are from Asia. Public debt, in local currency is highest for Japan, Italy, France and the US in the 70-130% of GDP range. The very high level of Japan's public debt is mostly a result of the banking crisis of the 1990s, and if added up with private external debt is in the over 200% of GDP range (Table 1 column 4).

Ideas towards a new international financial architecture?

Table 1. Old and new G7 comparative indexes (December 2008 and 2014)

	1	2	3	4	5	6
	International Reserves 2014 (Bns USD) (4)	General Government Net Public debt % GDP (3)	GDP (PPP) % Total World GDP	General Government Net Public debt % GDP* (3)	GDP per capita (PPP) (1)	GDP Growth 2010-13 Per annum (2)
	2014	2014	2014	2008	2008	
Japan	$1.268	227,70	5,7	129,49	34,831	1,9
Germany	$249	74,70	3,81	65,1	37,208	2,1
France	$185	95,00	2,87	68.1	34,945	1,2
Italy	$182	132,10	2,34	102.3	29,894	0,5
USA	$150	71,20	19,88	72,69	48,387	2,2
Canada	$69	92,60	1,8	33,5	40,107	2,4
Great Britain	$105	86,60	2,93	74,01	35,982	1,5
Old G-7	*$2.207*	*111,41*	*39,33*	*78,29*	*37,336*	*1,7*
China (1)	$3.341	22,40	13,98		8,304	8,8
Russia	$537	13,40	2,98		16,750	3,4
India	$298	51,30	5,48		3,563	7,2
Brazil	$373	59,30	2,91	35,5	11,805	3,4
South Korea	$327	37,20	1,97		31,404	3,9
Hong Kong	$341	37,00	0,43	0	47,634	4
Singapore	$253	106,70	0,35		59,582	6,9
New G7	*$5.470*	*46,76*	*28,1*	*5,07*	*25,577*	*5,4*

Sources: IMF, (Jan. 2011 report),
(1) CIA, https://www.cia.gov/library/publications/the-world-factbook/rankorder/2188rank.html,.
(2) http://data.worldbank.org/indicator/NY.GDP.MKTP.KD.ZG
(3) https://www.cia.gov/library/publications/the-world-factbook/rankorder/2186rank.html
* Public debt is measured in domestic currency
Table prepared January 2009 by Leonel Carranco Guerra, project www.OBELA.org, at IIEC UNAM and updated 13 May 2015
The long run (20 years) growth trend excluding 1985-2004 is 2,4 for the Old G7 countries and 6,2 for the New G7 countries excluding the Russian Federation.
Old G7 Estimated GDP p.c 2020 *41,899* USD

Globalization, international trade and international payments

New G7 Estimated GDP p.c. 2020 *38,489*USD before inflation

The new G7 countries are creditors in net terms save Brazil with a 35% national debt.

The situation in 2008 deteriorated as bank rescues were introduced, reduced consumption was forced through austerity measures and taxes were raised. The consequence is that the debt indexes look far worse in 2014 while growth perspectives wilted further.

The long-term growth perspectives for the old G7 countries will be one third that of the new G7 countries in the long run, 1.7% versus 5.4% *ceateris paribus*, until they balance out their fiscal and external accounts and reduce the weight of the national debt on the national budget, if the trend established between 2010 and 2013 remains. If they were to return to the previous long term trend it would be 2.4% versus 6.2%. In both cases, the convergence pattern in the total size of GDP is established and somewhere over the next two decades those two sets of countries will have the same size with different GDPs per capita.

The new phenomenon of slow growing highly indebted rich countries, to use World Bank criteria, has introduced a level of volatility in world currency markets non-existent before the 1990s as well as a new trend in the flow of funds conventionally read from the North to the South. It has also made the governance of IFIs obsolete as they were based on the old G7 country international economic structure.

However, the current governance of these Government international institutions reflects more the fact of the power highly indebted rich countries (HIRC) than that of a powerful economic community, which old G7 countries constituted up to the 1980s. The size of GDP per capita no longer reflects the potential of the economy. In fact, all things being equal, in ten years, if growth rates are maintained, both sets of countries will have the same GDP per capita in PPP and the 31% difference will have been covered. Might this be the success of the export led model? What happened between then and now was the generalized application of export led policies which inverted the creditor and debtor relationship, where developing countries turned into under-consuming major surplus economies and major developed countries turned into over consuming economies that borrow the difference from developing countries. To put it in terms of the Governor of Bank of China's words, never before has a reserve currency been credit based (Xiaochuan, 2009). The international system must reform to take these changes into account. The end of Bretton Woods and the transnationalisation of the world economy launched the world system beyond Bretton Woods. Any deal relating to Bretton Woods takes into account the past economic structure that is in the process of fading out.

4. Rethinking the national, regional an international interests for financial reform: the reserve currency

Ocampo (2009) and Xiaochuan (2009) deal with the issue of the US dollar as a reserve currency and refer to the Triffin dilemma as a major problem because national economic interests can be contradictory with international economic interests thus making the nationally based reserve currency a contradictory one. Both Xiaochuan and Ocampo underline the fact that what is good for the health of the national economy of the reserve currency nation; can be bad for the health of the international economy. They both refer to the extremely high deficits in the leading economies and their impact in the value of the reserve currency. This can be appreciated for example in the volatility of the USD-Euro exchange rate. (See graph 3) It has for example a standard deviation of 11.9% between March of 2008 and May of 2009 while ten years earlier it was scarcely 4.1%.[4] It is the result of active monetary policy by both the FED and the ECB in light of the financial crisis.

Both authors recommend an enlarged and renewed SDR mechanism that faces first of all US veto power to prevent this from occurring. But more importantly, the articles of agreement have defined the currencies recognized by the Fund in the said article XIII, 2, b. So introducing currencies currently not considered as reserve currencies into the SDR basket requires a major change at the IMF, that recognizes new actors and withdraws US veto power.

---

[4] Oanda builds a series of monthly Euro values from before the Euro came into existence. http://www.oanda.com/convert/fxhistory

Graph 3

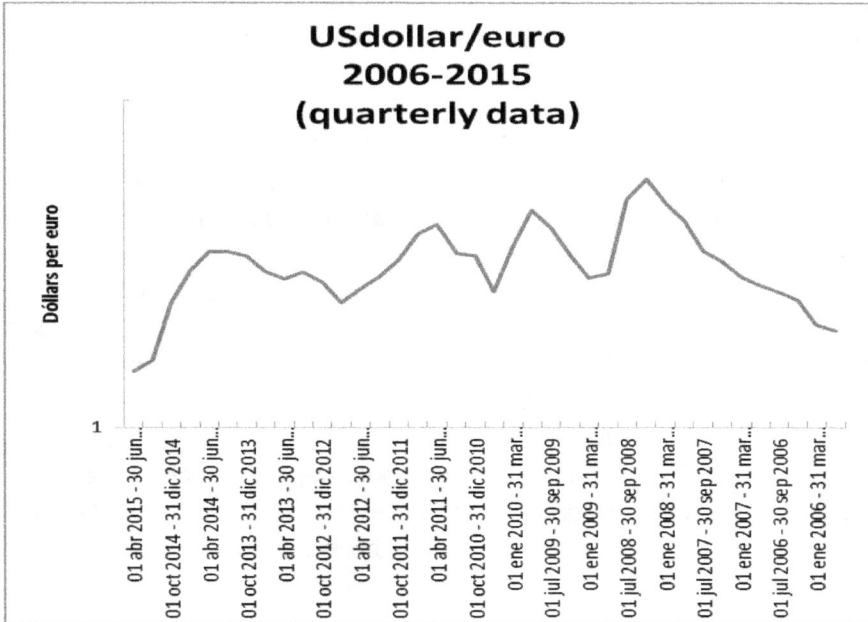

USdollar/euro
2006-2015
(quarterly data)

Source: OANDA

In December of 2005 the Fund said:

> "The criteria for selecting the currencies in the SDR basket
> are the same as in the previous (2000) review: The
> currencies included in the SDR shall be the four currencies
> issued by Fund members, or by monetary unions that
> include Fund members, whose exports of goods and
> services during the five-year period ending 12 months
> before the effective date of the revision had the largest value
> and which have been determined by the Fund to be freely
> usable currencies in accordance with Article XXX (f). In the
> case of a monetary union, trade between members of the
> union is excluded from the calculation."[5]

---

[5] "IMF Completes Review of SDR Valuation",
http://www.imf.org/external/np/sec/pr/2005/pr05265.htm

Ideas towards a new international financial architecture?

The definition in article XXX (f) is "(**f**) A freely usable currency means a member's currency that the Fund determines (I) is, in fact, widely used to make payments for international transactions, and (ii) is widely traded in the principal exchange markets."[6]

A new changed SDR basket would need to include China, India, Russia and Brazil with the new proportions emerging from international trade. For this to happen, those countries would need to trade in their own currencies and establish an international currency market for them. This has not happened before as international prices were set in USD and settled in that currency. China has taken a step in this direction by agreeing to trade in local currencies with a list of countries of Asia and two in Latin America, Brazil and Argentina. "To date (10-4-09), China's central bank has signed currency swap agreements totalling 650 billion Yuan with six monetary authorities, including Korea, Hong Kong, Malaysia, Indonesia, Belarus and Argentina."[7] Equally, Brazil has established an agreement to trade in *reales* with Argentina[8], China[9] and Colombia[10] and the issue was approved at the ALADI Board level.[11]

Any reform of Governance at the IFIs must take these elements into account and reflect it well. Otherwise the tendency for regionalisation will strengthen further and in the extreme make IFIs useless. The future of IFIs as it stands is that of the BIS in 1945 unless major reforms are made not only to the quota system but also to the articles of agreement. In March, 2008 reforms were introduced at the IMF and they said "the agreement will adjust quota shares to better reflect the relative weight of member countries in the world

---

[6] "IMF Article XXX - Explanation of Terms"
http://www.imf.org/external/pubs/ft/aa/aa30.htm
[7] "Chinese Cities Named for RMB Trade Settlement Pilot"
http://www.eeo.com.cn/ens/finance_investment/2009/04/10/134819.shtml
[8] "Comienza hoy el sistema de pago en moneda local entre la Argentina y Brasil"
http://www.lanacion.com.ar/nota.asp?nota_id=1056716
[9] "Dune Lawrence and Paul Panckhurst, "China, Brazil Yuan Trade Will Take Years, Bank of China Says", Bloomberg,
http://www.bloomberg.com/apps/news?pid=20601083&sid=abIG6z0BzwoY
10 http://www.dinero.com/noticias-comercio/colombia-brasil-pesos-reales/57061.aspx
[11] Latin American Integration Association (ALADI in Spanish) see
http://www.aladi.org/nsfaladi/Prensa.nsf/vbusquedaComunicadosweb/29374886CF9
1F958032575BE004ADC03

economy, particularly that of dynamic emerging countries" (IMF, 2008). Essentially what happened was a small increase in some members quotas, a fraction of a percentage point but all major actors remained essentially the same and no substantial changes were reflected (Bryant, 2008). Reforms like those introduced in March 2008 only serve to alienate further its constituents.

The criterion for introducing the Euro as a block currency in the IMF calculations of the SDR is that the process of European integration has given way to a supra national currency, the Euro. This process of financial integration has advanced to the point where it is a currency for a single national block, the European Community.

If we follow the same reasoning with other regions undergoing financial integration that reflect a process of economic and political integration there appears to be the NAFTA-CAFTA-Caribbean Community process, that also includes Colombia, Peru and Chile. This is left over from the Clinton FTAA initiative of the 1990s and might be referred to as the core US Dollar region. Asean+3 with the Asian Currency Unit follows; then come two African unions that use the French Franc as a common reference; then the Rand zone of southern Africa and finally the Emirates CCASG of the Middle East. In this logic, if we were to include a new rouble zone in the making, a new basket would need to include the following weights shown in the table 2 below.

Ideas towards a new international financial architecture?

Table 2. Regional weights of GDP and Trade

BASKET WEIGHTS OF TRADE AND GDP			
	GDP (%)	Trade (%)	Weight (%)
Euro Zone	15.49	28.52	22.00
US Dollar Zone*	25.53	16.18	20.86
Rouble Zone	3.64	2.84	3.24
ASEAN +3	21.27	18.46	19.87
CCEAG**	1.58	3.21	2.39
ECOWAS***	0.12	0.09	0.11
WAMZ****	0.56	0.46	0.51
COMESA*****	1.28	0.83	1.05
RAND ZONE	0.77	0.59	0.68
UNASUR	2.93	1.95	2.44
India	4.70	1.42	3.06
Pakistan	0.65	0.17	0.41
Other dollar zone	21.47	25.30	23.38
			100.00
*Is composed of NAFTA, CAFTA and Caribbean Community member countries.			

Source: CIA Factbook - UNCTAD

A starting point for reform is the monetary block issue. Having a monetary block in the current SDR but a quota system by countries on the board of the IMF does not seem to be consistent. The Euro zone is a monetary block that expresses the European Community and should thus have proportional representation on the board of directors while all the other blocks could have increased proportional representations. The table above is presented as an example and is not exhaustive of all zones nor of all-important independent countries. A more stable SDR basket could be built using partial regional baskets instead of local currencies or a mix. The four currencies included in the SDR belong to large over-borrowed, low growing economies and their weights do not reflect either their GDP or their trade weight in total world GDP and trade.

5. After Bretton Woods II: rethinking the private and public debt for financial reform

The accumulation of export surpluses over a twenty year period has allowed leading deficit countries to over borrow *in toto* private and public debt. The significant new role of Asia as a whole in both international trade and international finance calls for a reconsideration of the IMF/WB Board reflecting this major change and diminishing the European role. The democratisation of IFIs should include the use of the population weight in a basket that is now only designed with the weight of GDP. This should also lead to the elimination of US veto power established in 1944, which now makes no sense, and to a change of the mechanism by which each BWI has a director from Europe and the United States, respectively and never any from anywhere else in the world. This is hardly relevant these days, aside from being undemocratic, opaque and biased in favour of old economic and financial realities. A system where macroeconomic policy leads to massive surpluses that help finance massive deficits created by the model itself cannot work forever, as the 2007–2011 crisis has come to show. Finally, the creation of a new reserve currency designed in 1968, with the weights of the world economy as perceived in 1968 bears no relationship with the new realities.

The effect of export led growth for Latin America in general has been a process of deindustrialisation and specialization in new primary goods exports. For Asia on the other hand is has been an opportunity for export substitution. The difference between one region and the other is the role of the State and the process under which the transition from import to export substitution happened. Amsden (1989) and Wade (1990) in their important works on East Asia point out to the importance of the State as a guide in the process of industrialization throughout export substitution from primary to complex. Contrary to the evidence, the WB (1990) produced the *East Asian Miracle* that constructs the idea that laissez faire policies gave way to new entrepreneurship that led the miracle. It was a market led miracle according to them. Analysts point out in the direction of misrepresentation in the WB study and moreover of having fabricated a paradigm by fitting facts into a neoclassical theoretical framework (Wade, 1990).

Ideas towards a new international financial architecture?

The consequence of freeing the markets has been at least twofold. On the one hand productive activity was replaced by the financialization (Epstein, 2005) of the economies with the result of the 2007-2011 global financial crisis Secondly world income concentration grew even further (Wade, 2001). Thirdly we have seen the process of reverse aid mentioned earlier as poor surplus economies finance large deficit economies that has fed into the second (Ocampo, 2009).

6. The debt issues today and defaults

Sovereign defaults are not what they used to be when bank lending presided over international credit (1960–1982). The rebirth of the sovereign bond market in the 1990s after 60 years, came together with its insurance: credit default swaps (CDS). These are derivatives used as insurance by bondholders against what may be perceived as a high default probability. For example, when Ecuador's president Correa assumed power in January 2007, CDS where issued against Ecuadorian bonds betting that Ecuador would default. If Correa had defaulted, the CDS holder would have paid the market price for the bonds to the bondholder and assumed their ownership, thus leading to lawsuits to recover their nominal amount plus past due interest and charges. This has changed the manner in which defaults are faced today. "The $58 trillion notional market in credit default swaps – double the amount outstanding in 2006 – is regulated by no one. Neither the SEC nor any regulator has authority over the CDS market, even to require minimal disclosure to the market."[12] In the case of Ecuador it was not clear who had bought the CDS and the Government would have been well served to know if opposition party members where betting against the default, thus leading an international press campaign around the issue. The CDS market like all derivatives markets are made of bets which in turn raise the price of the derivatives if more agents enter the game. The CDS instrument works well when one debtor defaults with a limited impact on the market. If all major debtors default, like in the case of hedge funds in 2008, then CDS holders go bankrupt. This is partially what took AIG to the grave in 2008.

---

[12] Testimony Concerning Turmoil in U.S. Credit Markets: Recent Actions Regarding Government Sponsored Entities, Investment Banks and Other Financial Institutions http://www.sec.gov/news/testimony/2008/ts092308cc.htm

Globalization, international trade and international payments

The fact that sovereign defaults did not occur over the four years into the crisis (2007-2011) does not mean the elements for default are not present in 2015. There are nine different categories of countries in terms of wealth and debt according to the Wold Bank: rich, middle income and poor; highly indebted, medium and low. What has been observed is that there are now highly indebted rich countries (HIRC) with far more complicated problems than there opposite HIPC due mainly to long lasting fiscal deficits and an economic policy based on over consuming what other exporting countries are under consuming using external debt private and public to finance them. Problems have arisen mostly in Japan and Southern European economies were IFIs did not either foresee the problems or design a solution or a mechanism for such a solution. It was supposed that problems would be posed initially in those countries that suffer from "original sin", where all public debt is foreign held (Eichengreen et al., 2003). This is mostly Africa and to a lesser degree Eastern Europe that has not yet developed a domestic securities market. Latin American countries have to some extent replaced external debt for domestic debt thus becoming more resilient to balance of payments restrictions. These are the cases of Mexico, Brazil and Argentina, mostly but also from other countries in the region that have used the funds provided by domestic private pension funds to hold Governments bonds (Reinhart and Rogoff, 2008). Eastern European countries have been very affected but not as substantially as Iceland, Ireland, Portugal, Spain and Greece.

Nevertheless, these suppositions turned out to be wrong and HIRC are the issue, with not enough emphasis yet placed on either Japan, Great Britain nor the US that all have more than 80% of public debt to GDP which implies a major share of the national budget assigned to debt repayments while new bonds have higher costs with the restrictive implications in terms of government expenditure, public investment and public sector wages. The crisis has not hit neither Europe nor the US nor Japan seriously because interest rates are at near cero levels. A rise in interest rates with debt levels wondering the 100% level will mean 1% of GDP excess payment per 1% of increased interest on public debt.

Ideas towards a new international financial architecture?

This time increased international reserves have gone hand in hand with increased domestic debt in Latin America which is neither the case in Eastern Europe nor in Africa. Reinhart and Rogoff argue that:

> "First, domestic debt is large—for the 64 countries for which we have long time series, domestic debt averages almost two-thirds of total public debt; for most of the sample these debts typically carried a market interest rate, except for the era of financial repression after World War II. Second, recognizing the significance of domestic debt goes a long way toward explaining the puzzle of why many countries default on (or restructure) their external debts at seemingly low debt thresholds. In fact, when heretofore ignored domestic debt obligations are taken into account, fiscal duress at the time of default is often revealed to be quite severe.4 A third and related point is that domestic debt may also explain the paradox of why some governments seem to choose inflation rates far above any level that might be rationalized by seigniorage revenues leveraged off the monetary base (e.g., as in Cagan's classic, 1956, article on postwar hyperinflations)" (p.2).

Since 2011 falling export revenues in hand with falling tax revenues will press those poor and middle-income countries that have a total high indebtedness of both domestic and external debt. The external debt position alone is not sufficient to address the threshold of defaults because these can happen due to falling export revenues or falling tax revenues, or both, which is usually the case in major crisis, like the 1930's. The 1930s must be kept in mind because of the impact of the Hoover Year on European economies.[13] Reinhart's and Rogoff's paper stresses the need to have a full vision of debt, not only external, which is the most studied. In Ugarteche (2008) a discussion is made of the types of measurements required. Such an argument is made on the grounds of material developed in the 1920s when

---

[13] The Hoover Year was proclaimed by President Hoover in 1929 and later in the British Parliament as a way of deferring the charge of war debts to the US and between European countries. This prevented a moratorium or default but the effect was exactly the same (Ugarteche, 2007, ch 2).

the problem of domestic debt and external debt was in the open. This means domestic debt series must be constructed and made public for all IMF member countries in stock and flow series with GDP as a denominator so both external and internal public debt can be added. Currently, as the authors point out, it is a feat to find the data. The denominator is currently exports but total debt service is in the extreme paid with fiscal revenue. International comparative indicators then must be made adequate to this reality.

Sovereign debt problems burst usually when falling revenues meet with rising interest rates that usually appear when the monetary policy of the lending country is tightened due to higher inflation, as its economy starts to recover. This is true for both domestic and external debt as was seen in most works on the 1980s debt crisis and for the aggregate in the mentioned paper. The tightening of US monetary policy will have consequences in this field if history if is to repeat itself.

Aside from the metrics the issue is how to restructure those debts. This reintroduces the issue of international board arbitration for sovereign debt (Ugarteche and Acosta, 2007). A.O. Krueger made a proposal from the IMF. (SDRM)[14] in 2002 and before that Raffer (1990, 2010) who first elaborated on the concept after the 1930s (Helleiner, 2008). What is required is a global system and not one designed for developing countries, nor HIRC. Both creditors and debtors are new to the problems faced given it is emerging markets that bear the brunt of credit to leading economies in the form of reserves held in T Bills in the four reserves currencies. The new debtors are HIRC that previously have had no experience with debt other than the First and Second World War debt owed to the US and mostly condoned, including the German debt in 1952, thus a new global mechanism is required (Acosta and Ugarteche, 2007). The contrary debt solutions for the Greek and Ukrainian defaults in 2015 reflects the discretionary use of criteria for debt solutions rather than a more formal GDP growth based criteria.

---

[14] A.O. Krueger, *A New Approach to Sovereign Debt Restructuring*, IMF, April 16, 2002 http://www.imf.org/external/pubs/ft/exrp/sdrm/eng/index.htm

Ideas towards a new international financial architecture?

After the 2008 crisis the proposals made on debt negotiation by the South Centre with the Third World Network[15] aim at:

a. The right of developing countries that have been experiencing large and sustained capital outflows to exercise temporary debt standstills and exchange controls should be recognized, and statutory protection should be granted to these countries in the form of stay on litigation with IMF support and on lending.

b. There should be a moratorium on debt servicing by low-income countries to official creditors, including the World Bank and the IMF, at no additional costs.

c. The restructuring of sovereign debt should be based on negotiations with private creditors and facilitated by the inclusion of rollovers and collective action clauses in debt contracts.

d. A call for an international system of impartial debt arbitration needed to settle sovereign private and official debt disputes.

7. Future challenges for a financial reform

Since the beginning of the crisis there have been various efforts from the IMF and the regions to try and face the coming problems with swift mechanisms. The most advanced is the Chiang Mai Multilateral stabilization fund signed in November 2008 constructed with the previously established bilateral swap agreements amongst Asean central banks. The innovation is that it now includes China, Japan and South Korea in an Asean+3 arrangement. The backside to this is that it requires IMF approvals between tranches just as if it used the IMF itself.

In late 2008, the ASEAN member nations agreed to establish a multilateral Chiang Mai Initiative fund CMIM for 80 bn USD. This was expanded in February 2009 into 120bn USD that is almost the same as the IMF has for

---

[15] South Centre and Third World Network (TWN), "Policy Response to the Global Financial Crisis: Key Issues for Developing Countries", 20 May, 2009. Ms.

the entire world before the November declarations.[16] According to the FT the IMF, which has $142bn in quickly available resources and $50bn it can raise rapidly, recently finalized an agreement to borrow an extra $100bn from Japan and a further $150bn from other member governments adding up to nearly 450 bn USD.[17]

An Asian Currency Unit accompanies this initiative. (Graph 4) There exists a Japanese Asian Monetary Unit that is measured daily and gives an idea of the value of the regional currencies *vis-a-vis* the US dollar/euro average. There is a discussion on whether it is the AMU or the ECU that is more solid but the measurement exists and shows greater stability given the monetary cooperation agreements established within ASEAN to make this possible. The important part of the monetary agreements is that it facilitates growing intraregional trade thus stabilizing extraregional currency flows (table 3). The ASEAN process goes in the direction of a monetary block in the long run. In the short run it is an agreement to keep exchange rates stable within the region.

A similar process is in place in South America as was pointed out before. The various initiatives that are being discussed slowly range from the constitution of a new generation development bank, followed by a regional currency unit, and a stabilization fund, which would mean a strengthening of the existing Latin American Reserve Fund. More recently the announcement of the establishment of a UNASUR economic council points in the same direction of macroeconomic policy coordination. This could allow for the establishment of a Latin American Monetary Unit (graph 5) that could serve as a reserve currency made up of a basket of local currencies, much as the AMU concept and the SDR concept.

---

[16] ASEAN, The Joint Media Statement of the 12th ASEAN Plus Three Finance Ministers' Meeting Bali, Indonesia, 3 May 2009, http://www.aseansec.org/22536.htm
[17] Edward Hugh, "IMF Rapidly Expanding Its Balance Sheet, February 23, 2009". http://fistfulofeuros.net/afoe/economics-and-demography/imf-rapidly-expanding-its-balance-sheet/

Ideas towards a new international financial architecture?

Graph 4 Daily Value of AMU (Asian Monetary Unit) vs. US$ - Euro, US$, and Euro

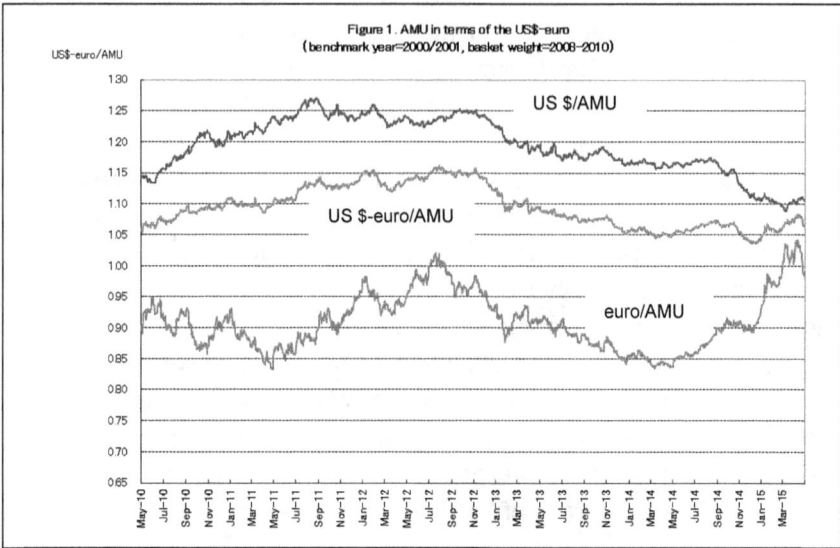

Figure 1. AMU in terms of the US$-euro
(benchmark year=2000/2001, basket weight=2008-2010)

Source: http://www.rieti.go.jp/users/amu/en/

Graph 5. Daily value of CAMLA – (Latin American basket of currencies) vs US$-euro, US$ and Euro (benchmark 2006-2007)

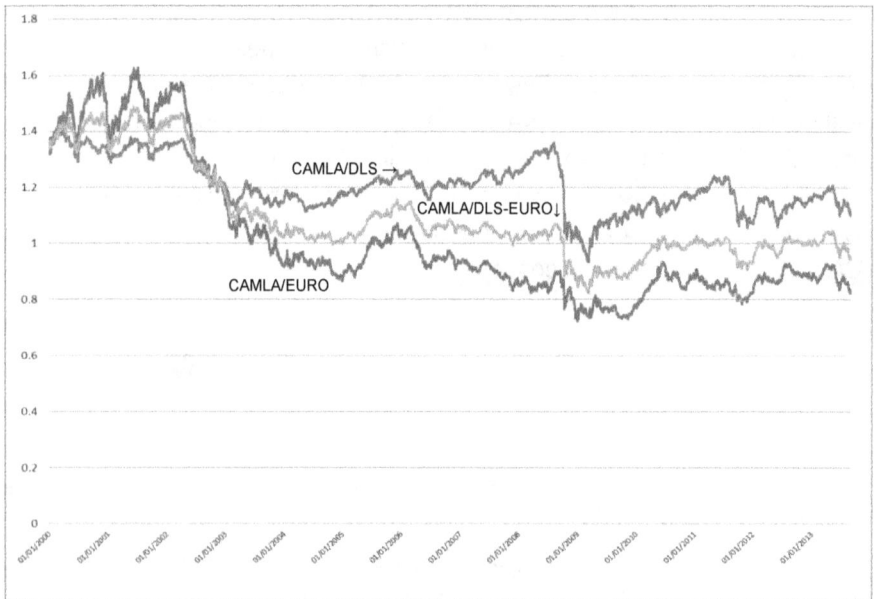

Data period: four years previous

200

Globalization, international trade and international payments

Source: Ugarteche, "La CAMLA un cesta monetaria latinoamericana", in Mantey and López La Integracion Monetaria en América latina, FES Acatlan UNAM, 2014.

The above currency basket initiatives follow the European currency union pattern and for the same reason, the stability in intraregional trade and capital flows. These are growing as fast over the past fifteen years as global trade and capital flows. When the Venezuela data is isolated in Latin America, it is much faster.

Table 3. Intra and extra regional Latin American growth rates before the crisis (1995-2007)

Annual growth rates of international trade of goods Weighted average				
Period	1995-2007		2000-2007	
Country	South America	World	South America	World
Argentina	6	8	8	11
Bolivia	18	13	24	19
Brazil	11	11	16	16
Chile	9	13	15	20
Colombia	11	9	17	13
Ecuador	14	10	19	16
Paraguay*	6	7	10	12
Peru	16	14	26	22
Uruguay	3	7	5	10
Venezuela*	-2	12	0.2	11
Total South America	9	11	13	12

* last available year 2006
Prepared by Aline Magaña Zepeda
Source: Anuario Estadístico de América Latina y el Caribe, 2008, CEPAL

The aggregation of all regional initiatives might be a way forward for a decentralised and more politically balanced international monetary system, biased today by US Treasury interests and power used through its veto power at the IMF. The persistence of procyclical policies after the G20

Ideas towards a new international financial architecture?

meeting announcements[18] on counter cyclical policies in their loans, only serves to alienate further member countries that are looking for a reform of the international financial architecture. It is very evident after the G20 Summit in London that there are two rules of the game and that the lack of change of the leading country in its policy makes institution reform even less attractive. It seems to centre on more funds with no policy change and above all without the inclusion of all member countries in its scope of action. It remains a North South institution as it was after 1975 and the formation of the G3.

What is shaping out is a group of regional institutions that might conform monetary blocks and give space for a reconfiguration of existing IFIs. Some regional institutions created have been the BRICS bank, The BRICS stabilization fund, the Asian Infrastructure Bank, The Latin American development bank, with 22 member countries instead of the Banco del Sur with seven; the European Financial Stabilisation Fund and the European Emergency Fund. In all cases, the change in the global economic structure changes completely the actors and their weights and introduces the need for a more dynamic and democratic system, with new institutions in the way. The IMF needs a democratic reform in exchange for the existing old fashioned system of "colonial countries elect their peers" system, left over from the *Pax Americana*.

A major shake-up at the Fund would also mean a descaling of the institution with more concentration in parts of the world where regional institutions are still not formed and more cooperation with those regional institutions that do exist or are in the process of being construed. The risk is that it may become irrelevant, as it already has turned since the start of the century. The proposed solution of changing the managing director and having one from the South might improve its image but if the same policies remain in place, this will not help multilateralism.

The position of the United States and Great Britain at the G20 meetings is centred on keeping the Fund as it is with more resources in the logic that this

---

[18] IMF First Deputy Managing Director John Lipsky Outlines Actions to Address Global Financial and Economic Challenges, IMF, http://www.imf.org/external/np/sec/pr/2008/pr0848.htm, March, 2008.

keeps US power and especially the financial sector influence, intact. "The agreements we have reached today, to treble resources available to the IMF to $750 billion, to support a new SDR allocation of $250 billion, to support at least $100 billion of additional lending by the MDBs, to ensure $250 billion of support for trade finance, and to use the additional resources from agreed IMF gold sales for concessional finance for the poorest countries, constitute an additional $1.1 trillion programme of support to restore credit, growth and jobs in the world economy. Together with the measures we have each taken nationally, this constitutes a global plan for recovery on an unprecedented scale" (2009, G20 London Communiqué).

The fact that US international economic policy has not changed after the Bush administration demise serves to point that it is a national policy and a show of power of the financial sector within the US Government That is why after the G20 meeting in Washington in November 2008, with Bush, the US position did not change under Obama and was supported by Great Britain in April 2009 in London. The point of discussion over the Stiglitz Commission Report and the place for discussing economic and financial issues if at the UN or at the G20 went to the G20. "The view that UN global reforms are a revolutionary group of ideas not only seems to be outdated in international affairs – aprés le mur – but also ignores the importance of a new multilateralism in a global world."[19]

The various initiatives for a reserve currency reform are a second bone of contention. The fact that a reserve currency cannot be credit based grounded on foreign aid makes the issue senseless. The way forward is a supranational reserve currency as both Chinese Central Bank Governor and Ocampo have suggested and for the additional reason of the Triffin dilemma which today is more poignant. National economic interest may conflict with international economic interests. More unbacked US dollars help the US economy reactivate but deteriorate the value of the reserve currency that by definition must be scarce.

---

[19] Neil MacFarquhar, "At U.N., a Sandinista's Plan for Recovery", New York Times, May 24, 2009. http://www.nytimes.com/2009/05/25/world/25nations.html?_r=1

Ideas towards a new international financial architecture?

8. Concluding remarks

The issues of financial market regulations are complex and must be addressed at the national level in international financial instruments issuing countries, and the global level, to keep pace of trade. No one can prevent a major crisis from recurring unless there is an agreement on new rules that regulate and monitor financial instruments of various complexities issued mostly in the US and UK and traded around the world. This implies that innovative financial instruments would need to be registered in an international entity before they enter the market and could not be used without control. This means new functions should be given to IFIs as well as a new design is made of the IFA. This is already reported by Edward Truman. (2010) President Obama took the first step in this direction in May 2009 when he announced the derivatives reform act and later the Dodd-Frank Wall Street Reform and Consumer Protection Act in the US in July 2010, opposed by derivatives traders[20] and bankers alike during the discussion period. However the fact that international financial instruments they are traded worldwide means that national regulation is important but not unique nor a replacement for global supervision of derivatives and other instruments. This was addressed also in London by the G20 but also ignored thereafter. Issuing countries must regulate financial issuers because they are their responsibility, but international traders and operations must be supervised as well in order to prevent the unsuspected contagion we have seen in the crisis started in October 2007.

> "Bankers and hedge fund managers are fond of saying, 'If you place restrictions on our activities in New York, we'll just move elsewhere – like London.' This makes attitudes toward the financial sector in other countries – particularly Britain – highly relevant to the American public policy debate on financial regulation."[21]

---

[20] Gretchen Morgenson & Don Van Natta "Even in Crisis, Banks Dig In for Fight Against Rules", NYT, May 31, 2009.
http://www.nytimes.com/2009/06/01/business/01lobby.html?ref=todayspaper
[21] Simon Johnson, "The Future of Finance: International Edition", NYT, Thursday, July15, 2010, http://economix.blogs.nytimes.com/2010/07/15/the-future-of-finance-international-edition/

Globalization, international trade and international payments

In the new global context, then, with a major leading role for Asia in the new international financial architecture and a new enhanced role for Latin America and the Middle East, Russia and its neighbours, in world financial and economic affairs, it is evident that the new debtor nations are in no position to place rules of the game, as other debtor nations learnt previously in the 1980s. Finally, given de global scope of the issues, United Nations is the only space for future discussions on global reforms.

References

Amsden, A. (1989) *Asia's Next Giant: South Korea and Late Industrialization*. Oxford University Press.

Boughton, J. M. (2004) The IMF and the Force of History: Ten Events and Ten Ideas That Have Shaped the Institution, IMF *Working Paper No. WP/04/75,* May.

Boughton, J. M. (2001) *Silent Revolution: The International Monetary Fund 1979–1989*, IMF.

Bayne, N. (1997) "History Of The G7 Summit: The Importance of American Leadership" Keynote address delivered at a conference on "Explaining Summit Success: Prospects for the Denver Summit of the Eight," sponsored by the University of Colorado at Denver and Metropolitan State College of Denver in co-operation with the University of Toronto G8 Research Group,", Denver, Colorado, June 19.

Bordo, M. and Eichengreen, B. (1993) *A Retrospective on the Bretton Woods System: Lessons for International Monetary Reform*, University of Chicago Press.

Bryant, R. C. "Reform of IMF Quota Shares and Voting Shares: A Missed Opportunity", Brookings, April 8, 2008,
http://www.brookings.edu/~/media/Files/rc/papers/2008/0409_imf_bryant/0409_imf_bryant.pdf

Dąbrowski, M. (1995) "The Reasons of the Collapse of the Ruble Zone", *CASE Network Studies and Analyses No. 58,* Warsaw
http://papers.ssrn.com/sol3/papers.cfm?abstract_id=1312324

Ideas towards a new international financial architecture?

Eichengreen, B., Hausmann R. and Panizza, U. (2003a) "The Pain of Original Sin," in Barry Eichengreen and Ricardo Hausmann (eds.), *Debt Denomination and Financial Instability in Emerging-Market Economies,* Chicago: University of Chicago Press

Epstein, G. (2005) *Financialization and the world economy* Cheltenham, UK; Northampton, MA: Edward Elgar

Helleiner, E. (2008) "The Mystery of the Missing Sovereign Debt Restructuring Mechanism" in *Contributions To Political Economy,* 27, OUP, pp.91-113

International Monetary Fund. (2008) "Reform of IMF Quotas and Voice: Responding to Changes in the Global Economy", 08/01 - April 2008, http://www.imf.org/external/np/exr/ib/2008/040108.htm

Keynes, J. M. (1943) "The Objective of International Price Stability", The Economic Journal, 53 (June-September): pp.185-87.

Lustig, N. (1997) "Mexico in Crisis, the U.S. to the Rescue. The Financial Assistance Packages of 1982 and 1995". En *Brookings,* http://www.brookings.edu/articles/1997/01development_lustig.aspx

Ohmae, K. (1990) *The Borderless World, Power And Strategy In The Interlinked Economy,* New York, Harper Collins.

Ocampo, J.A. (2009) "Reforming the Global Reserve System", Ms.

Pauly, L. W. (1997) *Who elected the Bankers? Surveillance and control in the World Economy.* Ithaca, Cornell University Press,

Raffer, K. (1990) "Applying Chapter 9 Insolvency to International Debts: An Economically Efficient Solution with a Human Face", *World Development* 18(2), pp.301-310.

Raffer, K. (2010) *Debt Management for Development Protection of the Poor and the Millennium Development Goals,* at Edwar Elgar

Reinhart, C. M. and Rogoff, K.S. (2008) "The Forgotten History of Domestic Debt," NBER Working Papers 13946, April. http://www.nber.org/papers/w13946

Securities and Exchange Commission, *Emergency Order Pursuant To Section 12(K)(2) Of The Securities Exchange Act Of 1934 Taking Temporary Action To Respond To Market Developments,* Release No. 58166 / July 15, 2008

Shubert, A. (1991) *The Credit-Anstalt Crisis of 1931,* Cambridge University Press.

Ugarteche, O. (2014) "La CAMLA, Cesta Monetaria Regional Latoinoamericana" en *La Integracion Monetaria de America latina,* FES Acatlan UNAM.

Ugarteche, O. (2011) "La coopération financière régionale, une alternative", Ceras – revue *Projet* n°320, Février 2011. At: http://www.ceras-projet.com/index.php?id=4801.

Ugarteche, O. (2009) *Historia critica del FMI.* IIEC UNAM, México DF, 2009.

Ugarteche, O. (2008) "Fuentes de financiamiento públicos e indicadores internacionales. La evidencia latinoamericana reciente." *Economía UNAM,* No. 13, enero-abril, pp.128–140.

Ugarteche, O. (2014) *La arquitectura financiera internacional: una genealogía,* IIEC UNAM

Ugarteche, O. (2007) and Acosta A., "Global Economy Issues and the International Board of Arbitration for Sovereign Debt (IBASD)", *El Norte – Finnish Journal of Latin American Studies* No. 2, December 2007, ISSN 1796-4539

Ugarteche, O. (2000) *The False Dilemma: Globalization: Opportunity or Threat?,* ZedBooks London.

Volz, U. (2010) *Prospects for monetary cooperation and integration in East Asia.* Cambridge, MA: MIT Press

Volz, U. with Aldo Caliari (eds.). (2010) Regional and global liquidity arrangements, German Development Institute, Bonn

Wade, R. (1990) *Governing the Market.* Princeton University Press.

Wade, R. (2001) "The Rising Inequality of World Income Distribution", *Finance & development,* 38 (4). ISSN 0145-1707.
http://www.imf.org/external/pubs/ft/fandd/2001/12/wade.htm

World Bank. (1993) *The East Asian Miracle: Economic Growth and Public Policy: Main report.* OUP.

Xiaochuan, Z. (2009) "Reform the International Monetary System", People's bank of China, http://www.pbc.gov.cn/english/detail.asp?col=6500&id=178

CONCLUSIONS

Ideas towards a new international financial architecture?

CONCLUDING REMARKS
A new world is possible and necessary

Alicia Puyana and Oscar Ugarteche

The ever growing integration of world economics demands a continued revision and renewal of institutions, norms and practices, a process that embeds both opportunities and risks. The opportunities consist in the possibility to take advantage of scientific and technological progress and the risk are the unequal distribution of the opportunities and growth effects which could increase concentration of wealth, income and political power. It is a task for collective organizations think and act to promote the best of this process, and control its damages.

The world has enormous experiences in how financial crisis erupt and damages social and economic fabric, let it be the Gold Standard collapse, which ignited a chain monetary crisis and impoverish-the-neighbor politics. When World War II was about to end, the US economy was undoubtedly established as hegemonic economic and military super porwer and the world split by the ideological and political divide between socialism and capitalism, new rules were adopted in the shape of the Bretton Woods, institutions, to rule the functioning of the world capital and goods markets according to developed countries interests. The Bretton Woods architecture created a system lasting for almost three decades. Its "stability" could be attributed to the several reforms undertaken to accommodate the rules to the deep changes the world was experimenting day by day: increasing numbers of new independent states; the economic and technological transformation of almost all developing countries and their growing share of global GDP and world trade; the IT revolution and the creation of the 24 hours functioning global capital market; finally but not least, the end of the Cold War with the collapse of the Soviet Union and end the West and East Europe divide. But the Bretton Woods crisis was evident already in 1971 and so far no other overall settlement has been put in full motion. Bretton Woods' institutions and organisms have continued to work, as zombies form a previous economic system. Some changes have been adopted, but they did not fully respond to the new realities. So, despite of the repeated claims of famous Nobel prize winners (Lucas 2003) declaring as solved, for many decades to come, the great problem of macroeconomic theory remains: the management or prevention of economic cycles.

These crises, were not, never were, limited to capital and financial markets. They spread to the entire economy, with severe effects on growth, employment and poverty. A new international financial architecture is needed fully aware of the fact that markets are far from efficient and do not suffer only from marginal imperfections but from endemic pathologies, such as long periods of deep unemployment or permanent sub-employment. In effect "… risk markets are incomplete and information is imperfect, markets are not constrained Pareto optimal… market failures, rather than appearing as isolated and easily correctable by government intervention, appear to be all-pervasive" (Stiglitz, 1991, pp.18-20). The Efficient Market Theory appears to have at least some major problems, information is nowhere near perfect and as Shiller points out, it is used for "phising phools" and fraudulent profit making. The 300 bn USD fines the SEC and CFTC gave nine major global banks between 2012 and 2014 penalizes Libor, commodity price and exchange rate rigging. The fines are in toto the size of the GDP of Peru plus Ecuador, to give a point of comparison.

The number of agents that concur the market is small and highly concentrated, giving way to such abuses as the gold price bubble (September 2008 to September 2012 from 800 USD oz. to 1920 USD oz). Few very large banks entered the market leading to a severe rise in the Gold price and at the 2000 dollar an ounce level, they sold, leaving all the small investors holding the bucket. With few and very large investment banks worldwide there is very little competition. Worse, the criterion that agents can be too large to fail has created a new category of financial agents, those that do not consider risk as a variable for measuring profit. The solution when those had problems in 2008 was to make them even larger instead of splitting them into "right size to fail" firms. Finally there is the problem of the irrationality of the markets. Rational choice did not show up when the irrational exuberance happened. The herd instinct seemed to lead the way instead. So, changes in financial institutions have to be undertaken *pari-*

A new world is possible and necessary

pasu with a new macroeconomic policy-frame able to tame the markets, and prevent and manage economic cycles. As Shiller (2015) suggests "...because we can be manipulated or deceived or even just passively tempted, free markets also persuade us to buy things that are good neither for us nor for society" (Shiller, 2015). The author adds "The reluctance to acknowledge the need for immediate intervention in a financial crisis is based on a school of economics that fails to account for the irrational... and that ignores the aggressive marketing and other realities of digital-age market... But adhering to an approach that overlooks these factors is akin to doing away with fire departments, on the grounds that without them people would be more careful – and so there would then be no fires" (ibidem).

Policies, macroeconomic policies have not and cannot be limited just to define the incentives to induce individuals to work and save: low taxes, moderate public spending, and stability. All in all, these changes have to take into consideration the integration of the world economy in all its levels (as Davidson and Passaris stated in their chapters). At least, the debate has to consider some central elements:

a) The fragmentation of production has changed the way to consider comparative advantage and change the definition of comparative costs, since production does take place in single space, in an old one nation – one product scheme. Segments of production process are distributed in countries all around the world depending of particular countries factor endowments and productivity. The allocation is taken by multinational corporations in line with their market strategy and not to the needs of recipient countries development needs. Transnational corporations have become global players with great power, and some kind of world-regulation of their activities is needed.[1]

b) The increasing deregulation of international commerce has multiplied consumers' choices, but has risked jobs and limited sovereign decisions in clue areas. For example, the derivative markets have allowed to speculate with food stocks and prices,

---

[1] For example, the Transnational Institute has studied this profoundly, and has some proposals on the issue. www.tni.org

which isn't neutral on famine debates, more than they have helped producers to reduce their risks.

c) Capital flows have largely surpassed real GDP, and in doing so have intensified macroeconomic instability. It is usual to be presented as an inevitable effect of scientific progress evident in information and communication technologies, as well as in transport capacities. But the process of science research and technological advance are not exogenous, and the technology market is not a competitive market. The foundation of the crisis widespread contagiousness was deregulation and the claims of the efficiency of the markets which allowed almost any agent to invest in anything. For example, it can well be discussed why commerce banks can buy in secondary capital markets, or why public funds can operate with derivate bonds. As well, it can be considered why countries should not have any control over its frontiers. This does not necessarily mean to enclosure national economies, but some information requirements to operate in any country should not be dismissed as medieval practices. What is the reason for discrediting any attempt register and to know who invests in our country? Minimum register standards, as well as minimum permanence requirements, are relatively simple proposals. The Tobin Tax is another old proposal which can be discussed. Finally, is it good for humanity wellbeing that every market, production or area can be used for private profit? Or at least some of them should be protected of different forms of speculation? Is it alright to leave water supplies or rainforests survival in private hands?

Such changes need international cooperation in which all parts are considered equal and debate and vote on equal terms. Such even playing field is a utopia today. Perhaps tomorrow the landscape will be different.... Perhaps. So there are some fields to be deeply changed:

i) *Tax havens*: these geographical spaces out of all regulatory frameworks have no justification, whatsoever. They work both for criminal activities and for legal firms as well.

214

ii) *National accounting:* as Knight explains, cross-national clearance could be developed in order to distinguish wealth creation from monetary transactions. The current system of national accounts was developed not that long ago, for a different world; why not start studying alternatives?

iii) *Central banks:* new roles and duties to redefine the banks independence, have to be designed. Neoliberal reforms have left central banks in the hands of the very same people they were supposed to control. The needed equilibrium between national democratic control and international coordination aims should be explored and instrumented. The Greek crisis is the fresher remains of how external financial institutions impose their interest over national democratic institutions.

iv) *Sovereign debt regulation:* recent scandals as Argentina and the so called "vulture funds" or the Greek restructuration left few doubts on both the role of international organisms and the power of few banks and financial funds. Argentina managed to promote a UN resolution on some principles to regulate sovereign debt restructuration, which was rejected by Canada, Germany, Great Britain, Israel, Japan and the US despite the mild nature of the commitments. The argument is that market mechanisms can solve debt problems, but as we have recently seen in Ukraine, Puerto Rico and Greece, it is not the markets but some either Government or financial agents that work out the debt problems. The lack of a sovereign debt arbitration mechanism puts in peril the use of public debt for financing development plans, as Lima and Brown have partially explored.

v) *The role of international organisations:* it seems urgent to first, clarify their functions and the reasons for the use of conditionalities, second, to democratize them as the asymmetric power a few countries show in the IMF or WB tilts these organizations to conform to the philosophy and interests of these few countries. It is not strange that many regional integration processes are rehearsing on how to play by their own institutions (as Ugarteche explains in his

215

Ideas towards a new international financial architecture?

chapter). The importance of the BRIC players cannot be dismissed as if the world has not changed.

Global financial problems posed by new instruments used worldwide and the increased contagion between markets, epidemics as they are referred, require new global institutions that reflect the new economic power structure. With Europe double counted in the G20 and the G7 countries keeping majority votes at the IMF while they really express a grouping of highly indebted, low growing countries that are losing weight in the international sphere, IFIs have little chance to regain legitimacy. The forcing of the IMF role is only pushing its credibility downwards. Regional responses are emerging and will continue doing so, but this should be a thought out process and not only the addition of spontaneous regional decisions, or in the BRICS case, a grouping decision. There is more information and more financial instruments but there is also an increased demand for more democracy at the international financial sphere. Blocking new global institutions for new market ones, does not take into account the new international balance of economic power. A new world is possible and necessary.

References

Lucas, R.E. (2003) 'Macroeconomic Priorities', *American Economic Review*, 93(1), pp.1–14

Shiller, R. (2015) "Fraud, Fools, And Financial Markets", Social Europe, September 21 available at: http://www.socialeurope.eu/2015/09/fraud-fools-and-financial-markets/

Stiglitz, J. (1991) "The invisible hand and Modern Welfare Economics", NBER, WP No. W3641, available at: http://www.nber/org/papers/w3642pdf.

About the editors and authors

Oscar Ugarteche Galarza is PhD in History and Philosophy from the University of Bergen, Norway, M. Sc. from the London Business School of the University of London, BS in Finance from the College of Business Administration, Fordham University, New York. Previously working at the Catholic University of Peru and international consultant on foreign debt issues, he moved to Mexico in 2005, and entered the Institute of Economic Research at UNAM as researcher- he is also professor at the Faculty of Economics in UNAM. He belongs to the Sistema Nacional de Investigadores since 2008. His career includes visiting scholarships at University of Newcastle, 2014; the Latin American Institut Frei Universität Berlin, 2011; Institute of Latin American Studies, U. of London, 2000; Centre for Development, U. of Bergen 1993 and 1995, St Antony´s College, Oxford, 1987. He published thirty five book chapters, nearly sixty papers And articles, and twenty two books (some of which are in multiple editions), mostly in Spanish, one in English. Some recent titles include: *Historia Crítica del Fondo Monetario Internacional; Arquitectura Financiera Internacional: genealogía 1850-2008; La Gran Mutación. El capitalismo en el siglo XXI.*

Alicia Puyana Mutis is PhD in Economics by Oxford University. Professor and researcher at Facultad Latinoamericana de Ciencias Sociales, FLACSO, 1997 to now, teaching economic growth for D. Phil courses at FLACSO. Member of: the Colombian Academy of Economics Sciences, the Mexican Academy of Sciences, the International Development Economics Association IDEAS, the Consejo Editorial de la Editorial Anthen Press (for the Anthen Studies on Globalization). Her latest book publications (as an author, coauthor, or editor) since 2012 include: *La economía petrolera en un mercado politizado y global. México y Colombia; México. De la crisis de la deuda al estancamiento económico; Diez años del TLCAN. Las experiencias del sector agropecuario mexicano; América Latina. Problemas del Desarrollo en la Globalización 1980-2013; Strategies against Poverty. Designs from the North and Alternatives from the South.*

Maria Alejandra Madi holds a PhD in Economics and a MSc in Philosophy. She is currently Avocational Lecturer at Steinbes University Berlin. She is also Chair of the Wolrd Economics Association Conferences, Co-editor of the World Economics Association Pedagogy Blog and Assistant Editor of the *International Journal of Pluralism and Economics Education*. She is also Director of the Ordem dos Economistas do Brasil and Counselor of the Conselho Regional dos Economistas do Brasil-SP. Former Professor at the University of Campinas, Brazil (1983-2012) and coordinator of the undergraduate course in Economics (2004-2006). Her career includes visiting professorships at the University of Manitoba (2008) and the University of Kassel (2010). More recently, she has co-edited the WEA book *The Economics Curriculum: towards a radical reformulation* and some of the Green Economic Institute books, including *The Greening of Global Finance* and *The Greening of Latin America*. Her latest publications include *Global Finance and Development*; *Small Business in Brazil: competitive global challenges*. Her research interests include finance, economic development and social justice.

Carlos Marichal received his PhD in History from Harvard University (1977). He is professor of Latin American economic history at El Colegio de Mexico, a leading research and postgraduate institute. He is author of *A Century of Debt Crises in Latin America: From Independence to the Great Depression, 1920-1930*, Princeton University Press, 1989 and editor of two dozen books in English and Spanish on Mexican and Latin American economic history. His most recent book is *Nueva historia de las grandes crisis financieras: una perspectiva global, 1873-2008*, Editorial Debate, Madrid, Buenos Aires and Mexico, 2010. He is a member of the Nacional Research System of Mexico, highest level 3. He was member of the Governing Board of El Colegio de México (2003-2008). He has been founder and former president (2000-2004) of the Mexican Association of Economic History. He was awarded the *Premio Nacional de Ciencias y Artes de México, 2012,* in the category Social Sciences, Philosophy and History.

About the editors and authors

Constantine Passaris is a Professor of Economics at the University of New Brunswick (Canada), an Onassis Foundation Fellow (Greece), a Research Affiliate of the Prentice Institute for Global Population and Economy at the University of Lethbridge (Canada), an Affiliate Professor of the Canadian Centre for German and European Studies at York University (Canada) and a member of the Academic Scientific Board of the International Institute of Advanced Economic and Social Studies (Italy). He is a prolific author whose scholarly publications have been published in monographs, books, encyclopaedias and academic journals. He has written extensively on economic issues dealing with public policy, globalization, economic governance, demography, immigration and multiculturalism. He currently serves as a New Brunswick Ambassador, a Fredericton Business Ambassador and the Chair of the New Brunswick Ministerial Advisory Board on Population Growth. He was conferred the Commemorative Medal for the 125th Anniversary of the Confederation of Canada in 1992 in recognition of his significant contributions to fellow Canadians, community and to Canada. He was conferred the Queen Elizabeth II Diamond Jubilee Medal in 2012 for his exceptional contributions to New Brunswick and Canada.

Gerson Lima is Doctor in Economic Theory by the University of Paris X (1992). Before assuming the academic position, he was a leading economist at some private companies and public institutions. After the doctorate degree, he became Titular Professor of macroeconomics at the Federal University of Paraná where he served the Economics Teaching Committee of the Federal Government, the National Association of Post-graduate Courses in Economics, and the Regional Professional Economists Council as vice-President. His major contribution to economic theory and teaching is the textbook *Economics, Money and Political Power* (in Portuguese) that has been successfully used to teach real world economics to non-economics students at colleges.

Tim Knight worked for over thirty years in analysis and re-engineering of payment processes. As a result of his professional background, he has applied the re-engineering experience, expertise and techniques to economic, welfare and democratic processes, and has also documented his insights, analysis, and proposals in a number of draft documents which have been presented at University conferences. He is currently working on research entitled the "Re-Engineering the Economic Processes" which aims to contribute with suggestions to overcome the current and on-going financial crises.

Ellen Brown is an attorney, founder of the *Public Banking Institute*, and author of twelve books, including the best-selling *Web of Debt: The Shocking Truth About Our Money System and How We Can Break Free*. In *The Public Bank Solution*, her latest book, she explores successful public banking models historically and globally. Her other books include *Nature's Pharmacy*, co-authored with Dr. Lynne Walker, which has sold over 285,000 copies; and *Forbidden Medicine*, on the success and tribulations of an alternative cancer healer. She has also written over 300 articles, posted on her blog at EllenBrown.com; and co-hosts a radio program on PRN.FM called "It's Our Money with Ellen Brown" (http://itsourmoney.podbean.com/).

Uli Kortsch is the Founder and President of Global Partners Investments, Ltd. In his capacity as president, Mr Kortsch has written a bill for Congress, reviewed by Congressional Legal Services, as well as Treasury, and the Senate and House Banking Committee staffs, and conferred with approximately 15 presidents, ministers of finance, and ministers of commerce during the course of business in over 50 countries. Mr Kortsch served as Managing Partner at Kolagg Investments, LLC, Executive Vice President of Asset Management Associates, Inc., Chief Financial Officer of Dream Builders, Inc., and National Director of Youth with a Mission (Canada), Inc. He has served on many boards, including MercyShips International, International Reconciliation Coalition, the University of the Nations, Dialogue Institute, and World Relief Canada.

Paul Davidson is Holly Professor of Excellence, Emeritus at the University of Tennessee. He is the Editor of the *Journal of Post Keynesian Economics*. He is the author, co-author, or editor of 22 books and over 210 articles. His research interests include: International monetary payments and global employment policies; monetary theory, income distribution, energy economics, demand and supply for outdoor recreation, Post Keynesian economics. He is listed in *Who's Who In Economics*, *Who's Who In The East*, *Who's Who In The South and Southwest*, *American Economists of The Late Twentieth Century*, *Dictionary of International Biography*, *Men of Achievement*, and *Contemporary Authors*.

www.ingramcontent.com/pod-product-compliance
Lightning Source LLC
Chambersburg PA
CBHW061158220326
41599CB00025B/4531